Narrative Inquiry

Narrative Inquiry

Philosophical Roots

Vera Caine, D. Jean Clandinin and Sean Lessard

BLOOMSBURY ACADEMIC
LONDON • NEW YORK • OXFORD • NEW DELHI • SYDNEY

BLOOMSBURY ACADEMIC
Bloomsbury Publishing Plc
50 Bedford Square, London, WC1B 3DP, UK
1385 Broadway, New York, NY 10018, USA
29 Earlsfort Terrace, Dublin 2, Ireland

BLOOMSBURY, BLOOMSBURY ACADEMIC and the Diana logo are trademarks of
Bloomsbury Publishing Plc

First published in Great Britain 2022

Cover design by Toby Way
Cover image © oxygen/Getty Images

A catalogue record for this book is available from the British Library.

Library of Congress Cataloging-in-Publication Data
Names: Caine, Vera, author. | Clandinin, D. Jean, author. | Lessard, Sean, author.
Title: Narrative inquiry: philosophical roots / Vera Caine,
D. Jean Clandinin and Sean Lessard.
Description: London; New York: Bloomsbury Academic, 2022. |
Includes bibliographical references and index.
Identifiers: LCCN 2021028871 (print) | LCCN 2021028872 (ebook) |
ISBN 9781350142046 (paperback) | ISBN 9781350142053 (hardback) |
ISBN 9781350142060 (pdf) | ISBN 9781350142077 (ebook)
Subjects: LCSH: Narrative inquiry (Research method)
Classification: LCC H61.295.C35 2022 (print) | LCC H61.295 (ebook) |
DDC 001.4/33–dc23
LC record available at https://lccn.loc.gov/2021028871
LC ebook record available at https://lccn.loc.gov/2021028872

ISBN: HB: 978-1-3501-4205-3
          PB: 978-1-3501-4204-6
          ePDF: 978-1-3501-4206-0
          eBook: 978-1-3501-4207-7

Typeset by Integra Software Services Pvt. Ltd.

To find out more about our authors and books visit www.bloomsbury.com
and sign up for our newsletters.

Contents

Section III Living within and on Landscapes

Section IV Imagination, Inquiry, Wonder and Playfulness: Opening into Liminality and Uncertainty

Section V Relationality

Acknowledgements

This book has been an idea in our minds for many years now, as we worked to develop and live out narrative inquiry as both a phenomenon and a methodology. Writing the book allowed us an opportunity to reread and revisit many books and articles that we had read over more than thirty years since Michael Connelly and D. Jean Clandinin published the article entitled 'Stories of Experience and Narrative Inquiry' in the *Educational Researcher*. Finding old references and searching our bookshelves for copies of books was an invigorating and generative process. 'Listen to this' we called out to each other, as we reread passages that we had forgotten. Many days we felt like we were engaging in conversations with old friends.

We were fortunate that, over the three years we worked on the book, we were able to spend many days writing together in Jean's home on Canada's west coast. Intense days of writing together were almost regular monthly occurrences. During these writing retreats, we read, wrote, talked, walked, shared meals, all amidst our ongoing lives. We imagined otherwise in what mattered in our lives as researchers and teachers. We know how much response and community matter to each of us and we know it is attending to our lives, and to the lives of others, that creates the possibilities of imagining what it means to think of lives narratively and to engage in research narratively. Finding ways to sustain our writing in the midst of the Covid-19 pandemic has been challenging and we are fortunate to have done this work together. It was through metaphorically visiting old friends that we were sustained during the pandemic, as reaching backwards allowed us to also look forward.

While our main focus in this book was on the theoretical underpinnings of narrative inquiry, this book would not have been possible without the extended periods of time, over many years, alongside research participants in various studies: youth who left school before graduating; mothers, fathers and children who arrived in Canada from Syria as refugees; Indigenous youth and families who we came to know in what was known as the U of A Art Club; young women who were composing lives amidst difficult circumstances of being HIV positive; young Indigenous people who joined

Growing Young Movers; Indigenous mothers and grandmothers who were preparing their children for kindergarten in urban schools; early career teachers who left teaching; and working alongside women and children who lived in precarious housing situations. These participants, many of whom we still hear from and who are characters in our lives as we are in theirs, have shaped us and have allowed us to understand narrative inquiry in more depth.

We have learned much from community members and Indigenous Elders, especially Elder Isabelle Kooteney, who graciously made spaces for us to learn with them as we engaged in different research projects. They shared their living knowledge of theory with us, as we worked alongside participants. They took us home both metaphorically and in actuality. We learned as we sat together at kitchen tables, surrounded by the beauty of rural surroundings, and as we engaged in shared long silent walks.

We also have been blessed to work with many graduate students both at the University of Alberta and in other universities across the world who continually share new ideas, wonders and readings. They engage with us in multiple conversations and push us to name what it means to think narratively. We also met, and worked with, colleagues in many places who share our passion for thinking narratively; many are also dear friends.

We have been supported by funding for multiple projects over many years, notably by the Social Sciences and Humanities Research Council of Canada, the Canadian Institute for Health Research, the Alberta Centre for Community, Child, Family and Research (now Policy Wise), the Women's and Children's Health Research Institute, and our home institution the University of Alberta. We would also like to thank Bloomsbury Publishing, particularly Mark Richardson and Evangeline Stanford, for their kind support of our work.

We acknowledge, as always, our families, especially our children and grandchildren who continue to inspire us to listen to their stories as they negotiate their lives in complex worlds.

Introduction

We sit together to dream ideas for this book, a dreaming that asks us to gather our thoughts, our lives and our writings to tell a story of the ideas that are part of, integral to, thinking narratively. What we dream calls us to write somewhat differently than we have in other works focussed on concerns of methodology and on particular research projects or around particular research puzzles. In this writing we return to the central ideas of narrative inquiry, ideas that emerged not only from living and inquiring alongside multiple participants in many research projects, but also from reading the work of scholars from diverse disciplines and professions, from different national contexts and from different times. In this book our aim is to make visible the philosophical roots of narrative inquiry as methodology and phenomenon. We take up these key ideas in individual chapters. The whole of the book will make visible the philosophical ideas in narrative inquiry. At the end of each section we include methodological notebooks in which we show the link to, and the relevance of, our thinking to narrative inquiry as methodology.

Why This Book, Now?

As we trace our reasons for writing this book, we name multiple. For many years now we have engaged in narrative inquiry studies and in naming the phenomena under study as narrative. We learned much along the way and, in this book, we trace some of our philosophical roots, as well as the ways in which we developed as researchers and worked to develop the field of narrative inquiry. We strongly believe that philosophical work is important to graduate students, yet few opportunities exist for them to engage with philosophical readings. Larger narratives are at play in academic institutions and in funding agencies that have shifted what we do over the past many years and have governed, both intentionally and unintentionally, how we spend our time. This is often evidenced in shifting work arrangements, increasing pressures to measure outcomes, as well as in research agendas that are no longer driven by a sense of curiosity. For us, engagement with philosophy speaks to a love of knowledge (understood in a broad way, and something we will return to in a later chapter) and inquiry, an engagement with ideas that exist in the world and that exist and shape the lives of people we engage with, as well as ourselves. For years we have been particularly interested in the philosophy of life and the philosophy of ethics as they shape how we understand experience, as well as in the practical consequences of our thinking about experience.

One of the challenges we face as we write about the philosophical roots of narrative inquiry is that we cannot lose sight of the beginning place of narrative inquiry as situated in people's experiences. Experience is where we begin and where we end in narrative inquiry. Woven into experiences are, always, the complexities of life and living. We cannot start with one aspect of experience and set aside the rest of experience, the rest of life, without doing damage to the person, the individual who is having the experience.

If we start with a concept, for example, identity or community or imagination or some other concept, the concept is unfolded, followed through to its complexities and, perhaps, to the ways the concept is lived in experience. It is the concept that provides the organizing frame. The concept is privileged, placed as the starting point for understanding experience. As narrative inquirers, our task is quite a different one. We cannot figure out the concept first and then see 'it' in experience. We start in the experience, at the outset seeing the messy interwoven threads, knowing each is important and needs to be addressed. But, as we pull one thread of an experience, we always know the rest of experience is present.

This makes this book especially difficult to write as we can neither select the concepts to develop and then see their application to understanding experience nor can we select a theorist or group of theorists within a particular discipline. And yet, our task is to show how theoretical our work is, how different theorists, and some of their writings, have become part of how we have developed narrative inquiry as phenomenon and methodology and ethics. We draw forward concepts and ideas from a range of theoretical sources, including feminist scholars, pragmatist philosophers and philosophies of resistance.

Given that we are situated in a large research intensive university, with large graduate programs, we have also paid close attention to graduate students and the intellectual communities of which they become part. We have noticed that increasingly graduate programs are more concerned with having students align and graduate with knowledge in substantive areas, as well as in ways that focus on what is determined to be fundable research programs. This often means that research methodologies and substantive areas of inquiry are organized hierarchically or pitted against each other.

Increasingly we see students and beginning faculty turn away from exploring the philosophical roots of the methodologies and phenomena under study. We are also deeply concerned about a trend we see in academia that often makes research a technical exercise focused on methods. There is an absence of philosophical discussion, in both academia and the public realm, about the ways in which we take methodological turns as well as about multiple ways to think about, and see, the world. Too frequently we gloss over matters of ontology and epistemology. Furthermore, we sense a lack of curiosity about the philosophical underpinnings and concerns that shape inquiries with a sole focus on the substantive questions. There is a turn towards the technical, a turn towards the instructive, the 'how to do research'. We know that others have noted similar concerns within different disciplines and in different global contexts. Our intention, in this book, is to respond to these concerns, as we make visible what we understand as key ideas in narrative inquiry, ideas that are grounded in theoretical, as well as practical, understandings.

Thinking with the ontological and epistemological underpinnings of narrative inquiry opens up possibilities to think about a complex and interconnected world. We offer ways to resist the turn to the technical and to think with philosophical ideas that help us understand and make sense of experience. Through continuous engagement with different scholarly texts, over time, we have resisted this turn to the technical and resisted a focus on technical undertakings of narrative inquiry as a research methodology with standard protocols, interview schedules and analytic processes. Our resistance comes from reminding ourselves that our focus on experience understood narratively is understanding the phenomena under study narratively.

Our interest as narrative inquirers is marked most strongly by a focus on lives and, consequently, on experience. While one might position theory in opposition, or contrast, to experience, or lives, or in contrast to practice, we see theory as much more interrelated with practices, with experience, with lives. Our hope for this book is that we are able to make visible how we think with ideas, how we work to be playful as we inquire, and how our ideas and experiences as researchers evolve over time when we engage with ideas.

Coming to the Book: Autobiographical Origins

The ideas for, and about, this book grew over years, spent, not only in academia, but also spent living in relation with people and communities who joined our research, who in so many ways helped us live up to possibilities. In as much as we write about ideas in this book, we also write about the ways in which we live our lives. While we write about the ideas and our lives now, perhaps as a way to shape forward-looking stories, we also know that ideas that we have come to think with, have been significantly shaped by our histories, by the places, and by social contexts we have lived within. Taking a step forward offers us the gift to look backwards and recall some of our earliest connections to the ideas and the people and places that have shaped them.

> The white little car my mom and dad owned was something! It was a car that got us to places on weekends and evenings, places of adventure and fun – like the pottery class where we crammed as many kids in the backseat as possible, or the swimming adventures at a local dug out that had turned into a lake. We were on the move! The car too got us to our weekly family gatherings at my aunt's house, that now, in my memory, turned into epic gatherings for they hold so much of who I have become. And as I think about that white little car, I have no memories of what happened to it – I have no idea when or where the car no longer was part of our way to get around. I remember that the car had a radio and that as we got older we would often ask my parents to turn it on – always the answer was the same: 'wo man singt, da lasse dich ruhig nieder, böse Menschen haben keine Lieder' [where you sing, let yourself settle down, wicked people have no songs] with my dad alway adding that 'böse Menschen haben ein Radio' [wicked people have a radio]. I don't think we ever played the radio, instead each request was followed by my parents breaking into song. After some hesitancy and eye rolling, we all joined in. Song after song until we finally arrived at our destination. Perhaps, neither my brother, sister, or I wanted to be considered wicked. I still recall the songs even now and the words still seem to hang in the air. What seems to be implicit in my father's words about singing, was that singing evoked and fostered social relations. You had to pay attention to multiple voices, to the rhythms, the words, and the sounds, but more importantly we had to pay attention to each other.

The importance of social relations was instilled in Vera early and lived out in the ordinary things she did as a family. It planted early in Vera's life an appreciation that social relations were established in the doing; they required commitment.

I sat in my grandson's grade 3 classroom in a school that borders a major US city on Thursday afternoon following the shooting in a Parkland, Florida high school where 17 students were killed. My grandson's school was having a lock down drill and I was a school visitor in the room with the teacher and the 20 or so 8 and 9 year old children. As they gathered on the small carpeted area after doors were locked, lights turned out and windows shuttered, their teacher spoke of the importance of staying silent, of stilling their bodies, of staying far away from the windows, of staying low to the floor, of trying to make themselves not visible to whoever might be trying to cause them harm. I, too, sat on the floor, quietly watching the teacher, as he tried to answer questions about guns and who should have them and about what should be done if a shooter came to their school. I felt the fear and apprehension of the children and recognized the enormity of the situation the teacher was facing. While I sat quietly, feeling the horror of what could happen, I thought about the teacher's responsibility, about the responsibility of each child to their classmates, about the responsibility we each carry as people in relation to each other.

The moment stayed with me as I walked quietly out of the school. My thoughts drifted back to my childhood spent on a small subsistence farm in a rural community in western Canada. My parents lived their lives, and taught me to live, in responsible ways with the land, the animals, and the people who lived around me. If neighbours were hungry, our family stretched meagre food supplies to share food; if animals were in harm's way on country roads, we worked to make sure they were guided off the roads; if the land was not producing, my parents worked to rotate crops to sustain the soil in the garden and in the grain fields. I was raised to live my life with a sense of responsibility to others, to seeing myself as part of larger communities, not focussed only on what was right or best for me and my immediate family. Part of that responsibility involved taking action, doing something when something needed to be done. It was not enough to know what needed to be done, what should be done. To live responsibly meant to do something. Not to act, not to do something that made a difference in the ongoingness of lives was not an option, even though action called forth going beyond self to those in the communities in which one lived.

I thought again about the message my grandson's teacher was giving the children, that is, that in moments when they might be in harm's way, they needed to be responsible for themselves and for others, to be quiet, to not draw attention to the class by talking or moving about. I liked his message but the horror and imagined scenes continually seeped into my mind. My stories to live by, shaped by my early years, called me to see the interconnections, the responsibilities to, and for, others around me. What, and to whom, were my responsibilities in this moment?

Thinking with Jean's story we can see how ideas of responsibility have shaped her life; from her early years within her family and farming community to her times now spent with her grandson in his school.

'On the road, the long narrow road, I am going back to the place where the waters flow'. I have written this small sentence over and over in my black travel journal. On planes or in vehicles on road trips, with my pencil in hand, I start at the same point in my writing. Each time the opening line expands in various directions, sometimes filling multiple pages, sometimes only partial word sketches. I start this line as a reminder of the importance of going back home to my First Nations community in the spring, when the ice breaks up on the lake and the water starts to flow in the many channels and to the place that I have come to know as the rapids.

Each year, for many years now, I make the long trip back home to honour this place and gather with my community. I make my way from the straight prairie roads and open fields, noting the geographical shifts to narrow gravel roads, as I come closer to my home community in Northern Saskatchewan. As I make my way closer to home I am surrounded by the comfort of pine trees on both sides of the road, welcoming me and greeting me into another familiar place that I have come to know over time. I enjoy this drive as it provides me with thinking time, and that opening fragment 'on the road, the long narrow road' begins to take shape. As it takes shape, I feel its meaning become fuller.

On this drive and with the shifting geography, the shift changes something in me and draws me into an important experience. I often wonder on that trip about the stories that are so present within this place. I think about the trees and the forest. I imagine the many animal relatives including the elk, bears, caribou, and wolves who are beginning to move differently at this time of the year, when the snow has started to melt and the ice begins to break. There are seasonal markers in this place that change everything. I think more clearly about my ancestors and relations that are also part of this place. I think of them watching over me in the trees and, when I am thinking with these experiences, I begin to wonder and let my imagination help me travel to what life might have been like for them in this place. I wonder about how, and where, they travelled through the tree line maze. I enjoy this transformational experience as I undo myself from the city and the urban landscape and begin to reconnect with this meaningful place. In the past few years I have been joined by my daughters, two new travellers who have come to understand the importance of this trip to the rapids and our homeplace.

I share this narrative to highlight the important places that shape my experiences and my stories. These looking back moments are within me, more than I know, even within the city life that I am currently composing. It is most likely the snow melting and the green grass starting to emerge through the yellow straw-like covering from the seasons past that evokes this memory within me. It is a geographical reminder and a sensory marker, that it is that time again, 'when the waters begin to flow'.

As we think with Sean's experience, we see the significance of the connection between place and memory. This significance is particularly important to the living of narrative inquiry as we can see how stories are planted in people's memories by being in place.

We share these brief fragments to give a sense of who we each are, as well as to provide some sense of our understanding about our philosophical commitments. They are fragments of our lives and how we have come to compose them. They are stories shaped by our lives, lives lived as people rather than as researchers or methodologists. We know our lives are shaped by larger social, cultural, familial and institutional narratives, as well as by place and time.

Situated within Pragmatist, Feminist and Indigenous Ideas

We intentionally began with brief autobiographical fragments to allow readers to understand something of who we are, and the ways that our life-making has shaped our coming to ideas that fit within pragmatist philosophies. We want, however, to make clear that what might be seen as only stories of our personal lives are deeply rooted within larger social, cultural and institutional narratives. We find the work of Erin McKenna and Scott Pratt (2015) helpful as we work to discern some of the larger social and cultural narratives that shape our lives.

McKenna and Pratt (2015) in *American Philosophy: From Wounded Knee to the Present* helped us see that, in part, the larger narratives we were born into were philosophical ones. McKenna and Pratt traced the history of pragmatist philosophy in the United States from 1894 to the present. They show how philosophical considerations were deeply entwined with political and social actions and events. Our lives have been situated in Canada and in Germany and not in the United States and, as we read their work, we found ourselves amidst national events and people who were not familiar to us. Different places and people in Canada, Germany and elsewhere have also shaped our understandings. We try, as we write this book, to draw in other events, people and places that are familiar to us.

The early philosophers about whom McKenna and Pratt (2015) wrote, Jane Addams, Kicking Bear and John Dewey, were ones who immediately captured our imagination. As we read of Addams and Hull House and of the life and work of Charlotte Gilroy Perkins, we were drawn to the ways they were thinking about life-making, about what mattered in a living out of philosophical ideas around community, responsibility, gender, inclusion and social action towards more equitable ends. We were wakeful to understanding that had we lived in the times of Dewey and Addams, we might have shaped our lives in ways consistent with their pragmatist philosophies. We felt their ideas, their life-making, were resonant with our own. As we compose our lives, we felt that sense of resonance with moral responsibility, and commitment to people and their lives. As they faced social and political consequences for their actions, grounded in philosophical stances, we, too, have also lived with the sense of otherwise, of struggling to shape different spaces with other possibilities, recognizing that what we do has practical life consequences.

Temporally, in relation to their book, we locate our lives in the years after the end of the Second World War, with the rise of logical positivism and American empiricism. We understand, however, that McKenna and Pratt (2015) draw forward the theories that reverberated and recurred over time from the 1800s to the present. As we read of the philosophical debates over time, interwoven as they were with the politics of war and nationhood following the Second World War, we note that what comes to replace a 'vision of activist philosophy is a vision of a neutral method focused on analyzing the formal logical structure of language' (p. 157). We see that it was this philosophical tradition that was taking hold. By the time we began our work as researchers, this tradition had taken hold in the philosophy departments with which we were familiar in Canada. This turn to logical positivism was something we had read before in Ellen Lagemann's (1989) classic text in which she observed 'one cannot understand the history of education in the United States during the twentieth century unless one realizes that Edward L. Thorndike won and John Dewey lost' (p. 185).

We turned away from philosophy to our work in education and nursing, in part, because we were unable to locate ourselves in the philosophical discourse of objectivity and neutrality. For example, Jean, when she worked in schools as a teacher, counsellor, and later in her work in the academy in teacher education, created spaces congruent with the ideas of the early pragmatists, ideas such as those of the classical pragmatists. Jean also sees her work as linked to what McKenna and Pratt (2015) call a tradition of resistance.

Charles S. Peirce, William James, and John Dewey tried to show the limits of established philosophies by reconceiving the practice of inquiry, the idea of self, and the nature of democracy. American Indian thinkers including Charles Eastman, Arthur Parker, Gertrude Bonin, and Luther Standing Bear challenged extermination and assimilation by proposing ideas of community and place that drew on North American indigenous traditions. W.E.B. Du Bois and Jane Addams challenged industrial capitalism and aimed to reconceive communities around an idea that Addams called 'lateral progress'. Josiah Royce, Alain LeRoy Locke and Horace Kallen offered a notion of community around a logic of borders that could inform experience in the context of lived diversity. This tradition of resistance has rarely found a place in discussions of American philosophy […, in part because it was] aimed to make the complacent uncomfortable and the dogmatic doubtful.

(pp. xii–xiii)

We were not familiar with many of these philosophers, although we were deeply steeped in Dewey's work. The ideas though, as we read them, called forth from each of us a deep resonance, a sense that we were shaped by these traditions of resistance in our lives and that these traditions shaped our work in schools, in community health, in Indigenous communities and in higher education. These philosophical ideas carried within them our spirits of resisting the status quo, our sense of composing our lives in ways that called forth relationality, and moral commitment to equity and social justice.

Structure of the Book

In narrative inquiry we focus on people's experiences, people's lives, situated and shaped by larger cultural, social, familial, institutional and linguistic narratives. However, this does not mean that theory is not integrally woven into narrative inquiry as we understand the phenomenon of experience. We draw on theories selected because they are relevant or helpful in understanding some of the key ideas in thinking narratively about phenomenon. We did not adopt one theoretical stance, as we thought narratively, but used the ideas from different philosophers as they helped us think with lives and the stories people lived and told.

Sometimes when others read our work, or the work of our students, they remark that the work is atheoretical, or not theoretical enough. 'Too much life, not enough theorizing', critics sometimes remarked. We have frequently responded that narrative inquiry is theoretical, pointing at different times to philosophers such as Dewey, Mark Johnson and David Carr; to psychologists such as Anthony Kerby and Theodore Sarbin; and to feminist scholars such as Addams, bell hooks, Carolyn Heilbrun and Maria Lugones. It was, as we continue to do this work, that we realize that perhaps the lack of recognition of theory is because theory stood in different relation to experience, to lives, in thinking narratively.

We are again reminded of McKenna and Pratt (2015) who wrote of broadening the canon of philosophy as they selected scholars to include in their text, scholars such as Addams and Gilroy Perkins, people who would not have been included as philosophers in the traditional canon of philosophy. We have also broadened the canon of theoretical resources to include Indigenous Elders, fiction writers, poets and essayists. We have included people of Indigenous heritage as well as authors and writers who name different places as homelands. We draw on a broad canon of scholars from different disciplines to ground our work theoretically.

Table of Contents

We divided the book into five sections grouped around a set of ideas. Each section includes a set of relevant chapters. Each chapter is written as a stand-alone essay on a particular significant idea in narrative inquiry. We make visible theoretical work that has shaped our understanding of each idea and how it is central to thinking narratively. We begin each chapter by tracing how these ideas, and subsequently certain authors, influenced our work over time. In each chapter we also situate our knowing in our own experiences. There are challenges in staying with singular concepts, such as place, or identity, or community. When starting with experience, it is impossible to see people as fragments, or as embodying or living conceptual ideas. At the end of each section (from two to five chapters) we write a methodological notebook.

Methodological Notebooks

In the methodological notebooks we make the ideas, and our understandings of them, visible by drawing on our most recent study alongside refugee families with young children from Syria. In this study we work with eleven families who recently arrived in Canada; that is, we met them less than two years from their arrival. We are interested in their experiences over time and as they interact with more formal institutions such as schools. As we spend time with families, we listen to their stories of experience, as well as live alongside them as they negotiate their ways in a place so foreign to all of them. In these notebooks we show how thinking narratively with the ideas is part of the methodology of narrative inquiry, and is expressed in our methods.

Section I

Starting with a Particular View of Experience

Experience is a central aspect of narrative inquiry. An inquiry into how humans experience the world highlights not just individual experiences, but also experiences situated within social, historical, linguistic, political, familial and other contexts. It is in thinking with experience that we understand the told and lived stories of people, and of people in relation. In this way, we understand narrative inquiry 'as an experience of the experience' (Clandinin & Connelly, 2000, p. 189) D. Jean Clandinin and Michael Connelly (2000) drew on John Dewey's work, to develop an argument that inquiring into experience is key to education. It is in reading Dewey's work that it becomes visible that experience, education and life can not be separated. In Chapter 1 our focus is on experience from a place of attending to the wholeness of an individual's life. Chapter 2 makes visible that knowledge, for us, is closely tied to experience. For Clandinin (1985) knowledge is 'imbued with all the experiences that make up a person's being. Its meaning is derived from, and understood in terms of a person's experiential history' (p. 362). While the work in narrative inquiry is often seen as relying extensively on speech or text, in Chapter 3 we turn towards the embodiment of narratives. This embodiment is visible in both the living and silences of our lives.

1

Experience

Abstract

In this chapter we make visible our understanding of experience. As narrative inquirers, experience is one of the most significant terms. One of the aspects that is important to us is that experience is a source of knowledge, but also carries what was seen in the fourteenth century as 'an event that has affected one' (Online Etymological Dictionary, np). The interaction between knowledge and implications that are reflected in the etymology of the word experience is critical.

The way we take up experience reflects the influence of pragmatist scholars, like Dewey. It is the work of early pragmatists that shaped our thinking; for many of the early pragmatists experience was a central concept. For Dewey (1934),

> experience occurs continuously, because the interaction of life creature and environing conditions is involved in the very process of living. Under conditions of resistance and conflict, aspects and elements of the self and the world that are implicated in this interaction qualify experience with emotions and ideas so that conscious intent emerges.

> (p. 36)

In this view of experience, there is always a sense that life is in the midst, that experience is always evolving and that experience builds upon experience. Experience, then, is something always in the making, being shaped and reshaped over time, as new situations are encountered. Experience is neither fixed nor certain.

Turning to Experience

Almost always do the events of my adolescent life blend into each other and it is impossible to recall my age or the school grade to determine the specific year of the events. It was a significant time of my life, a time that left many marks and has deeply shaped my understanding of the significance of experience – experiences of my own and also those of others. Feeling increasingly alienated within a school system that valued conformity, I turned towards people and places that allowed me to see and experience things in new ways. While much of these experiences were the consequences of unintentional encounters and relationships, they left me with a sense of serendipity and most certainly with a sense that there were worlds beyond those I had come to understand. In my search of these worlds I recognized that I was not only looking for new experiences, but that I was also most interested in the ways in which experiences unfolded.

On the days in Grade 7 or 8 when it became unbearable to remain seated in the hard and uncomfortable wooden chairs at school, I would leave the school grounds. Together with my then boyfriend Markus, who identified himself as a poet, we would head towards the marketplace. The marketplace had a large water fountain, as well as benches that allowed people to sit and gather throughout the warm and sunny days of spring, summer, and fall. At the edges of the marketplace were some of the first fast food places we had come to know. I still recall the spring rolls at the local fast food place. A place where the smell of grease filled our bellies despite not having eaten anything. We became regular customers, always ordering 3 or 6 or sometimes 9 spring rolls – always enough to share with the man whose watchful eyes followed us.

I do not recall the man's name and for now, in the retelling of my experience, I will call him Bruno. I remember Bruno's bicycle and the strapped-on bags of personal belongings that were very neatly tucked out of sight, as to not call forth attention. I remember the instability of his bicycle caused by the weight of the bags that were strapped to the frame. Bruno always kept his bicycle within close proximity out of fear that belongings could be stolen and not returned – belongings that were important to him, as I learned over time. Bruno was not from here, he had no deep emotional connections to people or places in the area – he was for months just passing through. Bruno was hard to ignore, his body was present in public spaces in ways that made many turn away from him. His presence in the marketplace was visible – he appeared out of place – and the smell emanating from his body became almost always overwhelming. Yet, Markus and I were drawn to him – perhaps what drew us in was that he lived in a world so foreign to us. Yet, the piece we shared with him was our interest in poetry and writing. Slowly over time, while sharing grease-filled spring rolls, Bruno began to tell us stories. Stories that spoke of his experiences as a young man growing up in postwar Germany, of a man who had become divorced and lost all family connections, of a man filled with sexual desires, and a desire to be a writer.

The times, while skipping school, that Markus and I spent sitting on the benches on the main market square suddenly weren't so empty anymore. We began looking for Bruno each day both during school and also after school. Bruno had a way with words that drew us into his world – a world filled with injustices, inequities, and few possible futures. There were times when he would whisper stories into Markus' ears, stories that were not intended for my ears, yet told loud enough that I could hear. Stories of women in his life, of mothers and daughters, of sexual encounters, and of desires and needs. Some of the stories became graphic accounts of his life that I found both revolting and also mysterious. Bruno seemed to thrive on what had become daily visits with us. While our daily visits never quite gained a sense of ordinary in my memory, I remember that I had a sense through listening to his stories of experience, that the ordinary experience of poverty and substance use had become more real, more tangible to me. Bruno tried hard to help us see that despite sleeping in foreign beds, of entering strangers' bodies as payment and not because of love, was somehow ordinary. Sitting on the benches surrounding the market place, I could feel the gaze of strangers – of people like my parents, whose world was so different from Bruno's.

There were times when we would accompany Bruno on his bicycle, on his way out of town, to places that provided temporary shelter or refuge to him. Places located near roads and ditches that were outside of the gazes directed at him at the marketplace. It was in these places that Bruno became more quiet and withdrawn. In these places he asked Markus to read his poems, and to tell him stories of who we were – a way to fill the silences, the quietness, and perhaps the desperation that was palpable at times. Bruno was getting older, his body more fragile, less resilient, and less able to get comfortable on the rocky ground that formed his mattress on the nights he did not enter the bodies of strangers, of mothers and daughters, who longed for the warmth of a body. At least that is the story he told.

One day, Bruno was gone. He disappeared, perhaps much in the same way, as Markus and I had suddenly appeared in his life. I remember the franticness of looking for his body, his bicycle, remnants of his belongings that would indicate that he was OK. Bruno's presence and sudden absence had a profound impact on my understanding of experience – it was my experience alongside him that called me to turn towards care and that allowed me to understand experience as a complex human endeavour.

Locating Experience: Calling on Dewey

In thinking with Vera's experience, we are reminded that our understanding of experience is grounded in Dewey's work and that the idea of experience has a sense of living. It is something we actively participate in, it is not an afterthought that comes through the telling and retelling of experience. As Vera points out her adolescence was '*a time that left many marks and has deeply shaped my understanding of the significance of experience*'. It is these marks that are left, that are not only inscribed into our skin and our bodies, but that are being shaped as our bodies and worlds grow in new ways.

Experience is something we do. It is something we are part of, much like the landscape we stand on. At the same time our understanding of experience is marked by change and an orientation towards the future. For Vera, her encounter with Bruno changed her; it shifted how she understood social differences and inequities. It is alongside Bruno and Markus that Vera first realized that experience is one of the most sensitive indicators of inequity – that when attending to experience we can not turn away from the social, cultural, political and historical positions we occupy and that shape each of our lives. Bruno's sudden disappearance remains troubling and calls Vera to be wakeful and to not take experiences or relationships for granted. His disappearance continues to shape her work; it is his absence that calls her to care. It is the experience of his disappearance that lingers, that is filled with questions about how relationships are sustained amidst adversity, social difference, and how relationships both in reality and in imagination are reflective of agency. Bruno has shifted and changed Vera's future experiences. *In my search of these worlds I recognized that I was not only looking for new experiences, but that I was also most interested in the ways in which experiences unfolded.* As Dewey (1938) points out 'no experience lives and dies to itself. Wholly independent of desire or intent every experience lives on in further experiences' (p. 27).

If this sense of experience living in further experience is the case, it also means that knowledge, which is closely linked to experience, is always changing and evolving. While this book is a turn towards the philosophical, it is important to recognize that 'Dewey's conception reorients what counts as philosophical practice by reconnecting it with experience' (Pratt, 2002, p. 17). This close link between knowledge and experience is important for us, as it makes visible that knowledge is common, that it is living amidst the ordinary. This sense of ordinary was evident in Dewey's (1958) writing in his work *Experience and Nature*,

[e]xperience includes *what* men do and suffer, *what* they strive for, love, believe, and endure, and *how* men act and are acted upon, the ways in which they do and suffer, desire and enjoy, see, believe, imagine – in short, processes in *experiencing*. 'Experience' denotes the planted field, the sowed seeds, the reaped harvests, the changes of night and day, spring and autumn, wet and dry, heat and cold, that are observed, feared, longed for; it also denotes the one who plants and reaps, who works and rejoices, hopes, fears, plans, invokes magic or chemistry to aid him, who is downcast or triumphant. It is 'double-barreled' in that it recognizes in its primary integrity no division between act and material, subject and object, but contains them both in an unanalysed totality. 'Thing' and 'thought' … are single barreled; they refer to products discriminated by reflection out of primary experience.

(p. 8; italics in original text)

In thinking with Dewey's words, it is important to recognize that Vera and Markus' actions were part of their experiences. Driven by a sense of curiosity, a sense of seeking the other, the unknown, the unfamiliar, their seeking of experience, was a way of acting. It was a way to understand the suffering, the love, the endurance and the desire to reimagine the world. Vera and Markus talked often about Bruno and, long past his disappearance, they wondered how he had shaped them. For Markus, Bruno had been one of the first people to take him seriously as a poet, as someone who was gifted with words, with an ability to evoke images between, and amidst, the lines and words written. In this way Bruno not only had shaped and affirmed a possible future for Markus, but also had extended a friendship that centred on their mutual love of words.

It is here that Dewey's (1938) words begin to make sense, as he writes

experience does not go on simply inside a person. It does go on there, for it influences the formation of attitudes of desire and purpose. But this is not the whole of the story. Every genuine experience has an active side which changes to some degree the objective conditions under which experiences are had.

(p. 39)

Bruno had changed the conditions under which experiences happened for Markus and also for Vera, and he, too, had given rise to new experiences. It is here that we can see that 'a transaction taking place between an individual and what, at the time, constitutes [their] environment' (p. 43) is central to experience. For Dewey, what marks experience are two criteria: continuity and interaction. Criteria that cannot be separated from each other, as they form 'the longitudinal and lateral aspects of experience' (p. 44).

Continuity

Experience is something always in the making, being shaped and reshaped over time, as new situations are encountered. Experience understood narratively is always in the midst and it is shaped in the making and remaking, in the recollecting of what is past, but also in what continues to live on in future moments. These ideas of experience continue to shape what we have drawn forward from Dewey's ideas of experience with the ways that interaction and continuity weave together to create situations. While Stephen Crites (1986) suggests that the present 'is the pivotal point out of which the "I" who recollects retrieves its own self, the present is not "a static point"' but 'is always leaning into the future, projecting itself into the future. [...] I recollect the past out of my interest in the future' (p. 163). As Vera sits in the marketplace alongside Bruno and Markus, it is the smell of grease, the taste of spring rolls, the eyes that follow her that hold her in the present; yet, it is Bruno's way of reaching back to the past that creates the possibility for Vera to think about and perhaps rethink the future. For Crites, 'we appropriate our personal past, in fact, out of the future' (p. 164). It is Bruno's presence that draws Vera's attention to the future, which in turn calls her to look backwards – to remember the hard wooden chairs, the inflexibility of what schools offered her, the moments in which her experiences were confined to narrow ideas of what counts as knowledge. It is in these moments that Vera is forced to reconsider not only her future, but also who she was and has been.

This sense of continuity allowed Vera to enter Bruno's life, and it, too, allowed her to make sense of his absence. Her experiences, alongside Bruno, showed Vera that '[g]rowth, or growing as developing, not only physically but intellectually and morally, is one exemplification of the principle of continuity' (Dewey, 1938, p. 28). Bruno shifted Vera's gaze away from looking at him, to thinking with his experiences. This shift has marked Vera's life since then; he has called her to see experience as a relational endeavour.

Interaction

For Dewey (1938) the second criterion that intersected with continuity was interaction, which speaks to the objective and internal conditions of an experience. This interplay between objective and internal conditions is important, as it calls us to look at not only what goes on around us, but also what happens inside of us. While the objective conditions are important and are often given much consideration, we cannot take the individual out of the situation. The interaction between the individual, the objective conditions and other people is important. The internal conditions speak to the needs, desires and turmoils that live within people, that shape how they see and experience the world – it, too, shapes what people learn.

Experience as Mis-educative

For Dewey (1938) experience was the means and the goal of education. He makes this clear when he states 'there is an intimate and necessary relation between the process of actual experience and education' (p. 25).

> The belief that all genuine education comes about through experience does not mean that all experiences are genuinely or equally education. Experience and education cannot be directly equated to each other. For some experiences are mis-educative. Any experience is mis-educative that has the effect of arresting or distorting the growth of further experience. An experience may be such as to engender callousness; it may produce lack of sensitivity and of responsiveness. The possibilities of having richer experience in the future are restricted.
>
> (pp. 25–6)

Vera turned away from school early on in her life, as from her vantage point schools focused predominantly on the objective conditions of experience. Students were replaceable in some way, bodies were talked to, rather than considered as living and breathing persons who held knowledge. For Vera schools were mis-educative; yet, as she felt pushed out of school, this push opened up new possibilities, possibilities of meeting Bruno. While the interactions between Bruno and Vera could be seen as educative, they too showed moments of being mis-educative. Vera still remembers when Bruno talked with Markus about his sexual relationships.

> *Stories of women in his life, of mothers and daughters, of sexual encounters and of desires and needs. [...] Bruno tried hard to help us see that despite sleeping in foreign beds, of entering strangers' bodies as payment and not because of love, was somehow ordinary.*

When Bruno shared the graphic accounts of his life, he did not ask or consider who Vera was. There was no recognition of Vera's vulnerabilities as a teenage girl, as someone who not only desired love, but also believed that love was possible and that love held a promise. Even now, Vera is called to re-read poems by Erich Fried (1979). Both Vera and Markus were reading Fried's work at that time, and his poem *Bei dir sein wollen* spoke of a sense of love that was marked by a desire to be together. Bruno planted doubts about the possibilities of love, in a way that foreclosed promises and desires. In Dewey's (1938) words, it had 'the effect of arresting or distorting the growth of further experience' (p. 25). It was only much later in Vera's life that perhaps what can be thought of as mis-educative at that age, became educative in her work as a community health nurse and, later, as a researcher. Perhaps it is here that we better understand that 'the quality of any experience has two aspects. There is an immediate aspect of agreeableness or disagreeableness, and there is its influence upon later experiences. The first is obvious and easy to judge. The effect of an experience is not borne on its face' (Dewey, 1938, p. 27).

Thinking about the Narrative Quality of Experience

Crites (1971, 1986) helps us see three critical elements which give experience a narrative quality: sacred stories, mundane stories and temporality. For Crites (1971), narratives, too, have an organizing function – it is through narrative that we can express coherence over time. This coherence is important in that it shapes our ongoing life-making. It helps us think who we are and are becoming over time.

Understanding Experiences: Sacred and Mundane Stories

Sacred stories, stories that carry a sense of authority, and that allow us to understand our ongoing stories in relation to them, are important to discern for Crites. While mundane stories are reflected within sacred stories, they are the ordinary stories. For Crites, stories offer us a moral compass. Through the acknowledgement of time, Crites (1986) also draws our attention to memory, yet he too warns us of the 'illusion of causality' (p. 186). While time is a critical element, it cannot be understood as a linear concept that shapes experience. It is these three elements: the sacred stories, the mundane stories and temporality that give experience a narrative quality. While we return to the work of pragmatist, and other, philosophers we are also influenced by people like Robert Coles. Coles (1989), in his early work, chronicles his experiences as a resident and becoming psychiatrist, which draws us into the living of experience. It is his unfolding experience and that of the people he works alongside, that remind us that we need to understand the wholeness of a life, that each life and each experience is shaped by others.

> *Bruno was hard to ignore, his body was present in public spaces in ways that made many turn away from him. His presence in the marketplace was visible – he appeared out of place – and the smell emanating from his body became almost always overwhelming. Yet, Markus and I were drawn to him – perhaps what drew us in was that he lived in a world so foreign to us.*

Both Coles and Crites helped Vera see that the ordinary or mundane parts of experience are indeed critical to experience and to who we are and are becoming.

Attending to Cover Stories as a Way to Understand Experience

It was not until some years later that we found more of Crites' (1979) work, writing that offered us new ideas for continuing to think narratively about experience. In the early years we wondered sometimes about the stories people told, stories that in the telling could cover over, or cover up, lived stories, the person's experience. There were many who argued that people with whom we engaged in research were deceptive and would not tell the 'truth' about their experiences. It was Crites (1979) who helped us think about what he called 'the aesthetics of self-deception' (p. 107), the ways that people told cover stories when they wanted to fit into dominant or required narratives. However, he warned us of the dangers to ourselves, to the narrative coherence of our lives, when we told cover stories often enough that we came to believe them, that is, to have deceived ourselves into believing that the cover stories told were the lived stories. These cover stories could overwrite our more coherent stories and betray our embodied experiences, those experiences that we had lived.

> *Bruno began to tell us stories. Stories that spoke of his experiences as a young man growing up in postwar Germany, of a man who had become divorced and lost all family connections, of a man filled with sexual desires, and a desire to be a writer.*

The stories, which may have initially been told with a purpose of fitting into dominant narratives, a kind of way to keep ourselves hidden, became stories that we believed were 'truthful' tellings of our experiences. Reading Crites made Vera wonder about the stories Bruno told and lived. Were the stories of his constant moves, of sleeping in ditches or strangers' beds, cover stories for a deep loss and a longing of something otherwise?

Searching for Narrative Coherence

> 'Without memory, in fact, experience would have no coherence at all.'
>
> (Crites, 1971, p. 298)

Years later we again found Crites, this time in a 1986 book edited by Sarbin and entitled *Narrative Psychology: The Storied Nature of Human Conduct*. Crites' chapter in the book entitled *Storytime: Recollecting the Past and Projecting the Future*, drew on his earlier work on temporality and experience. He returns to the concepts of self which emerge from his narrative conceptualization of experience as embodied, ideas woven into the 1971 article. He plays with an idea of identity that we draw forward in our narrative conceptualization of experience.

> 'I'–this self who speaks now–have memories that go back to early childhood, fragmentary and intermittent, but forming enough links with a past to give this present self a sense of having existed over time. The chronicle of memory has many lacunae, yet it gives access to a past that the one who remembers claims as his own, an identity through many metamorphoses.
>
> (Crites, 1986, p. 156)

His ideas about identity, that is, that identity is not 'simply a matter of the organic continuity of a body' (p. 156) through maturation emerge also in our narrative ideas about experience. Visual images of one's face, one's familiar surroundings from earlier times, one's auditory memory (what he calls the experience of the ear) contribute to one's sense that '"I" am rooted in a past with which I remain in some sense identical' (p. 156). However, he helps us argue that 'a self-identical self is not a precondition of experience, but its consequence' (p. 158).

He argues, as do we in our narrative understandings, that 'experience is itself mediated by coded sound, image, language, all presupposing a vast social processing of such forms' (p. 158). For Crites, as for us, 'the remembered past is situated in relation to the present in which it is re-collected' (p. 158). Place, both in where the experiences happened and in the place where experiences are re-collected, shapes the ways that experience continues to be lived, told, relived, and retold.

> By such aesthetic means this 'I' that now says 'I' actively forges, gathers, re-collects its continuity of experience out of the inchoate intersubjective stream of memory. ... story-like narrative establishes a particularly strong sense of personal continuity, because it can link an indefinite number of remembered episodes from the single point of view of the one who recounts or merely recalls the story. This single point of view is the 'I' who now speaks or recalls, and this 'I' which situates my story and distinguishes it from others also anchors which I call my self in its identity over time.
>
> (Crites, 1986, p. 159)

As we draw Crites' ideas into our conceptualization of experience, we, too, see that experience is not, as he wrote,

> [a] coherent life of experience is not simply given, or a track laid down in the living. To the extent that a coherent identity is achievable at all, the thing must be made, a story-like production with many pitfalls, and it is constantly being revised, sometimes from beginning to end, from the vantage point of some new situation of the 'I' that recollects.
>
> (p. 160)

> The 'I' who speaks and recollects is a thoroughly bodily presence, but the self it recollects out of the past, which 'I' own as my own is indeed unphysical, not because it is a soulish substance but because it is a narrative recollection of what no longer physically exists, is no longer present.
>
> (p. 162)

Crites (1971) argues that different strategies are at play when we anticipate the future and appropriate the past. He offers us a more complex understanding of the relations between telling stories out of our past and, even in telling, continue to live stories in our present.

While Crites helps us see the importance of time in relation to narrative coherence, it is Carr (1986) who calls us to further inquire into the link between narrative structure and our experiences and actions. Carr takes 'the conception of narrative structure a step further by attempting to show that it is the organizing principle not only of experiences and actions but of the self who experiences and acts' (p. 73). This sense of narrative coherence is a central aspect to our lives. Vera's return to her experiences alongside Bruno and Markus is calling attention to this in ways that only slowly become visible. Vera's own son is the age at which Vera met Bruno and recalling these experiences has called forth questions for her. It is now that Vera asks herself often what are the people and places that her son can turn towards to allow him to see and experience things in new ways. Who is Vera alongside her son to open up these new spaces?

Experience as a Moral Compass

As we call forth attention to experience, we do so knowing that experience can also act as a moral compass. Attending to experience can change the stories we tell and live.

> If experience has the narrative quality attributed to it here, not only our self-identity but the empirical and moral cosmos in which we are conscious of living is implicit in our multidimensional story. It therefore becomes evident that a conversion or a social revolution that actually transforms consciousness requires a traumatic change in a man's story.
>
> (Crites, 1986, p. 307)

As we contemplate the extraordinary and difficult experiences in people's lives, we are reminded of Eva Hoffmann's (1994) work. In her writings she returns to her family's experience of the Holocaust. She notes that '[t]he experience of the Holocaust, [...] should lead to a deeper sense of what it is to be human, an enlargement of vision, not a lessening of it' (n.p.). It is here that we can sense the deep connection between life, experience and action. We are called to consider the future in ways that account for the past. This turn to story 'makes it possible to recover a living past, to believe again in the future, to perform acts that have significance for the person who acts. By so doing it restores a human form of experience' (Crites, 1986, p. 311). Vera recognized by returning to her experiences alongside Bruno that, for her, care was grounded in experiences, in the stories people told about their lives. Experiences, in this way, act as a moral compass to care.

Summary

In this chapter, we laid out our narrative view of experience drawing centrally on Dewey's view of experience. His criteria of continuity and interaction are significant to our narrative understandings. It was, however, the work of Carr and Crites who more closely linked narrative to experience. Further on in the book, we return to Carr and Crites but, before we do so, we turn to the links between narrative, experience, knowledge and inquiry.

2

Knowledge

Abstract

In this chapter we make visible our ideas of knowledge and knowing. We are, once again, drawn back to pragmatist scholars such as Dewey and Donald Schön. As we inquire into the link between knowledge and experience, we connect knowledge to the personal, to action and ultimately to narrative. At the same time we came to understand that knowledge is continuously unfolding and is embedded within larger contexts that are shaped culturally and socially. As our understandings of knowledge evolved, we drew increasingly on feminist scholars and, later, on Indigenous scholars.

Turning to Experience

The small windowless seminar room was crowded, overfilled with a big table and too many chairs. I took a chair on one side and immediately felt restrained in what was starting to feel like a room with not quite enough air. My first doctoral class after too many years working in schools, I thought, as I glanced around the crowded room. After the mandatory introductions, Michael Connelly, the instructor, began to speak of John Dewey and his theory of experience. I recollected reading Dewey's (1938) Experience and Education as an undergraduate. Maybe I already knew some of the content of this course, I thought hopefully. The instructor went on to talk about his work with Freema Elbaz, work focussed on understanding what they called practical knowledge, a kind of knowledge that was experiential. I sat up a bit straighter, paid a bit more attention. This was not what I had learned was knowledge in my long ago philosophy classes.

Practical?

No, I had been taught that knowledge was definitely analytical, conceptual.

Oriented to practice?

No, I had been taught that knowledge was about logic, about clarity, about truth.

Experiential?

No, knowledge was not about people and their lives when philosophers talked about it.

What is he saying? What is this view of knowledge? How can this be knowledge?

My thoughts drifted out of the seminar room back to growing up on a small farm. It was to my parents that my thoughts first drifted. Somehow, something from what I was hearing triggered memories of my parents. Now, as I revisit this moment, I awaken to the possibilities that there was a link between knowledge and what I had seen my parents living. This connection resonated for me.

Walking in the newly plowed fields with my father in the spring, I remember how he knelt down and ran the soil through his fingers, feeling the moisture, the temperature, the grain of the soil. Speaking softly he spoke of when it might be seeding time, of what crop might best thrive in this field this year, of what the soil might need to enrich it. I listened and wondered at how he knew, what he knew, how he came to know what he knew. But neither he nor I spoke of knowledge.

I remember finding pictures in old magazines and catalogues of new clothes I wanted. I took the photos to my mother, knowing she was busy with all it took to feed a family of 7 on a subsistence farm. She and I both knew there was no money to buy the clothes I was admiring from the shops and catalogues. 'Could you make me one like that?' I asked, pointing out a favored dress. She stopped what she was doing and looked intently at the picture, wondering aloud about the kinds and amounts of fabric required to sew such a dress. 'Was that corduroy or velveteen?' she wondered. 'Is that a check or a plaid? What kind of fabric drapes like that?' She spoke of how the kind of fabric and the printed pattern on the fabric influenced what would be required to recreate the dress. What fabric would work? How much fabric was needed? As she spoke of yardage and cost and difficulty of sewing such a dress, she created pictures in my mind. As I followed her words and gestures, the dress began to take shape in my imagination. And in my imagination, the dress became something I wore to school, to a country dance, to a family gathering. I wondered then at how she knew, what she knew, how she came to know what she knew. But somehow while I heard her knowledge expressed, this seemed a long way from what I would later study of what counts as knowledge.

As my thoughts returned to the cramped seminar room, for the first time I began to see that if we thought of knowledge in the ways that I was just learning about, it became a way to story my parents as holding knowledge. Within such a view of knowledge, knowledge became a kind of living knowledge.

These concepts of knowledge live at the heart of narrative inquiry, of thinking narratively about phenomena that we study as researchers. While in that seminar I first awakened to another way of thinking of knowledge, over time I learned this view of knowledge was grounded in the work of many philosophers, philosophers such as Dewey, Schön, Michael Polanyi; psychologists such as Jerome Bruner; feminist scholars such as Virginia Woolf, Carol Gilligan and Nel Noddings; and Indigenous scholars such as those discussed in the books of Pratt (2002) and McKenna and Pratt (2015).

A Turn to Linking Knowledge and Experience

As we think with ideas of knowledge within narrative inquiry, we are drawn to some of the pragmatist scholars, most importantly, and in the first instance, to Dewey's work. For Dewey knowledge is created by focussing on, and engaging in, processes of knowing – it is through processes of inquiry that we get closer to knowledge. For Dewey knowledge becomes something we do. Within Dewey's philosophy there is a link between knowledge and action. Rather than something separate from action, knowledge is composed in the processes of inquiry and doing.

What Jean learned that day in the seminar room helped her see that knowing/knowledge did not need to be separated from doing, that is, knowing or knowledge was in the action, not separate from the doing. In earlier undergraduate philosophy courses, she had learned that knowledge was pre-determined by patterns of logical analysis.

Working within a Deweyan concept offered Jean the possibility of beginning to see knowledge not as something separate from life and living. As Jean drifted back to memories of her parents, she, for the first time, had a way to think about their 'doing' as embodying their knowing. They held knowledge that lived in their practices, that was their practice.

Knowledge, according to Dewey (1938) and other pragmatist scholars such as Schön (1983) and Johnson (2007), was always in the making, on the way. It was not fixed and frozen but was always in process and always in context. As a person lived in the world engaging within their changing contexts, their knowledge also changed. For Jean, what she heard in the seminar room that day allowed her to begin to think about the knowledge that lived in her father's careful actions in relation to the soil in which he planted his crops. As he knelt down to touch the soil, the knowledge of all of his other experiences of planting and growing and harvesting crops over his lifetime was brought forward. McKenna and Pratt (2015) drawing on Dewey wrote that

> 'every problem that arises, personal or collective, simple or complex, is solved only by selecting material from the store of knowledge amassed in past experience and by bringing into play habits already formed' (Dewey, LW 11, p. 37). Yet, in order to be successful, this 'store' needs to be modified to meet the new conditions that have arisen [...].
>
> (p. 91)

As Jean's father felt the soil and considered the weather, he drew on his experiential knowledge to know what crop to seed in the field and when to begin the seeding. He drew on his knowledge of other years and other crops and called forward habits already formed. He knew he also needed to consider new conditions such as the germination ratio of the seeds he had saved or purchased to plant this year and the current weather patterns. He was carefully modifying this 'store of knowledge amassed in past experience' in order 'to meet the new conditions' (McKenna & Pratt, 2015, p. 91).

The view of knowledge that we begin with in narrative inquiry is congruent with that of Dewey and other pragmatist scholars who had a 'commitment to a dynamic, pluralistic world of experience in which knowledge is a product of ongoing investigation, always limited in scope, subject to failure, and liable to be overturned as the problems of the world change' (McKenna & Pratt, 2015, p. 4). In narrative inquiry we understand knowledge as emerging from ongoing inquiry into lives and living, knowledge which is 'always limited in scope' (McKenna & Pratt, 2015, p. 4). Within narrative inquiry, we shared pragmatist understandings of knowledge which placed the person's knowledge in their actions and their actions within their knowledge. Each person's knowledge was in their action.

Jean wonders now, as she writes these pages, about the conversations about knowledge that she did not have with her father. She did not wonder with him about how his father who grew up in Cornwall in Britain taught her father about how to know soil, climate and particular crops that would grow in western Canada's northern prairies. She did not wonder about the other sources of knowledge from which her father learned. Consideration of how he was taught was a pedagogical concern but is closely tied to questions of the nature of knowledge. Experiential knowledge lives over time and place, is shaped by new conditions for knowledge and is expressed in new contexts.

Connecting Knowledge and the Personal

As we continued to develop understandings of what we meant by knowledge in narrative inquiry, the personal was initially a central focus. Polanyi was the first philosopher who explicitly drew our attention to considerations of the person, the personal, in knowledge. His direct statements on how each person's participation shaped what the person knew were helpful, as we named knowledge as personal, as in the person's actions. His 1958 book was one that Jean recalls being particularly powerful, especially his statement that 'into every act of knowing there enters a passionate contribution of the person knowing what is being known, and that this coefficient is no mere imperfection but a vital component of his knowledge' (pp. vii–viii).

As Jean thought again about her father's knowledge that lived in his actions of growing crops, she knew that there was 'a passionate contribution of the person knowing what is being known' (Polanyi, 1958, p. vii). What, and how, her father knew was very much part of his person, of all of his experiences of living as a child growing up on a farm with newly 'settled' farmer parents who had immigrated from England and of his subsequent experiences of seeding and growing crops. The personal was part of his experiential knowledge. Woven into conceptions of personal knowledge was Polanyi's understanding that knowledge was also tacit.

Polanyi drew attention to creative acts, and, in particular, intuition, guesses and hunches. For him these were expressions of passion, the passionate contribution of him, as a person, knowing what is being known. Tacit knowledge, knowledge that lives in action, gestures, movements, guesses and feelings also shape our narrative understandings of knowledge. Jean's father's knowledge, as lived in his actions, was expressed by smiles, nods, frowns, wonders and speculations. Was the soil warm enough for planting?

Was it moist enough? Was rain part of the weather forecast? What lived in the moment in his actions was not always verbalized and that knowledge was part of his processes of discovery.

Connecting Knowledge and Action

Understandings of tacit knowledge were also reflected in the work of Schön, a pragmatist scholar whose work on reflective practice is also significant to/for our understanding of knowledge within narrative inquiry. Schön (1983) saw 'a kind of knowing is inherent in intelligent action' (p. 50). Schön describes knowing-in-action, 'the characteristic mode of ordinary practical knowledge' (p. 54), as having properties such as 'actions, recognitions, and judgments which we know how to carry out spontaneously' (p. 54) without prior thought separate from the action. The knower is 'unaware of having learned to do these things' (p. 54), as the knower is 'usually unable to describe the knowing which our action reveals' (p. 54). Jean describes that observing her father, as she came alongside him as he knelt in the field, allowed her to understand experiential knowledge as having a tacit dimension. The knowledge was silent but visible if the action, the living, was understood as knowledge. Like Dewey, Schön called us to attend closely to action in order to recognize, understand, the knowledge in the action.

These ideas of knowledge as experiential, personal and practical, our beginning ideas of narrative knowledge, were described in 1985 with ideas such as 'action and knowledge are united in the actor, and our account of knowing is, therefore, of the actor with her personal narratives, intentions and passions' (Connelly & Clandinin, 1985, p. 178). Connelly and Clandinin argued that personal practical knowledge is 'complex because it embodies in a history, in the moment and in an act, all modes of knowing aimed at the particular event that called forth the … act' (p. 178). Returning again to Jean's memory alongside her father, we see that his personal practical knowledge embodied in his history over time, perhaps even intergenerationally, in the moment as he knelt to feel the earth, and in the act of deciding what, when and where to plant is expressed. In that moment, Connelly and Clandinin argued that actions such as Jean's father's action were 'a re-collection, a process of crystallization, out of the narrative unities of life experience' (p. 184).

Connecting Knowledge with Narrative

Bruner's work in psychology was a kind of parallel work to our emerging narrative ideas about knowledge. Bruner wrote that 'knowledge is a model we construct to give meaning and structure to regularities in experience. The organizing ideas of any body of knowledge are inventions for rendering experience economical and connected' (Bruner, 1962/1979, p. 120). Bruner, in *Narrative and Paradigmatic Modes of Thought* (1985), offered a view of two modes of thought that people use in interpreting and understanding their experiences. While the paradigmatic mode attempts to fulfill the ideal of a formal scientific description and explanation by employing systematic categorizations and conceptualizations, a narrative mode of thought is concerned with meanings that are ascribed to experiences through stories. They capture people's own explanations about what they want and how they go about achieving their wants. At the same time as Bruner was offering the concept of a narrative mode of thought in psychology, Connelly and Clandinin's (1988) ideas of knowledge within narrative inquiry, termed personal practical knowledge, were defined as

> a particular way of reconstructing the past and the intentions for the future to deal with the exigencies of a present situation .... a narrative, curricular understanding of the person is an understanding that is flexible and fluid, and that therefore recognizes that people say and do different things in different circumstances and, conversely, that different circumstances bring forward different aspects of their experience to bear on the situation.
>
> (pp. 25–6)

Within their narrative view of knowledge, the situational or contextual nature as well as the temporal nature of personal practical knowledge became more visible and pronounced. Personal practical knowledge was defined as context dependent and in constant composition as life experiences, both personal and professional, were woven together. Personal practical knowledge was moral and emotional knowledge and actively carried each person's being into interaction with events. Living out personal practical knowledge intimately connected each person with the personal and professional narratives of their life. Somewhat later, Polkinghorne (1988) offered an affirmation that narrative knowledge with its 'temporal, schematic linking of events ... is the kind of knowing that is used to understand personal action and autobiography' (p. 111). Drawing attention to the temporal unfolding of life events and actions over time, perhaps intergenerationally, is part of what we see as knowledge within narrative inquiry.

Knowledge as Unfolding, Contextual, and as Culturally and Socially Shaped

But if we leave the understanding of knowledge within narrative inquiry with only these dimensions, we have not yet done enough to show what we know as knowledge in narrative inquiry. Perhaps returning to Jean's experience with her mother's knowledge will help us show a strengthened view of knowledge within narrative inquiry. In Jean's story of her experience alongside her mother, Jean spoke of checking catalogues and magazines for ideas for favoured clothing that her mother could create for her. These were publications that came from within Western narratives showing, for the most part, white women and girls wearing dresses, skirts and blouses situated within European and North American dominant cultural and institutional narratives. They were made with fabrics and in fashions that fit these dominant narratives, narratives that were part of the knowledge that Jean and her mother embodied. Understanding knowledge as shaped by larger cultural and social narratives is part of narrative knowledge and it is always attentive to how knowledge is shaped that is part of understanding knowledge narratively.

In Jean's story with her mother, and with her story of her mother as someone who holds knowledge of design and dressmaking, and with Jean's desire to have clothing to wear that allows her to live out her desired story of herself, we see the ways that knowledge is always shaped by cultural and social narratives. Knowledge, understood within narrative inquiry, is always knowledge that is in context, both immediate contexts such as the relationship between Jean and her mother, and larger contexts such as social and cultural narratives of fashion and women.

Considering knowledge as embedded within, and shaped by, cultural and social narratives is informed by our readings of Lugones' work. Lugones wrote of worlds which people inhabit and of the possibility of travelling between the multiple worlds that each person inhabits. In Lugones' (1987) description of worlds and 'world'-travelling', she described that 'those of us who are 'world'-travellers have the distinct experience of being different in different 'worlds' and of having the capacity to remember other 'worlds' and ourselves in them' (p. 11). For Lugones, world-travelling involved shifting 'from being one person to being a different person' (p. 11). Travel is being constructed, and constructing oneself differently, in different worlds. Lugones' theories on worlds and world-travelling helped us understand something about how we see knowledge in narrative inquiry. We know ourselves, and others, within particular worlds and we can know ourselves, and others, differently in different worlds. Our knowledge shifts and changes and is multiple within the multiple worlds we may inhabit. As we revisit Jean's remembered story of her experiences with her mother, we see her knowledge within the multiple worlds she inhabits: one of Jean's mother's worlds is one in which she knows the skills of European dressmaking: fabrics, design, creation, as well as the technical skills of sewing but she knows as well her daughter's world of wanting to fit into her school and community worlds as a young woman.

As a young girl, Jean's worlds of school were not shaped by feminist ideas even though in the 1960s and onward, feminist understandings of knowledge began to be taken up in the North American academy. Now as we return to reread and think with Jean's stories of her mother's knowledge we are informed by our more complex and historical understandings of knowledge in narrative inquiry.

Some of the ideas about knowledge that we work with in narrative inquiry were, as Ben Okri (1997) wrote, 'planted in us early and along the way' (p. 46) without our consciousness. We learned, for example, from reading McKenna and Pratt (2015) and from reading Pratt (2002), that Dewey's ideas were strongly influenced by early feminists. Pratt shows how feminist ideas of knowledge within pragmatism were grounded in the work of feminist pragmatist scholars such as Addams, Gilroy Perkins and others. Scholars such as Addams were known by Dewey and her ideas were an influence on Dewey. As we read Dewey, the work of early feminist scholars infused our understanding of knowledge in narrative inquiry. As we developed our understanding of knowledge within narrative inquiry, we were unaware that we were being influenced by other early pragmatists who had drawn on ideas from the work of Indigenous peoples and early feminists. Without her awareness of these interrelated ideas about knowledge, Jean, in that first doctoral class when she confronted new ways to think about knowledge in Connelly and Elbaz's work, was also meeting feminist ideas of knowledge embedded within Dewey's conceptions of experiential knowledge.

The ways that early feminist scholars working within a pragmatist tradition took up Indigenous ways of understanding knowledge are also now evident as shown by Pratt (2002). Pratt draws on 'a logic of home', noting that a feminist pragmatist view of knowledge has a starting point within place rather than within character or temporality. Drawing on the work of Lydia Maria Child (1845), Pratt (2002) shows that

> [h]uman knowledge, like being, is a matter of particulars. While it is useful to recognize the connections among things, what they are and how they are known will always be plural and a matter of interaction.
>
> (p. 267)

Early feminist scholars such as Gilroy Perkins and Addams saw the importance of understanding knowledge as grounded in place and in interactions. Pratt draws attention to Addams (2002) book *Democracy and Social Ethics* to show how she

> adopts a logic of home where problems must be understood in terms of their circumstances and where solutions are to be found literally in the situation itself. [...] the only response to the problems of one's place is a method that will find a solution in the place, its people, history, lands and interests.
>
> (pp. 280–1)

When Addams co-founded Hull House with her friend Ellen Gates Starr in a poor immigrant neighborhood in Chicago, her work instantiated the ideas carried in the tradition of Neolin and Sagoyewatha, Johnston Schoolcraft and John Ross. Meaning is, they said, a matter of place, and the flourishing of the place, that is making a home, will depend upon establishing fit relations in the interactions of the place.

> (pp. 281–2)

For these early pragmatist scholars, knowledge is always within each context, each set of interactions, each situation. Pratt brings forward the work of Child to show that

> [i]n the logic of home as Child developed it, the principle of interaction served as the starting place, ontologically and epistemologically. In a context of domestic detail, things gained their meaning and character. By attending to the context, Child could take seriously the role of differences and their value. Understanding and action also required recognition of one's own home and the existence of other homes that served as alternative centers of meaning.

Such homes were not simply other isolated individuals, but complex relations among people, land, histories, and interests.

(pp. 270–1)

As we reread and became aware of these ideas of knowledge that date back many years, we return to reread Jean's stories of experience to see how our ideas of knowledge within narrative inquiry are shaped iteratively, by returning to theoretical works with new insights as well as returning to remembered stories to see anew what we know about knowledge in narrative inquiry. We see the ways that Jean's mother's knowledge was shaped by a particular familial context, a rural farm in mid-twentieth-century Western Canada. Her home was nested within 'complex relations among people, land, histories, and interests' (Pratt, 2002, p. 271) although as she lived out her knowledge alongside Jean, neither she nor the young Jean was awake to the ways their knowledge was nested in these relations. Even in the seminar room, as Jean first recollected her awareness of her experience alongside her mother, and began to name her mother as a knowledge holder, she was not awake to how what was emerging became a view of knowledge within narrative inquiry.

While we can see the influences of the early feminist pragmatist scholars' work on the view of knowledge within narrative inquiry, we were more aware of drawing on other feminist scholars such as Virgina Woolf, Gilligan and Noddings, as we developed our understandings of knowledge. There were, of course, many feminist scholars who shaped our understandings of knowledge in narrative inquiry. We highlight only three here, who, over time, continued to challenge us. Woolf (1977) helped us name the importance of having the safety of time and place to claim one's knowledge in writing, and in so doing helped us see again the intricate ways in which time, place and relationships shape an individual's knowledge. Who each person is, and is becoming, as shaped by, and expressed in, gender, privilege, geography and relationships is part of how we understand knowledge. Gilligan's (1982) work on understanding women's voices as shaped by experience, time, place and gender, as well as by social and institutional contexts, became another theoretical resource for our emerging understanding of knowledge. Reading Noddings' (1983) work on an ethic of care as expressing a particular feminist view of knowledge was also significant to developing ideas of knowledge in narrative inquiry. In her writing, she showed how stories are an expression of caring, a relational way of making sense of the worlds in which each person lives.

As we turned back on Jean's stories alongside her mother and Jean's awakening to how her mother held experiential knowledge, we see how Jean was surprised by the possibility that within this new way of seeing knowledge, her mother was knowledgeable. As we revisit Jean's opening stories we see how her mother, a woman, was almost invisible in terms of being seen as a holder of knowledge that lived in her and in her actions. It was, as Jean named her mother as a knowledge holder, that her mother became visible to Jean in new ways. As we revisited Jean's stories now, we see, over many years, how we understand knowledge in narrative inquiry is shaped by seeing diverse people, people who have been invisible, are now visible. What counts as knowledge in narrative inquiry has shape-shifted to understandings of knowledge as situated in people, and in their relationships with each other, with their communities, with the material world and with themselves.

As we became aware of Indigenous scholars and their writings, we began to see how their views were woven into our views of knowledge in narrative inquiry. Returning to Jean's story of her father, we now reread that story with insights gained from Indigenous scholars who have shaped our work. As Sean reads and rereads Jean's story with her father as a knower, he pulls forward how Elder Isabelle Kootenay has taught him to think about knowledge. Elder Isabelle is a teacher of the land: she turns to her knowledge of the seasonal patterns and rhythms to teach and to tell stories of the medicine wheel. Her stories are of plants and animals from a particular territory, native to her geographical and familial homeplace. Elder Isabelle teaches us to understand knowledge as both intergenerational and contextual to particular places and relationships. She shares how her knowledge is transactional through the stories of her mother and grandmother, both gifted storytellers within her community. She reminds us that the stories passed down are imbued with language and ceremony and are particular to place. Her life is shaped by earlier experiences that are animated by traditions that she has been taught as a female Stony knowledge holder within her community.

Jean's early stories of the farm alongside her father and in relationship to the intergenerational stories of Elder Isabelle resonate with Sean, as they highlight a seasonal rhythm and a very particular relationship to the land that goes beyond the annual routines of seeding time and harvest time. When Jean recollects her early experiences on the farm, she tells of how intimately her father understood the land and his knowledge of growing crops and how his knowledge was shaped by the fine details of geography, soil and weather. As Sean considers Jean's stories alongside Elder Isabelle's stories, he sees how Elder Isabelle is teaching us about knowledge and is pushing us to think in multiple ways of how we view and take in knowledge, ways that disrupt standardized interpretations of a singular or dominant narrative.

Summary

In this chapter, we explored knowledge and its links to experience, as we drew on the nature of experience as unfolding and imbued with cultural and social contexts. The chapter outlines early influences exploring the multiplicity in which knowledge might be considered. Various works on knowledge were discussed including Dewey's works as well as the important influences of early feminist scholarship and Pratt's work on native pragmatism. We laid out our narrative view of knowledge, drawing on diverse scholarly traditions including pragmatism, feminism and Indigenous scholarship. Drawing on these traditions shifted our ideas of knowledge as analytical and logical to knowledge as experiential, personal, practical and narrative. These ideas around knowledge appear and reappear in the book. In the next chapter we pick up threads of knowledge and experience in conceptualizing embodiment.

3

Embodiment

Abstract

By 2000 Clandinin and Connelly had turned to the idea of embodiment, where they think with experiential, embodied metaphors put forth by Johnson. Johnson's (2007) work was shaped by the idea that embodiment is central to cognition, and that it is situated within ongoing interactions with the environment. Embodiment is a social process that draws attention to how we embody stories and experiences. Our emotional expressions reflect our experiences and are seen as embodiments (Neumann, 1997; Sarbin, 2001). Often these embodiments provide us with insights into experiences that cannot be expressed verbally, or are carried in our bodies over generations (Young, 2005). Audre Lorde (1984) drew our attention to the connection between body and text and of the possibility to read the body as a text.

Turning to Experience

I know when I am getting closer to this home place. I can feel it within, pulling on my memories. At the edge of town I am met by a beautiful valley where the North Saskatchewan river winds through the sage hills and prairie grasses, carving out a path of perfection from North to South. I recall the physical geography with fondness as I travel to stories: early stories of First Nations ancestors who lived in this place long ago, before farms and settlement, before busy towns, before travel in this contemporary way. I think about the physical markers when I drive down the highway to this home place. I recall many similar trips home, travelling back ... thinking about this early place in memory. I could feel it within me once again today, senses awakening, taking over as I returned home. It has been too long.

My dad was a farmer who grew up in this prairie town. He had a small farm north of the city, near what the locals call the 13 mile corner. As I turn back in memory to early moments of home, this place stays with me. At an early age my family adopted me. I am from a northern community called Montreal Lake Cree Nation.

Images … I am surrounded by trees, long tentacles, creeping out over the ice rink in this prairie place, the moon watches over me at night pushing back the darkness. Snow piled high, early mornings, it is still dark in this place. I can spot him. He is out there in a fog of memories that stay with me in my much later adult moments. Misting, flooding, tending to the ice, it is so cold out there this morning. Casting shadows now, I can see him moving back and forth with a sense of direction, a certain cadence. I can see him through the farm light, one bulb hastily hung from the telephone pole. I am watching from the bay window at the kitchen table. I heard him get up early and waited until he was well along the way. I used to watch him often from that kitchen table performing this weekly ritual. I wish that I could go outside and help him, maybe play just one more game before school starts.

That ice rink of my childhood was giant in my mind. He constructed it with old wooden boards from the fencing no longer needed. At 6 A.M. the water show starts, frozen particles splinter across the air, spraying, projecting, from the black hose. I can still see it. I can still feel how these early experiences travel within me conjuring and pulling … nudging me back to the outdoor places of my childhood. He promised he would build it and he did, every winter, year after year.

no bumps on that ice, smooth carefully crafted,
weathered makeshift boards, humble boards keep the puck in play,
soft touch, a ricochet watching the puck skip across the frozen surface,
blades glide dancing in this way

My dad was the iceman, and my goalie. He did not know how to skate. We played on that sheet of ice nearly every night during the long lull of winter in this prairie place. I can still see when I close my eyes; his big black boots with yellow tattered laces; this image I can recall looking down, as he held me up going forward. I was only 4 when I first started. He was moving me around the ice … balance … careful step by step through the silence. Grey parka, no toque, faux fur, coldness weathered. These are the early memories of places in childhood that stay with me.

Seasons changing time, with the first snowfall. Running down the lane after school to get to our skating rink I recall. 'Let's go, hurry up, it's getting dark, we gotta play, Dad'. I am thinking it must have been difficult some days for him to follow me, effort needed, slowly bundling up. I can tie up my own skates now. I am getting stronger. I don't need as much help. I will be alright now.

Faster, smoother, gliding edges over time. I am the only one out there most nights. My dad was tired, he could no longer stay out like he used to. I only begin to understand this much later.

These early memories stay with me in the present and are called forth through the sprinkles of snow, ice forming, sliding forward through the sounds of children laughing on an outdoor rink of their own. I hold my own daughters upright now as they begin to move tentatively across the ice. I am on my skates and I hold them carefully, remembering my father's arms on me. These are the good stories, the shaping stories. I wonder as I write about the commitment to care take, taking care of me in this way through the experiences on an ice rink. A physical object between us, the ice rink, a relational place in a different way. We were learning to move in a different way in this place. I close my eyes now. I can still see that rink in my mind taking me home always.

Linking Embodiment to Narrative Inquiry

I close my eyes now. I can still see that rink in my mind taking me home. Sean writes of his experiences on a childhood skating rink alongside his father. He writes of returning to the experiences of a 'home place' and the memories that are pulled forward within his body as he revisits what it means to return home, to travel home, as a physical expression and a metaphor that manifests itself through responses within his whole body. Johnson (2007) encourages us to think beyond metaphor as defined by language when he calls on us to think about it as making meaning in the everyday and mundane experiences that shape and influence our actions.

It is through the everyday realities that we draw on Sean's experience of returning home as much more than a physical rink and the experience of skating on the ice with his father or the physical travel between geographic places. The metaphor within the *taking me home* stories where home and the concept of home and returning home through travel has multiple and layered meanings that continue to shape his experiences in the present. It is in this way a concept to make sense of his world and the interactions that he has within it.

Connecting Embodiment with Metaphor

We came early to the importance of thinking about embodiment in relation to narrative inquiry. Johnson, a Deweyan philosopher, helped us think about embodied metaphors as central to narrative inquiry and to developing understandings of knowledge in narrative inquiry. For Johnson, metaphors were experiential and embodied knowledge. Johnson (2017) argues that if Dewey were alive today he 'would have rightly insisted on always remembering that mind, thought, and language are grandly multidimensional, requiring not just a functioning brain, but also a functioning body that it is serving, which in turn is continually interacting with complex environments that have physical, social, and cultural dimensions' (p. 56). It was with these possibilities of understanding embodiment that we followed our Deweyan view of experience to the ideas of embodiment that Johnson offered us.

Johnson, in his influential book with Lakoff (1980), wrote

> [w]e have found, on the contrary, that metaphor is pervasive in everyday life, not just in language but in thought and action. Our ordinary conceptual system, in terms of which we both think and act, is fundamentally metaphorical in nature. The concepts that govern our thought are not just matters of the intellect. They also govern our everyday functioning, down to the most mundane details. Our concepts structure what we perceive, how we get around in the world, and how we relate to other people. Our conceptual system thus plays a central role in defining our everyday realities. If we are right in suggesting that our conceptual system is largely metaphorical, then the way we think, what we experience, and what we do every day is very much a matter of metaphor.
>
> (p. 3)

Johnson drew our attention to the ways that experiential knowledge is metaphorical and shapes how we live, how we orient ourselves in our thoughts and actions. We were taken with his ideas of embodied knowledge expressed in *The Body in the Mind*, his 1987 book. For Johnson, it is necessary to involve our whole being as we live in the world and come to know. Our understanding, therefore, involves our whole being – our bodily capacities and skills, our values, our moods and attitudes, our cultural traditions, the way in which we are bound up with a linguistic community, our aesthetic sensibilities and so on. In short, our understanding is our mode of being in the world. It is the way we are meaningfully situated in our world through our bodily interactions, our cultural institutions, our linguistic traditions and our historical contexts (Johnson, 2007). Johnson's ideas resonated with our emerging narrative views of knowledge, the embodiment of a person living in the world.

It is Sean's embodiment in his experience that comes forward as he drives into the river valley and contemplates its beauty, its perfection, as he recollects his early life growing up on the farm with his father. The geography of place, the winding river, the farm and the ice rink constructed and lovingly tended by his father shaped his bodily experience and shape who he is, what he knows and how he lives in the world. His body shapes his mind and his mind shapes his body. Embodiment is central to cognition and is situated within ongoing interactions with the environment (Johnson, 2007).

The imagined geography provides meaning for him as he thinks about his own First Nations community, his ancestors and his early experiences within the physical spaces and what this might mean in relation both to the past but also as he imagines forward with his daughters. As Sean writes of returning home he offers glimpses of his childhood home places, which in this way includes his experiences of having multiple homes in his early life, and looking, searching, to find meaning when returning home to the farm of his youth, as well as his First Nations community alongside his daughters in the present.

We see the centrality of embodiment in narrative inquiry in Sean's story as he describes his father beside him on the ice. Sean recollects memories of looking downward at his father's boots as his father held his four-year-old body upright on the ice; he recollects his father moving him slowly around the ice and teaching Sean what it feels like to stand upright on skates and then to be able to move on the slippery ice surface. In one way the story is powerful as it takes us back to another time in Sean's experiences, to another place, a father-made skating rink, and a powerful loving relationship between father and son. We see the relational between Sean and his father, the skates, the lovingly made and tended ice rink made on a farm each winter of Sean's childhood. Johnson (2017) reminds us that embodiment is a social process; it helps us see how story and experiences are embodied.

Attending to Bodies

Sean's story draws attention to what it means for bodies in relation to learn. Sean's body remembers what he learned from those moments on the ice with his father. Sean still skates, his body still remembers how to move on the slippery ice surface, what it means to move and balance. What the body remembers is what Sean remembers as he skates now as an adult and as he teaches his young daughters to skate. What he learned from his father's gentle hands guiding his body across the ice, slowly and carefully, are embodied now in Sean.

As we return to Sean's story, we see Sean's father inscribing his love for Sean on Sean's body through his practice of each year building a skating rink for Sean and tending it carefully. Each winter day for many years he spent time with Sean, first patiently guiding him as Sean learned to skate and patiently teaching him to handle a hockey stick. His dad became Sean's goalie as each winter day, after school and on weekend days, he and Sean spent time on the ice. Even when Sean's father grew older and it was more difficult to spend long hours on the ice with Sean, he still spent some time each day with Sean. On one level we could see this as a hockey-crazed father teaching his son to play hockey. But as we return to the story, and Sean revisits the experience, we see that Sean's father is using these experiences as a way to inscribe his love for Sean on Sean's body. And yet neither Sean nor his father speaks of this story in words. Sean's words *Let's go. Hurry up, it's getting dark. We gotta play Dad.* are words inviting his dad to the game. His words do not speak to his experience. And Sean's father is mostly silent, at least as Sean recollects his experience. His dad does not speak of what he is experiencing in all of these moments, over years and years of daily winter activities.

While it is our stories that are called up in narrative inquiry, our attention is drawn to embodiment by scholars such as Sarbin (2001) who write that a 'complete narrative theory of emotional life must incorporate the observation that narratives are embodied, that such embodiments as crying and laughter are important features of a story. I discuss crying as a rhetorical expression of the embodiment of emotional life' (p. 217). For Sarbin 'the meaning of "organismic involvement" is synonymous with the contemporary meaning of "embodiment" and is the means through which narrative-inspired imaginings can influence belief and action' (p. 217). We take him up to mean that it is the body's involvement through emotion in imagination (see Chapter 9) that is a prelude to action, to change. While we take up Sarbin's work again in Chapter 9 on imagination, we think it is important to note at this point the ways that embodiment is central to Sarbin's narrative conceptions of identity.

Attending to Embodied Silences

Anna Neumann (1997) helps us theorize the ways that embodiment is expressed often, not so much in words but in lives, in the living.

People live their stories as much as they tell them in words. They live them in what they do not say. They live them in attending to the words of others rather than their own. They live them in the gaze that comes with inward thought and inward talk while others all around are conversing. They live them in the feelings that come to surround them, that they give off in sighs and looks and gestures, or simply in the feeling that their presence evokes in others. All of these are forms of telling, though without words, and they are forms of telling that we can begin to read and hear through also without words.

(pp. 107–8)

As we read Neumann's words which speak of living lives, of expressing the relational and the social in silences rather than words, we can see Sean's father inscribing his love for his son on Sean's body each day. And it comes in his living, in the ways he composes his relationship with Sean, how he teaches Sean to attend to who he is in the world. And it is Sean who now embodies that knowledge of the love of his father in his skating. It is as Sean writes his story and as he reads his story with Jean and Vera that 'we can begin to read and hear through also without words' (Neuman, 1997, p. 108). We revisit Sean's story over and over, searching through what is not said, what is silent in Sean's story as we understand embodiment in narrative inquiry. Neuman's words that 'with every text that's told comes a silence that cannot be converted into words or understanding that is fully shared' (p. 92) help us understand that silence lives in all of our stories, silences that cannot convey what lives in the body. Further we understand that 'even in the silence of a story that lives without words, there exists a text to know and to tell, though its telling may occur in unexpected ways' (p. 92). In the silences of Sean's story lives his story with his father and his father's story with him. In the unexpected writing of Sean's story, Jean, Vera and Sean learn there 'exists a text to know and to tell'. We three learn of the embodiment of experience in stories and know anew that 'in every effort to imagine another's life, that accompany every gesture of empathic imagination. It taught me that the stories I hear of others' lives are composed only partly of text; they are also composed of silence for which no text can exist' (p. 92).

Attending to Intergenerational Silences

The silences that live in bodies and in their experiences can become visible in intergenerational ways as Mary Young (2005) so vividly shows us. Young, an Anishinabe scholar, tells of returning home from many months in a residential school where she was only allowed to speak English, where she ate dormitory food, slept in dormitories, wore school uniforms, and was not allowed to unpack her clothing, photographs and artifacts from home. When she returned home to join her family in her northern Manitoba community, she describes the first evening meal with her family.

> As far back as I can remember, we always ate together as a family and that night was no exception. After we (my father, three of my sisters and three brothers, I remember we had a visitor but I do not recall his name) were seated, I asked my older sister to pass the salt and pepper in English. Without looking at me my father said, 'Intanishinabemowin niin awind oma biiting.' (we speak Saulteaux in this house)
>
> My father was a very quiet man but when he spoke we all listened. Before he even finished his sentence, my immediate thought was 'I know we speak Saulteaux in our home. Why would I forget?' But in that moment I did forget. I wonder why it is that I remember clearly when I switched from speaking English to *Anishinabe* and not the other way around. In his caring way, my father reminded me of who I was. The nuns wanted me to forget who I was and to become who they wanted me to be. How could I have unraveled what I had been taught at the residential school for ten months in a few hours?
>
> (p. 18; italics in original text)

Young shows us that her experience in the residential school was an attempt to write over what had been inscribed on her body, what she embodied, from growing up within a loving Anishinabe home. In the moment her father reminds her of her language and calls her to remember what was inscribed on her body, that is, the family language and family stories.

Returning to the Body

While it is scholars such as Johnson who we often think of as first shaping our ideas of embodiment in narrative inquiry, we know the profound impact of the work of women of colour on the conceptualization of narrative inquiry. Writers such as Lorde, Maya Angelou, hooks and Toni Morrison were instrumental in shaping the intertwined ways that embodiment is part of narrative inquiry. Lorde (1984), in her book *Sister/Outsider*, emphasizes the profound influence of the body in mediating all knowledge and shows how people's feelings, or senses, teach each of us about our lives. Novelists and poets help us see that stories are inscribed on, and in, our bodies in ways that can both shape our forward looking stories and limit the possible dimensions of them. Shauna Singh Baldwin (1999) reminds us that we know what our bodies remember. John Prosser (in Ahmed & Stacy, 2001) highlighted that 'skin re-members, both literally in its material surface and metaphorically in resignifing on its surface, not only race, sex, and age, but the quite detailed specificities of life histories. [...] Skin is the body's memory of our lives' (p. 52).

Our lives are shaped by the shades, hues and shapes of our skins. Our bodies shape who we are. Sara Ahmed and Jackie Stacey (2001) in their edited book, *Thinking through the Skin,* are helpful in narrative inquiry with their understanding of embodiment as thinking not only '*about* the skin, but also to think *with* or *through* the skin' (p. 1; italics in original text). Thinking is, in this view, 'implicated in the passion, emotions and materiality that are associated with lived embodiment' (p. 3). Ahmed and Stacey draw on Merleau-Ponty (1968) and his emphasis on embodiment, not only as fleshy and material but also as 'worldly', as being in an intimate and living relationship to the world. As narrative inquirers we, too, attend to the relationships which are worlds made up of other bodies. As Ahmed and Stacey (2001) remind us, narrative inquiry emphasizes the need to always attend to the relationship 'between touch and the sociality of embodiment: one is always touched by others, not all of whom are necessarily human' (p. 5).

These are old ideas within narrative inquiry, ones that have been with us for many years. As we unpacked the ways we understand embodiment in narrative inquiry, we realized the impact of artists and scholars but also redirected our attention to Indigenous Elders and what they help us consider.

Being alongside Elder Isabelle Kootenay, a Stony Elder, helped shape conceptualizations of embodiment in narrative inquiry. Elder Isabelle has been alongside us for many years in research and in friendship. For us, research and friendship are often part of the relational aspects of being alongside. It was through her kindness, patience and openness that she allowed us to deepen our understandings of embodiment in narrative inquiry as she co-composed experiences with us that are rooted in language, intergenerational teachings and ceremony. She showed, rather than told, of the ways she thinks and lives, teaching us gently through stories of animals, plants, and seasonal teachings, through walks that are silent, through prayers in her language, through stories that were planted within her long ago. In these ways she showed us how she pays particular attention with her whole body to the seasonal rhythms and to the plants and animals that are interconnected with her. Her teachings and her ways of teaching show us how embodiment is part of narrative inquiry. She offered us multiple opportunities to reflect on our experiences of growing, living and remembering intergenerational experiences that continue to pull and shape how we, as narrative inquirers, understand embodiment in the present.

Summary

These ideas learned from philosophers, psychologists, novelists, poets, artists and Elders shape our knowledge and have shaped the ways we understand embodiment in narrative inquiry. As Johnson (2017) writes,

> [t]aking our embodiment seriously is a fairly radical existential act. It situates us firmly in our world and emphasizes our relations with other animals who share some of our capacities and actions, and who lack others. It shows us how who and what we are arises from our ongoing engagement with our environments (material, interpersonal, and cultural). It reveals how intimately and viscerally we are in touch with our surroundings, and this contrasts profoundly with traditional skeptical arguments that we are alienated from our world and cannot bridge the gap between mind and world. Finally, it explains how many of our most marvellous acts of imagination and creativity – in morality, the arts, politics, religion, science and philosophy – are possible for embodied creatures like us.
>
> (p. 228)

These concepts of embodiment, resonant through Sean's story, are present in his retelling of stories of his early experiences alongside his father. He vividly recollects the images of the outdoor rink and, more importantly, the centrality of relational connections, stories planted in him early. The experiences live in his body in the present as he shapes similar experiences with his own children and his body recollects how and what he came to know from his experiences with his father. These experiences are still active within his whole body, in some ways serving as reflective guides that, at times, unknowingly and in tacit ways, call him to remember to live out similar actions in his experiences as a father.

Section I

Methodological Notebook

In 1990 Connelly and Clandinin published an article in the *Educational Researcher* in which they first named a way of thinking about research as narrative inquiry. Working together during, and after, Jean's doctoral work, they attempted to find narrative ways to make sense of experience. At that time they outlined their understanding of the possibilities of narrative inquiry.

> The study of narrative, therefore, is the study of the ways humans experience the world .... It is equally correct to say 'inquiry into narrative' as it is 'narrative inquiry'. By this we mean that narrative is both phenomenon and method. Narrative names the structured quality of experience to be studied, and it names the patterns of inquiry for its study ... Thus we say that people by nature lead storied lives and tell stories of those lives, whereas narrative researchers describe such lives, collect and tell stories of them, and write narratives of experience.
>
> (Connelly & Clandinin, 1990, p. 2)

The 1990 article, which described narrative inquiry as both a way of viewing experience and a way of studying experience, was quickly taken up as a methodology, often without an acknowledgement that it was also a view of the nature of experience. This push towards methodology opened up new ways to engage in educational research. Connelly and Clandinin noted that narrative inquiry 'has a long intellectual history both in and out of education' (p. 2) that draws together scholars from diverse disciplines and histories. Even in their early writings, Connelly and Clandinin were clear that experience, lives in the making, was the starting point for thinking narratively. In their book *Narrative Inquiry*, published in 2000, they outlined what shaped their thinking over time, as they engaged with different scholars and in different academic and practice-based contexts.

In the five methodological notebooks in this book, we turn away from our central focus on the theoretical roots of narrative inquiry in order to link our view of narrative inquiry as phenomena under study to methodological concerns. We make these links visible by drawing on an ongoing study in which we narratively inquire into the experiences of Syrian refugee families with young children as they enter Canada and enrol their children in preschools.

Turning to a Particular Narrative Inquiry

As we try and discern a starting point for the narrative inquiry alongside Syrian refugee families, we are unable to name a single event. Instead a number of things collided that brought us to this research and, subsequently, shaped the unfolding study.

Jean calls Vera back to events in 2015 that shaped their work in significant ways.

> Jean: Do you remember Vera when we were at the 'Negotiating Neglected Narratives' Conference in Bergen, Norway in October, 2015? I remember how much the title of the conference spoke to us with its attention to stories that were left untold, pushed to the edges. At that conference we spoke about the work with the Indigenous youth we had been working alongside. We were invited by Elin Eriksen Ødegaard and Geir Aaserud, Norwegian scholars, whose interests are in early childhood and narrative inquiry. The work with the Indigenous youth seemed appropriate for a conference about neglected narratives, stories of people who were frequently not heard. Writing the paper for the conference allowed us to inquire further into the work we had been engaged in. We got to know many people who attended the conference during our time in Norway.
>
> Vera: Yes, I remember we felt resonances with some people and we hoped for some ongoing research relationships. Do you remember the taxi ride to dinner when Suzanne Garvis asked us about working with her on a narrative inquiry study into the experiences of Syrian refugees in Sweden? I was interested. I remember how Suzanne's invitation called forth images that

were part of the news reports of Alan Kurdy's death just a few weeks earlier. At the time of the conference, many people knew something of his story, the small boy and his family fleeing Syria in a boat. He was often referred to as the boy on the beach. It was a tragic, tragic story at the height of what was called the Syrian Refugee Crisis. The image of his small body lying motionless on the beach raised thoughts about the neglected narratives we had been talking about at the conference. He became a human face of a humanitarian crisis. I wondered, in the moment in the taxi with Suzanne, if we would come to know him and his family's story one day.

Jean: I was also watching the news reports and thinking about this new wave of refugees coming to Canada. Years ago, as a doctoral student intern, I was involved with the Ontario government response to the wave of refugees referred to as 'boat people', the people who fled from Vietnam and Laos. I knew there was much wrong with the Canadian response. I was hoping there was going to be a more informed response this time, one that took into account the complex and diverse lives of people. Mostly, I hoped we had learned to see people and not categories of people. When Suzanne asked as if we wanted to be part of a narrative inquiry, I began to consider the possibility. And Vera, right around that time, weren't you getting involved in that new group started by the Multicultural Health Brokers?

Vera: Yes, a few months earlier I began to attend the group that became known as COSI (Coalition on Social Inclusion). It was a group of people who came together to figure out ways, across disciplinary sectors, communities, and government sectors, to form a response to the Syrian refugees arriving in Edmonton. Members of COSI were guided by the aim of achieving social inclusion. One of my graduate students was part of the group and I was initially invited to attend alongside her.

Jean: Vera, I knew that you would be part of the multicultural work. You were so involved for so many years in work with people who were new to Canada. I remember the stories you told me about your aunt leading a home for women who had arrived as refugees in Germany. I think much of your childhood and adolescent years were marked by her work alongside them. As I listened to Suzanne, I knew you would have some insight into the European context.

Vera: Sometimes it seems that things collide, don't they? It seems the colliding of our autobiographical understandings, being amidst a global refugee crisis, and thinking about neglected narratives created a spark. Before we knew it, we were planning a multinational study of the experiences of refugee families in Canada and elsewhere.

The taxi ride, in which our conversation with Suzanne Garvis occurred, led to many more conversations and also to preparing grant applications. We decided that those researchers, who agreed to join in the research, would each apply for national funding from their own country but we would each build in elements to allow us to better understand how experiences unfolded in different social-political and cultural contexts.

As we designed the study when we returned home, our specific focus became on understanding families' sense of belonging, agency and identity as they composed their lives in Canada. We are particularly interested in the lives of young children and their families as they make sense of unfamiliar institutional settings, including schools. Engaging in a narrative inquiry alongside children, teachers and families, our intent is to offer insights into questions of identity-making and agency, particularly framed within what it means for Syrian refugee families to experience social inclusion and belonging. In keeping with the idea of neglected narratives, we knew the experiences of refugee children and families were not the focus of many large studies. For us, however, it was important to study the experiences and the knowledge of the families. We knew from Jean's long ago experiences in Ontario when people from Vietnam and Laos fled to Canada, that the focus was on policies and practices and not on the lives of the people. Vera's experiences within the COSI group also spoke of responses that were often marked by an immediate crisis, rather than understanding how lives unfolded over time. Members of COSI were most interested in what happened over time. It was important for us to consider the processes that marked social inclusion.

Since we understand that experience and life are deeply intertwined (Dewey, 1938), we use narrative inquiry methodology to explore the experiences of refugee children and their families with preschools. Clandinin and Connelly (2000) explain 'narrative is the closest we can come to experience [... The] guiding principle [...] is to focus on experience and to follow where it leads' (p. 188).

Furthermore, the lives of refugees are embedded in social circumstances that are 'puzzling, intractable, [and] no longer amenable to existing theoretical frameworks and social discourse' (Connelly et al., 2003, p. 366). When waves of refugees arrive in countries fleeing from political instability and danger in their countries of origin, there is a tendency to create a dominant story. This dominant story is most often based on limited knowledge about the past, present and possible future lives of refugees. Often the uniqueness of the lives of refugees is obscured and the stories told are told in relation to unknown cultural, political, institutional, familial and linguistic narratives. Despite a strong sense of a global world and a world in which no country has been untouched by the arrival of refugees, the ordinary, intimate and diverse life of refugees remains obscured. At the same time refugees often draw on the memories of their homelands to define who they are and are becoming.

To study forced population shifts of children and their families through narratives of experience, many types of understandings are needed. According to Clandinin et al. (2006), 'we need to understand […] embodied, narrative, moral, emotional, and relational knowledge as it is expressed in [context]' (p. 172). In order to make sense of refugees as culturally situated, and shaped, people who have been geographically displaced, we must pay attention to place, and to culture, which is 'the sum of the stories we tell ourselves about who we are and want to be, individually and collectively' (Maxwell, 2001, p. 1).

Cultural stories, Maxwell claims, are the 'staging ground' (p. 1) for identity narratives or stories to live by (Connelly & Clandinin, 1999), the narrative inquiry term for identity.

From the Methodological to Methods

We are in the midst of a five-year narrative inquiry study with eleven families. We have, with university ethics approval, engaged in months of volunteering in a weekly English language program with mothers and their preschool-aged children. With the assistance of two community-based Arabic-speaking women, who work as cultural guides and translators, we are engaged in conversations with families. We invited each of the eleven families to engage in this research over one to two years with a focus on the experiences of at least one child in each family who is in preschool/ kindergarten and at least one parent.

Coming alongside families in a narrative inquiry consists of writing field texts and, through a collaborative process of interpretation and analysis, research texts. Diverse field texts (data), including tape recorded conversations, informal conversations and play, family photographs and other texts were composed to inquire alongside participants as we attended to the temporal unfolding of their lived and told stories of experiences. Diverse forms of field texts invited participants into the research in ways that enabled them to actively document their unfolding lives so that the complex connections between their experiences in particular times and places can be understood. Field texts included photographs, memory box artifacts, field notes on events or activities to which researchers were invited, researcher journals, work samples, art work and family conversations. Field texts were interpreted alongside participants from within the three-dimensional narrative inquiry space (Clandinin & Caine, 2008), with attention to temporality, the personal and social contexts, and place.

Section II

Temporality

In this section we take up ideas of temporality that are woven into thinking narratively. We first grounded narrative inquiry within Dewey's ideas of temporality understood as the criterion of continuity of experience. Dewey offers a view of experience as over time and shows the unfolding and enfolding nature of a person's experience, experience as in time and over time. This notion of experience is one in which being in the midst, and on the way, is central to thinking narratively. We take up these ideas in Chapter 4. In Chapters 5 and 6 we turn to explore the ways memory is also a central concept in thinking narratively as resonances in experience reach into and over lifetimes, even over generations. These ideas, which point towards what is sometimes called rememory, allow us to see that memories are written in and on bodies, and in and through told, written and visual stories of experience.

4

In the Midst

Abstract

The idea of understanding experience as in the midst of a life is central to narrative inquiry. Experience for a person is always on going, each person is always a work of becoming. We speak of this notion of temporality within experience as showing the making of a life over time, as a process of being 'not yet' as Greene suggested. It is impossible to think narratively if one is thinking of each life as somehow fixed and frozen or as somehow finished and complete. While Dewey is a central resource in thinking of life as a composition over time, we also turn to other theorists such as Carr and Kerby to help us develop the ideas of lives as emboding temporality and in constant becoming. Alasdair MacIntyre offers further insights into this view of experience as narrative construction. Lives are always nested within social, cultural and institutional narratives within which each individual's experiences are constituted, shaped, expressed and enacted. This latter point draws attention to the unfolding and enfolding nature of temporality in that social, cultural and institutional narratives are also always in the making.

Turning to Experience

I worked for a while early in my career as an elementary school counsellor. Elementary schools in Canada are schools which include kindergarten to Grade 6 classes. In the schools where I worked students spent most of their days in one classroom with the same teacher. Some subject matters such as music education and physical education were taught by specialist teachers. I understood my place in the school as one in which I worked in classrooms with teachers and children, and with children and their families in settings outside of classrooms and sometimes outside of the school. I always thought of my work as a kind of coming alongside, standing alongside, teaching alongside, with children, teachers, and families.

Because I worked alongside many children from different grades and different classrooms over several years, I watched children grow and change. I watched them in the midst of their lives. When one school year ended and another began, I was still with children, teachers, and families who continued to want me to be alongside.

I was positioned differently in the school. I did not have one class of children nor did I have a physical classroom. Most teachers were with children from September to June. Over the ten months of a school year, test scores and other assessment measures were made. Late in the school year final assessment measures, including district-wide assessments, were made. The focus was on how each child changed from September to June and on their achievement levels in different subject matter areas. Report cards were written with summary scores and final cumulative comments. In June, as report cards were distributed, teachers said goodbye to children and, in September, new children came into their lives and classrooms. A few teachers kept in touch with some children. However, the contact was usually quite superficial and infrequent as teachers were busy with their new students.

However, I often saw the same children over more than one year, often over two or more years. I saw them in the hallways and classrooms in the spring of one year and then in different classrooms in the fall. My longer term relationships with them made sense to me, as I watched children compose their lives, and as I came to know them in somewhat changed circumstances. I was still alongside as they changed in physical ways as well as in their interests and relationships, in their desires and dreams.

I remember one little girl, I will call her Sandra. Sandra was in grade 2 when I first met her. She was filled with joy and wonder and I could tell she was loved in school and at home. No one ever 'referred' her to me but I met her in the hallways, on the playground, and sometimes outside of school. The school stories about her were of a child filled with promise, as well as stories of her as a kind and generous child, and as a high achieving student. Sometime in grade 4 something changed. She was 'referred' to me. She was missing school, her performance was not what it had been. She had lost some of her joy. It did not take long to learn that Sandra had been diagnosed with a terminal illness. The teachers knew, her parents knew, Sandra knew. I encouraged everyone to make spaces for Sandra to continue to compose her life in ways that sustained her, brought her joy. And, for the most part, other teachers, children, and families did just that, ensuring that Sandra was included, invited to parties and gatherings, and continued to be welcomed as an important person.

However, as June approached, there were those report cards that needed to be written. I suggested no report card be written for Sandra. We all knew that she would be gone sometime in grade 5 or 6. But the report card was a concern that was raised by the teachers and the administrators. What to write? What to say? I suggested writing about what she loved to do, what brought her joy, what her favorite books were, what music she loved. I knew that Sandra would not find it easy to read that she was no longer earning 'excellent' grades. I knew that this report card would be something that her parents would hold as precious when Sandra was no longer alive. I said 'no grading' for what was that about when we knew that her life was almost over. But grades were apparently 'needed' on that report card. So grades there were, grades that were not as high as in other years. While she was in grade 5, she passed away.

A View of Temporality Grounded in Dewey's Theory of Experience

As we wrote in Chapter 1, one of Dewey's criteria for experience is continuity, the idea that experiences grow out of other experiences, and experiences lead to further experience. 'Wherever one positions oneself in that continuum – the imagined now, some imagined past, or some imagined future – each point has a past experiential base and leads to an experiential future' (Clandinin & Connelly, 2000, p. 2). Each experience takes up something from past experiences into future experiences, as one becomes otherwise into the future. This idea of continuity over time, albeit with breaks, gaps and ruptures, is a key idea in narrative inquiry. At any point in time, experience is always something on the way. Time, therefore, is something in the midst.

While we also turn to other authors to understand temporality as in the midst, it was Dewey's idea with which we began. Following Dewey, our lives are temporal. This view of lives as temporal, as situated in time, which is itself unfolding and enfolding of experience, is central to narrative inquiry. The idea of lives as composed over time rather than as fixed and frozen is foundational. We see this unfolding sense of temporality at work as Jean describes her life in the school at two moments within time, the moment when she and Sandra were in the school and the moment, as Jean turns backward to understand her experience with Sandra, a child who was dying.

Jean reminds us that, within narrative inquiry, people are understood as always in the midst. We are, all of us, composing lives that are on their way. 'We are what we are not yet' said Greene (cited in Pinar, 1998, p. 1).

Jean recollects that she entered into her work as a counsellor with tacit knowledge that lives were always in the making, that temporality was interwoven with experience. Crites (1971), in his view of temporality, reminds narrative inquirers that 'the formal quality of experience through time is inherently narrative' (p. 291) and that narrative is 'capable of expressing coherence through time' (p. 294). For Jean, in her experience of being alongside Sandra and her family, we see narrative coherence in the midst of a present moment, situated within a past moment, and leading into a future moment.

Understanding temporality in this way, that is, as not a straightforward linear progression of time, is echoed by Kerby. He notes that 'our lives are temporally determined both by the beginning and the end that our physical being exhibits and by the history that threads between, and even beyond these two poles' (p. 15). Kerby's view is similar to Dewey's (1938) in that 'every experience enacted and undergone modifies the one who acts and undergoes, while this modification affects, whether we wish it or not, the quality of subsequent experiences. For it is a somewhat different person who enters into them' (p. 35).

Donald Spence (1982) offers helpful theoretical distinctions on how we understand temporality in narrative inquiry. He distinguishes between narrative truth and historical truth. Cheryl Craig (2005), drawing on Spence, argued that historians draw on a sense of temporality that explores time-event correspondence, while in narrative inquiry temporality is understood within the context of lives being lived in personal and social contexts. While temporality is present in both historical inquiry and narrative inquiry, the starting point for understanding the unfolding of time is different. Both historians and narrative inquirers see the importance of seeing temporality as in the midst but what temporality is in the midst of differs: for historians the focus is on a more linear linking of time and event with a search for patterns of events, while for narrative inquirers the focus is on a more unfolding, enfolding 'in the midst' sense of lives being composed. While a more linear understanding of Jean's life alongside Sandra would focus on the time-event correspondence, Jean offers an account of how she was attentive to Sandra's life composing. It was the temporal composing of Sandra's life both inside and outside the place of school that mattered to Jean in her account.

Temporality as More Than a Linear Unfolding

Hayden White also helped narrative inquirers sharpen the 'in the midst' sense of temporality. White's concern was with three kinds of historical representations.

These three kinds are: the annals, the chronicle, and the history proper. Needless to say, it is not narrativity alone which permits the distinction among the three kinds, for it is not enough that an account of events, even of past events, even of past real events, display all of the features of narrativity in order for it to count as a proper history .... The events must be not only registered within the chronological framework of original occurrence but narrated as well, that is to say, revealed as possessing a structure, an order of meaning, which they do not possess as mere sequence.

The annals form needless to say, completely lacks this narrative component, consisting only of a list of events ordered in chronological sequence. The chronicle, by contrast, often seems to wish to tell a story, aspires to narrativity but typically fails to achieve it. More specifically, the chronicle usually is marked by a failure to achieve narrative *closure*. It does not so much conclude as simply terminate. It starts out to tell a story but breaks off *in medias res*, in the chronicler's own present; it leaves things unresolved or, rather, leaves them unresolved in a story-like way. While annals represent historical reality as if real events did not display the form of story, the chronicle represents it *as if* real events appeared to human consciousness in the form of *unfinished* stories.

(White in Mitchell, 1980, p. 5; italics in original text)

What White helps us see is that for narrative inquiry, we understand the living and telling of stories as in the midst. Because our interest as narrative inquirers is always on the living and telling of each person's life, we do not understand life as finished but understand it as always in the making, as on the way. In many ways our understanding of temporality stops with the chronicles and we work against a sense of an ending, a finished story, even in the research texts. We try to stay with notions of annals and chronicles in our understanding of temporality.

Life, Experience and Temporality Intertwined

Kerby (1991) provides further theoretical insight into a view of experience as

> *at once part* and whole. The concept of experience can be used to cover the
> whole of a life. [...] and also the parts of a life. Another way of saying this
> is that experiences come to one not in discrete instances but as part of an
> ongoing life, *my* life. Experience gains its density and elusiveness precisely
> through a continuous contextualizing or meshing of part to changing whole;
> the relating of itself to itself.
>
> (p. 16; italics in original text)

In this way, narrative inquirers understand temporality as more than an
unfolding process but as an enfolding process in which each person changes
over time. Time also enfolds us and allows us to make a different sense of
past experiences as one lives into future experiences. Jean's opening narrative
allows us to see how time was at work in the living moment alongside Sandra,
Sandra's family and Sandra's teachers, as well as in the living moment as Jean
composed her storied account for this book. In Jean's account, she recollects
her experience and represents her memories as a told story, one which she
retells with hindsight (Freeman, 2010). Mark Freeman writes that hindsight
is 'a vehicle of narrative reflection, binding together the disparate episodes of
our lives into story' (p. 8) While she lived the moment temporally alongside
Sandra, Sandra's family and Sandra's teachers, it was temporally in hindsight
that Jean could 'pause, look again' (p. 15) and see the ways that temporality
shaped her life and those around her.

Temporality Understood within Narrative Coherence

Considerations of temporality in narrative inquiry return us to considerations
of narrative coherence. Narrative coherence, while part of Crites' view
of temporality, was first introduced within narrative inquiry through
MacIntyre's (1981) concept of narrative unity. Drawing on MacIntyre's
definition of narrative unity, Clandinin (1985) writes,

> as a continuum within a person's experience which renders life experiences
> meaningful for the unity they achieve for the person. What we mean by
> narrative unity within narrative inquiry is 'the union in a particular person
> in a particular place and time of all that he has been and undergone in
> the past and in the past of the tradition which helped to shape him. The
> notion of narrative unity is not merely a description of a person's history
> but a meaning-giving account, an interpretation of one's history. We can see
> within the history of an individual a number of narrative unities. The notion

of narrative unity allows us the possibility of imagining the living out of a
narrative as well as the revision of ongoing narrative unities and the creation
of new ones.

(p. 365)

In this way MacIntyre's notion of narrative unity helped us to further
develop a sense of temporality as embracing a sense of composition over
time. As we return to Jean's stories alongside Sandra and her family, we see
that Jean's sense of temporality as in the midst of Sandra's life was shaped
by her sense that Sandra's experience as a young girl with high achievement
should be allowed to continue, that her report card should either not be
completed or that it be composed in ways that honoured what Sandra
continued to experience in her life such as much-loved books, music
and activities. Assigning her failing or low grades was an interruption of
her narrative unity, a lack of acknowledgement of her experience as in
the temporal midst from birth to death. Carr (1986) reminds narrative
inquirers that narrative unity is an achievement, that for humans, the unity
of self is not an 'underlying identity' but is 'a life that hangs together, is not
a pregiven condition but an achievement [...]. What we are doing is telling
and retelling, to ourselves and to others, the story of what we are about
and what we are' (p. 97). As Jean considered Sandra's experience, she was
searching for a way to, if necessary, still have a report card for Sandra, but to
have one that made it easier for Sandra to continue to tell a story of herself
that made sense to her.

Each social and cultural narrative within which our personal experiences
are lived is also temporally in the midst. Clandinin and Connelly (2000) wrote
something of this sense of the temporal nature of institutional narratives as
they described their first narrative inquiry at a Toronto, Canada school.

Curiously, perhaps we feel a kind of intimacy with the school building and its
institutional narrative. People have come and gone, and we have observed, and
merged, narrative histories with them. But the school building remains and so
does its neighbourhood, though both go on and have their own stories. [...]
the narrative inquiry space pulsates with movements back and forth through
time and along a continuum of personal and social considerations. The
school and community, and the people that come in and out of them, take
on a dynamic interactive sense. The community is experienced as infusing
the school and the school as infusing the community. Histories too have
this sense [...]. The school and the community, the landscape in its broadest
sense, have taught us that they too have narrative histories.

(pp. 66-7)

We need to understand the temporality of actual physical artifacts, such as buildings, resources, books, desks and so on. The physical artifacts, too, shape our sense of narrative coherence.

Temporality Shaped by Social, Cultural and Institutional Narratives

Theoretically, within narrative inquiry, we see temporality as having an 'in the midst' quality. Time is always on its way, always in the making, always unfolding and enfolding. Carr (1986) reminds narrative inquirers that it is necessary to understand time within the larger social, cultural and institutional narratives. For Carr, the narrative structure of lives 'constitutes the unifying form common to two sets of possible oppositions: it is on the one hand the unity of the *lived* and the *told*, and on the other hand the unity of the *individual* and the *social* or *historical*' (p. 184; italics in original text). Carr reminds us that we need to understand our own lives within a unity of the lived and told but that we also need to understand our lives as individuals within the larger institutional, social and cultural narratives.

For example, narratives of school are composed around temporal cycles of yearly grade levels. As Clandinin (1989) showed the institutional narrative of schooling exhibits a periodic cyclic temporal order. Time in schools is organized cyclically into schools cycles such as yearly, daily, between holidays, reporting and Monday to Friday cycles. These cycles are embedded one within the other and are marked by characteristic features such as a certain duration. Each part of the cycle, beginning, middle or end, has certain characteristic features. These cycles are experienced by parents, children, teachers and others as being temporally in the midst. Those who work and live in schools experience time as in the midst of these nested cycles. In Jean's story, she shows how she was positioned, both within and outside of the temporal cycles which shape the institutional narrative of schooling. While she was bound within the annual cycle assigned to each grade, and within the autumn to summer annual cycle, she was outside this temporal cycle of knowing children. Neither the children's, families', teachers' nor her life 'ended at the end of June when a particular grade ended'. Lives continued.

While Jean draws our attention to her experience of temporality in her own life, she also shows her understanding of the temporality of Sandra's life. Jean knew that Sandra's life was framed by a medical condition, one that did not fit comfortably within the temporality of the institutional narrative of schooling. Sandra was a child whose life had an early end point in what is considered a life span. We do not know from Jean's story how Sandra was living and telling her stories but we do know how teachers, and Jean's experience of the clash between an unfolding 'in the midst' sense of Sandra's life, was not congruent with the annual temporal cycle marked by final year-end assessments and reporting.

The institutional narrative of schooling has a strong temporal sense as it shapes curriculum planning, grade levels, assessment policies and final reports to, and for, children and parents. Jean's life, situated as a school counsellor within the institutional narrative of schooling, is shaped by a different institutional temporality than her teacher colleagues' lives. The teachers' experiences were shaped by the need to assess and write a report card that reported on Sandra's progress on the kindergarten to Grade 12 temporal cycle, and the annual grade temporal cycle, not on Sandra's experiences in the midst of a foreshortened life.

It is when the institutional narrative of schooling bumps into an individual's life that does not fit the normal cycle that dis/continuity occurs. What the institutional narrative required of teachers no longer allowed Sandra's life to be seen as being shaped by a different temporality than the normal temporal cycles.

In the Midst of What? Shifting Institutional, Cultural and Social Narratives

Temporality is central to understanding the experience as a narrative composition. As Freeman (2010) argues, 'narrative, rather than being imposed on life from without, is woven into the very fabric of experience' (p. 123). As we awaken to the nested sets of temporality shaped into institutional, cultural and social narratives, Jean's experience with Sandra and with Sandra's teachers drew attention to other temporal narratives, ones that are grounded in natural cycles, in the narratives of nature, of other cultural experiences.

Alvine Mountainhorse, a Kanai Elder and Knowledge Keeper of the Blackfoot First Nation, told Sean, one day in conversation, that when schools and teachers were winding down with June graduation ceremonies and with cleaning and storing classrooms, schools and resources, that the institutional narrative of school with its ritual endings was not in sync with the temporal cycles of many Indigenous people's lives. Alvine explained, 'that it is just starting now Sean', as she spoke of the temporal cycles shaped by nature and land and marked by important ceremonies such as powwows and preparation for sundances, and gathering times such as the ripening times of berries and medicines.

Alvine was reminding Sean of different experiences, shaped by nature and culture. These experiences also interrupted the temporal orderings that shaped institutional narratives so common to our Western institutions such as schools. While teachers were focussed on temporal endings of a year of schooling, many Indigenous peoples were focussed on important cultural narratives grounded in experience. Temporality is still understood as fluid and unfolding, but is shaped by different cultural experiences, ones unfamiliar to those who lived by the school calendar.

As Sean and Alvine spoke, Alvine was eager to get home to her family and community in the South, as there were many preparations for the upcoming summer months. There was anticipation, and longing, for the sustaining seasonal rhythm that was so connected to Alvine's life composing, shaped by narratives outside the structures and schedules shaped by institutional narratives of schooling. Alvine was naming that she lived within different temporal narratives.

While Alvine gently guided the conversation with Sean, she was, in many ways, interrupting an understanding of temporality shaped only by standardized institutional narratives. As we showed in Chapter 2, our bodies feel the shaping influences of temporality and when there are interruptions we feel their power. Sandra's body, wracked by disease that interrupted her life, created a disruption for her teachers. It was difficult to break out of what the teachers' bodies knew as the annual cycle of schooling to focus on Sandra's life. As we wrote in Chapter 3, embodiment is understood as a social process; stories and experiences can be seen as embodied (Johnson, 2017). The teachers' bodies were shaped by their stories and experiences lived within the ways temporality was structured within the institutional narrative of schooling.

These conversations around rhythms and seasonal times continued to unfold for Sean, as Elder Isabelle Kootenay also draws on the notion of temporality using different cycles, cycles around the seasonal times. The seasonal times Elder Isabelle teaches and lives within bump with the institutional temporal narratives of school calendars. Elder Isabelle and Sean met as they both worked within a school board setting and then later as they collaborated in a large urban high school with over 2500 students.

Elder Isabelle came to work with Sean to help him think of other ways to consider student lives beyond subject matter and programming that existed within most large urban high schools. Sean wanted to learn, as well as have Elder Isabelle help other colleagues think of different ways to engage and work. Sean looks back at these moments that present themselves as teachers and guides in the present. When Sean describes Elder Isabelle and their time spent in the busyness of a large urban setting he looks back and recalls students and some staff over time paying attention to the sharp contrasting images of an Elder walking in the midst of young people's lives.

He speaks about seeing her physically trying to negotiate the busy terrain and the literal bumping in the hallways as student traffic moves quickly in and around her as people travel to get to the next class in relation to a daily schedule and timetable. The imagery stays with Sean when he looks back at how Elder Isabelle was teaching them all to think and pay attention differently in the ways we move in relationship to each other in institutional places like schools. Elder Isabelle was first overwhelmed by the hustle and the noise of the hallways between classes but over time some students and staff started to understand and pay attention by literally making physical space by carrying her bag or offering a helping arm. It was a shifting image that marks a clever disruption to the dominant patterns that are manifested in places like schools. Slowly walking and a gentle shuffle alongside others is a physical disruption that caused changes in the ways people physically and figuratively moved over time. This was a teaching in a different way that is connected to a temporal shift that is noteworthy.

At first glance the narrative of Elder Isabelle walking in the hallways of a large urban high school may come off as disconnected but it is the physical response that created a space for understanding the differences within temporal cycles and other meanings attached. When discussing the narrative with both Jean and Vera and how this stays with Sean, he spoke of the image of 'not belonging' and 'radically standing out' in the institution. Sean felt worried about how or if Elder Isabelle would be taken care of when he was not present. He felt a deep sense of responsibility and worried about the toll it might take on her as they together tried to bridge a structured legacy of time and patterns in a school that held very little openings for flexibility or seeing otherwise. This was the first time an Indigenous Elder had worked within this particular traditional sports-oriented school or even walked within the spaces of the hallways. This was a physical disruption to what one in this space would normally experience. It is through the physical disruption to the uncontested and unquestioned temporal structures that other opportunities for learning and paying attention became visible for the first time.

Summary

In this chapter we laid out our sense of temporality marked by a sense of becoming. Becoming is part of an unfolding over time and a lack of linearity. We know that temporality is not only intertwined with the telling and living but is closely linked to narrative coherence. Temporality is shaped by, and lives within, social and cultural narratives. In the next chapter we show that our ideas of temporality also shape our ideas of memory.

5

Memory

Abstract

In this chapter we take up a narrative concept of memory. While in many ways Dewey's concept of continuity of experience remains central to thinking narratively, we draw on other theorists who also show memory as part of narrative temporality. In particular we are drawn to the work of Kerby (1991) and Crites (1971). In Chapter 4 we drew forward Kerby's idea that 'our lives are temporally determined both by the beginning and the end that our physical being exhibits and by the history that threads between, and even beyond these two poles' (p. 15). Yet, he acknowledges that the significance of experience shapes our sense of time. Memory is not a chronicle of events, reflective of a 'simple temporality of succession, of duration, of before and after', instead 'memory, containing the past, is only one modality of experience, that never exists in isolation from those that are oriented to the present and the future' (Crites, 1971, p. 301).

Turning to Experience

While I hardly remember the coldness of the blustery winter day in 2016, the day in the beginning of February would be forever etched in my body. It was my first visit to the surgeon's office – just days after I had been told that the large lump in my right breast, I had first felt days before Christmas, was cancerous. The news, given to me over the telephone by my family physician, was an unwelcome disruption to my life, and our life as a family with a young child.

I was filled with a vague idea of what might unfold, drawing on my experiences as a Registered Nurse, but more so on my experiences alongside Julie. Julie, a friend and colleague, had passed away just months earlier as her breast cancer had metastasised to her brain and eventually her entire body was riddled with cancer. Sitting in the waiting room of the surgeon's office, I vividly recalled the time after Julie was admitted to the palliative care unit. It was a time where each breath had became so hard to take and where in each moment when someone carefully and gently stroked her body, her eyes would fill with pain. Her words were no longer audible and the room echoed with silences, the kind of silences that amplify suffering.

In these moments the only possible act to care was to read out loud the books Julie so loved, to tell the stories of her and our lives, to make visible connections to a life once lived, to people and places that mattered – a life that became increasingly tentative and a painful reminder that suffering can be profound, agonising, and devastating. And while her physical pain was controlled, it was the emotional and spiritual pain that filled each breath.

Memory: Thinking with Temporality

Recalling Julie's experience with cancer remains difficult for Vera. Each time it is a reminder that Julie's death came too soon, and that suffering can and is part of life. Yet, despite these difficulties, it is important to remember. It is important to remember, as this 'is a necessary mark of being human, […] being capable of having a history' (Crites, 1971, p. 292). Remembering Julie's experiences then is a way of acknowledging both Julie and Vera as being human, as 'capable of having a history'; remembering, while making visible suffering, also resists and avoids their erasure. Memory then plays a significant and critical role in creating narrative coherence across time. As Crites (1971) points out,

> [b]ut already in memory alone there is the simpler temporality of sequence, of before and after. Without memory, in fact, experience would have no coherence at all. […] It is already significant that experience has, in its present, this sheer momentary quality. But it is memory that bestows the sense of temporal succession as well as the power to abstract coherent unities from this succession of momentary percept.
>
> (p. 298)

To achieve this sense of narrative coherence Crites acknowledges that we require a sense of order – a sense of what comes before and after. And to achieve this sense we call forth or consult our memory. At the same time we are aware that only some experiences have been impressed upon our memory, which calls forth our sense, at times, that something is missing. While Crites helps us look backwards, memory for him and others is also about a future. 'Almost every place that his memory wishes to rediscover bears "traces of what has to come", as he [Benjamin] puts it at one point in *Berlin Childhood*. And it is no accident that his memory encounters a personage from his childhood "in his capacity as a seer prophesying the future"' (Szondi, 2006, p. 19, as cited in Brockmeier, 2009, p. 129).

In this way thinking with temporality in relation to memory raises questions about what and whose narrative we tell. What events of a life do we cover? And what do omissions of events within life stories signal (Bruner, 2004)? As Bruner pointed out: 'Even if we set down *annales* in the bare form of events (White, 1984), they will be seen to be events chosen with a view to their place in an implicit narrative' (p. 692). And while the temporal form of narrative is critical, Crites (1971) reminds us, as pointed out in Chapter 1, that 'the narrative quality of experience has three dimensions, the sacred story, the mundane stories, and the temporal form of experience itself: three narrative tracks, each constantly reflecting and affecting the course of the other' (p. 305).

It is in Vera's experiences that we can see the temporal unfolding of her experience of cancer, that was preceded by Julie's death. That the mundane experience of waiting rooms and quiet mornings was marked by memories and silences that foreshadowed a future.

The cancerous growth in my body, brought forth memories of Julie, of the quiet mornings and the dark evenings at the end of a long day. Sitting in the waiting room, I too was reminded of the emptiness of the palliative care room when Julie's body had vanished and the possibility to caress her body was taken on a day that signalled spring, not death. The cold and blustery winter day in February, had brought with it shadows of Julie, shadows of the possibilities that life was unpredictable and precarious at best – that I had no choice, but to live with this uncertainty.

As I imagined what would happen, I imagined that there would be moments where I would have to rely on others to read to me, that there would be moments where it would be impossible for others to care for my body without causing pain, that there would be silences. In this moment lived a deep recognition that for the first time in my life, my body had betrayed me, much like Julie's body had betrayed her.

Memory: The Connection to Continuity

Picking up on ideas of temporality, the connection to continuity becomes important. Memory reflects the routes we have created in our lives, yet as Bruner (2004) reminds us 'a life as led is inseparable from a life as told – or more bluntly, a life is not "how it was" but how it is interpreted and reinterpreted, told and retold' (p. 708). This connection between living and telling is important to our thinking about memory and continuity – in parts because '[d]ays or years are no valid currency in the realm of remembrance' (Brockmeier, 2009, p. 115), but more importantly, as we construct our history, '[w]e make up our lives as we go along, and then go back and turn them into coherent stories' (Oakley, 1992, p. xxiii). Coherence provides us with a sense of continuity.

> *My aunt died well over 20 years ago now – her bones brittle from cancer, she had turned towards her youngest sister, my mother. She was afraid to die alone and asked if she could live with my parents. Over time, I had forgotten the difficult moments, of blood transfusions, hospital visits, physicians who infused hope to avoid the difficult conversations about death. The moments that seemed easier were the times where we sat together to contemplate the text of her obituary, the invitations to the coffee after the funeral, the decision about what kind of cake to order, and the disbursement of her belongings. We knew that time was no longer infinite. I was called back to work just days before my aunt passed away and had made the long trek back to Canada's north where we lived at the time. I could not afford to return for my aunt's funeral.*
>
> *When I received my cancer diagnosis, my aunt's funeral blended together with Julie's death and created a sense of dis/ease and worry about how my life with cancer would unfold. I had neither my aunt nor Julie to turn to. Their stories lived in me, they were more than the memories I carried of each of them.*
>
> *Each time I return home, I visit my aunt's graveside, tend to the flowers and weeds that inevitably grow between visits. It really was only yesterday that the funeral hall stood empty again, the last crumbs of cake were eaten, and the dishes washed and put away. It was only this early morning that I sat by Julie's bedside.*

The sense of time is irrelevant to memory – Vera learned this the day she kissed her aunt goodbye, the day she left her mother to care for her dying sister. Being diagnosed with cancer was not an event in Vera's life, it was not an occurrence that was marked by dates or times. Instead, sitting in the waiting room of the surgeon's office disrupted Vera's sense of time and continuity. Questions arose for Vera: Who would visit her Aunt's graveside? Who would pull the weeds? Water the plants? Perhaps, continuity is recognizing that 'our spiritual life is at bottom simply the effort of our memory to persist, to transform itself into hope … into our future' (Miguel de Unamuno in *Tragic Sense of Life,* as cited in Kerby, 1991, p. 21).

Paul Ricoeur (1992) states that 'there is nothing in real life that serves as a narrative beginning; memory is lost in the hazes of early childhood [...] As for my death, it will finally be recounted only in the stories of those who survive me' (p. 160).

But who will survive me? Who will be at the funeral, the graveside tending to the weeds and plants? Can my death be recounted without knowing my early childhood? Whose memories will create continuity? Will a stranger stop by and reach out to remove the weeds that will inevitably grow?

Understanding who we are requires us not only to ask about the events and timelines of other people's lives, but must entail a recognition of who we are becoming. It is here that it is evident that

Our families serve as social repositories for autobiographical recollections from many times in our lives; we revisit favorite episodes, stories, and momentous occasions during holidays and other family gatherings. [...] The beginnings of our life stories are written in our families and when we try to make sense of these stories near the ends of our lives, it is often to the family that we return.

(Schachter, 1996, p. 279)

While memory is the central focus of this chapter, we begin to see how we can not talk about memory without contemplating time and continuity and how our lives are situated in different familial contexts. Contexts that can make time stop all together. This sense of stopped time can only be interrupted by memory.

Suddenly, while sitting in the waiting room, home felt so distant and continuity seemed an impossibility.

Recollecting Experience: Challenging Factual Recountings

In 1999 Patricia Hampl wrote: 'If I approach writing from memory with the assumption that I know what I wish to say, I assume that intentionality is running the show' (p. 28). Yet, we see in Vera's experience that we can not assume this intentionality. Likewise, a narrative understanding of memory acknowledges the ways that experience shapes each of our memories so that memories do not become reduced to factual recountings of events but become more like a recollection of experiences as Crites suggests. While Crites and Eva Hoffman help us to argue for these narrative understandings of memory, we also pull forward other arguments such as those of Mary Catherine Bateson (1994) who suggests that when we tell a story, our retelling of it makes a connection 'from one pattern to another' (p. 11). Thinking narratively is, in this view, a process of making connections, of making memories which are triggered by various senses and which stretch across, over and in time to recollect experience.

> *Walking into the surgeon's office I had no details, other than that the large lump in my breast was cancerous. I anticipated that a stranger, a man, I neither knew nor wanted to know, would look at my body and touch my breasts – and that his touch could betray me, for I had no certainty that he cared. I had no sense of who he was. I remember sitting close to the edge of the chair in the waiting room, wondering if it would be better to leave now.*
>
> *It has been months now that I finished the last radiation treatments that came once the surgery and chemotherapy was completed. There were many times where I felt lost, where the feeling of being betrayed by my body persisted, and where the uncertainty on how life would unfold became overwhelming. There are many moments that I cannot remember, where the stories are forgotten, repressed, or perhaps remain too difficult to tell.*
>
> *Yet, I do remember clearly the first sentence spoken by the surgeon on entering the exam room on that cold and blustery day in February. Without looking at me, he opened the door with such force that I moved back in my chair, and as he sat down with gusto, he proclaimed, without yet looking at me, 'I am on your team! We got this!' I recall, thinking in that moment with great certainty, that I should have left the waiting room.*
>
> *I had never asked for a team, nor was I certain that he saw me as being part of the team. I wondered briefly about whether Julie had had a team, and if so who had been part of her team? I too wondered if it was her team that had failed her – that had allowed death to happen at a time when her two young children still called for their mother. In the brief moments in which he told me about the treatment options and the accompanying odds of survival, I wondered who he was. What shaped his notions of team? What was a team to him? Did he think that being part of a team would make me feel more comfortable? Did he think that the survival rates would be easier to accept amidst a team? I wondered what were his experiences of, and on, a team? Why did it matter to him that there was a team?*
>
> *While these were all important questions, what I wanted to ask him most of all was if there were times when his body had betrayed him. And if indeed his body had betrayed him, what did it feel like? How was his life different after the betrayal? I too wondered if he would be willing to read out loud to me when his sense of 'We got this!' would prove to be untrue. When his team had failed.*

The surgery date came and went and, not long after the surgery, I left the hospital. The tumor, which turned out to be multiple tumors, was removed and the surgeon, perhaps, was right in that he 'got this one!' – I wonder if perhaps his focus on the tumor was his way of coping. Rather than working with me, he was able to remove himself from the possibility of betrayal and the pain that this could call forth. Perhaps the constant talk about survival rates, called forth battle scenes, of wars lost and won – and most wars have armies – teams perhaps, that know what to do when, where one soldier or surgeon is necessary, yet replaceable. Where we are better off to not know who the other is, where we do not have to face our own vulnerability or precariousness. I wonder what Julie would have said to him? Would she have asked him about his sisters, aunts, or mother? What would have happened if he would have thought about them, while he cared for me? And I still wonder if he really thought that treating cancer was like fighting a war.

There are moments where Vera wonders how the surgeon she saw would have recounted his interactions with her. Would some of his sentiments be the same? Would he recognize himself in Vera's retelling of her experience? Would it matter that the accounts of their experiences are different? That they each might carry different memories? It is Kerby (1991) who helps us see that '[t]he question concerning the veridicality of memory, however, is not cleared up by simply saying that the past is relived or remembered, for there is always the influence of the present perspective to contend with' (p. 24). Being alive, for now, allows Vera to tell her story differently. She makes no claim that her knowledge of, or recounting of, her experiences is an objective and warranted claim. Vera recognizes that her past experiences alongside her aunt and Julie are intertwined with her experiences; they shape the ways in which Vera comes to know. Jean-Paul Sartre (1964a) points out that

> For the most banal event to become an adventure you must [...] begin to recount it. This is what fools people: a man is always a teller of tales, he lives surrounded by his stories and the stories of others, he sees everything that happens to him through them; and he tries to live his own life as if he were telling a story.
>
> (p. 39)

If Sartre is right, then we need to inquire into the stories that live around Vera's surgeon. What stories is he telling himself? What stories does he live within? Does memory, in some contexts, become 'a curious amalgam of fact and fiction, experiences and texts, documentary footage, dramatizations, movies, plays, television shows, fantasies, and more' (Freeman, 2010, p. 101)? Or is it as Bruner (2002) suggests that what stories do is like that: we come to conceive of a 'real world' in a manner that fits the stories we tell about it, but it is our good philosophical fortune that we are forever tempted to tell different stories about the presumably same events in the presumably real world.

(p. 103)

While we challenge the factual recounting of experience, and echo Carr's (1997) scepticism of historical accounts, we are also mindful that

> [...] to deny the truth of memory in order to disarm moral and ethical power [...] is an efficient way of controlling masses of people. It doesn't even require much bloodshed, as long as people are entirely willing to give over their personal memories. Whole histories can be rewritten.

(Hampl, 1999, p. 32)

Yet, can we give up our personal memories? Memories seep through the scars on our bodies that mark some of us as survivors of cancer.

> *The scar on my right breast is visible – I neither cover it or hide it. That day in the swimming pool the eyes of the young girl in the change room see my scar and she can not help but remember her aunt.*

Can these marks, visible to the young girl in the change room of the swimming pool, be rewritten? Or can we write our lives between the lines of life and death, between fact and fiction?

Memory and Forgetting

While the young girl remembered her aunt, there was also an acknowledgement that she had forgotten the unfolding details of her aunt's life. Her memory had failed and a sense of forgetting settled in. At times forgetting is like disremembering; yet, as David Rubin (1986) points out, '[f]ailures of memory [...] have the potential to teach us a great deal we would not learn easily in other ways' (p. 16).

At other times, the link between memory and forgetting speaks to the trauma people have experienced. It is here that we see the close link between remembering and forgetting.

> [C]ertain traumatic events cannot – or cannot readily – become narrativized; they may be incomprehensible, unspeakable. And insofar as the event *is* narrativised, it may lose the intensity and force of the recalled trauma precisely

by trying to render it comprehensively. 'The danger of speech, of integration into the narration of memory', she [Caruth, 1995] writes, 'may lie not in what it cannot understand, but in that it understands too much' (p. 154).

(Freeman, 2010, p. 7)

While narrative has the ability to show complex temporal experiences (Brockmeier, 2009), there is a need to understand that '[t]he remembered self is unavoidably intermingled with the remembering self' (p. 121). Narrative in this way shapes remembering. Kerby (1991) further expands on this idea and draws our attention to differences between remembering and memory.

But if retention is part and parcel of present consciousness, then what we normally mean by the word *remembering* must be distinguished as a second form of memory. *Remembering,* or *recollection,* refers to acts which intend a content that is no longer an operative part of the living present. [...] There is, however, one condition built into memory, and this is the 'nowness' of the 'then', or the fact that memory implies a present act of recollection that is temporally distinct from the time which is recollected. If one has, in such an experience, lost the awareness of the present in which the recollection occurs, then one can no longer talk of memory but rather of hallucination, delusion, or some such state.

(pp. 23, 24; italics in original text)

Remembering and forgetting are complex processes; they are not fixed accounts of memory. As Vera points out they live in our bodies, they are called forth through the scars on our bodies, through smells and images that call forth memories. A reminder for us that to think narratively is to think with embodiment. '[R]emembering is not simply a process in the head!' (Crites, 1971, p. 301). When the young girl in the change room of the swimming pool sees the scar on Vera's breast we can see that the

disentanglement' of others' memories from one's own, of the actual from the fantastic – which presumes that it is somehow possible to extricate ourselves from history and, in essence, to reconstruct our identity anew and afresh, without spectral adornments – cannot be brought to completion.

(Freeman, 2010, p. 111)

It is here that Freeman helps us see that 'the work of hindsight must go beyond the particularities of 'my history', into the larger history in and through which one's life assumes its distinctive form' (p. 112).

It is only a few days ago that Robin e-mailed my husband and asked if she could talk with me, that there is something. Without saying the word breast cancer,

I have a sense that this is why she is reaching out. I know I am still weary and tired from the past two years – knowing that I have yet to regain my energy and strength, that I still do not trust my body, that I still understand so little about those who have come to provide care to my body, but who so rarely, if ever, knew me beyond the number on my red card, the card that has marked me forever in a system of care as having lived with cancer.

As I carefully respond to her email, I am mindful that in rare moments we have a choice about who is on our team. That in rare moments we can ask the young and energetic surgeon: who are you? And why do you care?

While I responded to Robin with a sense of care, knowing she too has young children that still call for her, I failed to tell her about my ongoing struggles. Each day when I look at my body, I notice the black inked dot just slightly to the left of my sternum. The inked dot, marked the careful calibration of where to place the radiation – the careful placement is necessary to avoid potential damage to the heart and to body parts untouched by cancer. And as I notice the dot my eyes are drawn to the scar on my right breast and I remember the deep blue eyes of the young girl at the swimming pool locker.

As we contemplate notions of remembering and forgetting, we are reminded that 'a man is always a teller of stories, he lives surrounded by his own stories and those of other people, he sees everything that happens to him *in terms* of these stories and he tries to live his life as if he were recounting it' (Sartre, 1964b, p. 64). We see this connection in Vera's experience alongside the young girl with the blue eyes in the swimming pool. Remembering and forgetting are connected to a community of life stories, to listeners and those who attend to our lives in ways that grasp or perhaps hear what we have experienced (Bruner, 2004).

Retelling Connections: Making Memories

Memories are more than a string of events or a chronicle of one's life. Memories, like histories, are about possible sets of relations and '[t]hese sets of relationships are not, however, immanent in the events themselves; they exist only in the mind of the historian reflecting upon them' (White, 1978, p. 94). We read into the events and make connections and in turn make and remake memories. At times this is done in an effort to create narrative coherence. Carr (1986) points out 'to attribute narrative coherence to real events is, according to some theorists, wishful thinking at best' (p.13), or put otherwise '[a]t best narrativization dresses up reality, reflecting our need for satisfying coherence, and, if we really believe it, derives from wishful thinking' (p. 15).

Playing with the idea of making memories recognizes the capacity of others and ourselves to imagine our future. It calls us to anticipate what is yet to come (Carr, 1997). Making memories requires us to be wakeful to a complex temporal structure (Carr, 1997) – one that can and does forever change. This idea of being playful is emphasized by Carr (1997) when he notes:

> Louis Mink was thus operating with a totally false distinction when he said that stories are not lived but told. They are told in being lived and lived in being told. The actions and sufferings of life can be viewed as a process of telling ourselves stories, listening to those stories, acting them out, or living them through. [...] Sometimes we must change the story to accommodate the events; sometimes we change the events, by acting, to accommodate the story.
>
> (p. 16–17)

And, as we begin to engage in playful ways with memory, Dillard (1987) reminds us that the writing of memoirs can impact memories.

The Emotional Meanings of Events: A Turn towards Memory

And as we make and remake memories, it is important to see memory as palpable and precise and that it allows the emotional meanings of events to be recognized. Hoffman (1994) in her *New York Times* book report develops a notion of resonant remembering which 'allows people to look at not only what happened to them, but, primarily, at what happened within themselves' (n.p.). She reflects on Mr. Appelfled's work and states:

> The need, he thinks, is for the kind of palpable, precise, personal memory in which the emotional meaning of events is recognized, for subjective thought, and for the probing of survivors' own internal journeys. [...] Therefore, Mr. Appelfeld believes, it is necessary to bring the past into the sphere of full and felt memory, 'to remove the Holocaust from its enormous, inhuman dimensions and bring it close to human beings.'
>
> (n.p.)

Some of these memories call forth emotions that speak to a deep pain, while others remind us that '[we] all live in the midst of memories of rickety chairs, first kisses, and painful separations, irrespective of their age and ours and of whether we want to or not. [And we must recognise that for] some, involuntary memories are a precious gift' (Brockmeier, 2009, p. 115).

We also draw on writers such as Clark Blaise (1993) and Baldwin (1999) to show that memory within a narrative inquiry view is also written on, and in, bodies, inscribed by larger social, cultural and institutional narratives. The idea that memory, emotions and embodiment are linked was taken up in Chapter 3. And as we return to Vera's experience we also see the link to imagination.

> *Yet, the inked dot is more than a carefully placed marker. While the ink dot holds memories, the permanent marker also continuously reinscribes my experiences in and on my body. While the operating room, the chemotherapy ward and the radiation chamber have become more distant in my memory, the failure of my memory has become increasingly troublesome. I no longer can remember the names of people I should know. I no longer can recall the names of places important to the stories I tell or live. I can no longer remember the dates of events, or place events in carefully constructed sequences. I no longer can remember. It is in more recent times where I have had to acknowledge the importance of my memory. I no longer attend social functions alone, or walk busy hallways at work out of fear that I should have recognized someone I did not. I carefully construct social encounters, and if at all possible avoid them.*
>
> *There are times when people smile at me, call my name, or come forward to touch my arm or give me a hug and I can neither recall their name, nor the reasons why I should know them. I dislike hugging strangers.*
>
> *Yet, perhaps the greater betrayal is the sense that while I sometimes remember people's names, I can no longer rely on this information out of fear that my encounter with them has never happened in actuality. I dislike hugging strangers.*
>
> *It is in these moments that I realize that my imagination fills in the blanks, where once my memory was.*

Summary

In this chapter we laid out how we think of memory in narrative inquiry. Our thinking is marked by notions of temporality that connect and draw forward continuity while, at the same time, challenge factual recounting. We show that memories are complicated as they are shaped by forgetting, emotion and imagination. In the next chapter we consider temporality from an intergenerational perspective.

6

Intergenerationality

Abstract

Temporality within thinking narratively is also intergenerational as stories are told across generations and become part of family and community stories. These lived and told intergenerational stories also shape the places in which we live. Thus temporality across generations, and as taken up in thinking narratively, has social, physical and familial expressions within a person's stories. We turn to writers such as Heilbrun and Young to show how these intergenerational reverberations are part of each of our stories. Writers such as Elizabeth Stone help us see how temporality is woven into family stories that shape individual's identity making, including stories of a person's place in the world. Stone, Bateson, Elder Isabelle Kootenay and Elder Francis Whiskeyjack address the power of intergenerational stories in thinking narratively as they shape our becoming and reverberate through our life-making.

Turning to Experience

I am a Settee and a Kingfisher
  These names are filled with meaning,
  A son and grandson from northern woodland places.
  In this place, surrounded by trees and lakes, grasses and plants, I know I am Woodland Cree.
  When I go back home to early places, the stories are always in movement, shape-shifting compositions. I am recalling stories each time I return home.
  Carrying them back, carrying the stories with me each time,
  they fill my body,

caring for them in this way can be heavy

I wonder who I am in these places, home-places, home-communities I have come to know.

Bits and pieces of a life is what I come to understand each time. I am trying to put the pieces of me together over time.

Meeting my Grandfather Jim Settee

There is a story told of my grandfather that I first heard through a documentary entitled Jim Settee: The Way Home *by filmmaker Jeannie Corrigal. In the film, she shares a story of a young boy who has gone missing in the northern forests of Saskatchewan. I recall my feelings as I listened to this story for the first time, recalling how it resonated with my own experiences, how it stays with me in the present. In the story of the lost boy, family and community members were starting to panic after two days of searching in the dense forests of northern Saskatchewan. They had not found him; they were starting to lose hope. My grandfather was away at this time and the community was hoping he would return soon to help with the search, as he was a well-known guide in the area. When Jim Settee returns to the community, he asks the family and the searchers where they had been looking and, more specifically, he asks where the boy had entered the forest.*

He tells the people to stay back. He will go alone. My grandfather tells his story in Cree. He recalls, in the film, how he entered the forest and how he stopped, listened carefully in silence, looked around, attending to what is both seen and unseen. He paid particular attention to the moss and, still speaking in Cree and through gestures, he showed how the moss moves differently and how it is marked by the imprints of humans and animals. He explained how to notice the markings that humans and animals leave and told of how, from his earliest memories, he, as a young boy, had been taught to read the forest. As he continued to tell, he explained how he walked straight into the forest, guided by the moss markings and the knowledge that he carried with him from these early teachings. He recalls almost walking right over the lost boy because of the dense forest covering. When my grandfather found the boy, he was so scared he could not even talk. He was shivering and huddled over. My grandfather told how he sat there with the little boy and held him for a long time with no words before he picked him up in his arms and walked him back to his family and the community. He helped him find a way home again, he said.

The story resonates with many in the community as well as with me. I, too, was finding my way home. I draw forward meaning from my grandfather's story, shared in the film, into my present life. The story speaks to the possibility of finding a way home that moves beyond understanding home as a physical place. I draw often on that teaching. My sister now caretakes the place where my grandfather lived.

I think, now, about the stories that continue to be shared with me. My grandfather was a trapper, guide, and hunter. As I learned through the stories shared in his community, I learned he was also a firespotter and advocate of our Woodland Cree community throughout the North. He could write and read in English, Cree, and syllabics. He believed strongly in the Creator and, later in his life, became the oldest ordained Anglican Minister in the North. He worked tirelessly to create work opportunities for people and sovereignty for his people through political and land rights advocacy.

Sliding back: Meeting my Grandfather for the first time

The story of the lost boy resonates with me, as I think of going home to my community for the first time at the age of seventeen and anticipating meeting my grandfather, Jim Settee. In the early moments of meeting him, I recognized how important he was to my family and to the larger community. I remember him sitting on the couch at my auntie's house during our first meeting and watching family members bring him tea; it was clear they took care of him in good ways.

I recall him asking, in Cree, for me to come sit beside him. I understood what he was saying. I still remember the feelings that rushed over me: everyone looking at us, everyone waiting for a response. A space suddenly cleared. I moved alongside.

He was a kind and welcoming man. I knew that, in my whole body, from how our initial meeting felt. He had a soft voice and gentle mannerisms that settled me. His face was marked with lines, aging memory markers. He had white hair, carefully combed. I remember, for the first time, that I could see myself in someone. It was an experience that stays with me. I remember clearly that sense of seeing myself in someone else. Our eyes are both brown, matching replicas. His eyes pulled me in on that first encounter. His presence made it easier for me to sit with him, to sit with what I did not know, and to embrace the discomfort with my full body. I remember his glasses resting softly in the pocket of his flannel shirt.

I remember myself, a young man with flowing hair, sitting beside him. I wore a long grey checkered shirt and blue jeans. I hoped I looked presentable to him. I pushed my hair respectfully out of my eyes but, even so, I had a hard time looking up. It was easier to keep looking down.

I recall Grandpa Jim holding my hand … he put his hand on my face. He did this like he could not see me or, perhaps, it was in a way that showed that, while he had not seen me for a long time, he still recognized something in me. No words were said between us. Tears began to well at the corners of my eyes; it was more difficult to breathe.

He spoke in Cree, barely audible … to my sister. She explained what he was saying.

'I was too old to keep you. I am sorry. You are home now.'

These early memories are captured in a picture taken by my sister that day I met Grandpa Jim Settee. The moment was filled with intensity. Even now, as I write these words, I feel the way my body felt that day. I saw Grandpa only one more time before he passed in that first year of my re-turning home. I wish our time could have been longer.

Intergenerational Family and Community Stories

Temporality is understood as stretching across generations in gendered ways, that is, in the available form and plot lines of stories. Heilbrun (1988), in her writing on women's autobiographical writing, showed how particular storylines, over generations, have shaped the kinds of stories available for representing women's lives and, perhaps, for the ways women can live their lives. She writes '[w]omen writing of their own lives have found it no easier to detach themselves from the bonds of womanly attitudes' (p. 22). She writes that such storylines handed down temporally have shaped the stories that women can write, and questions whether women can tell and live their lives outside the handed-down storylines.

> What matters is that lives do not serve as models; only stories do that. And it is a hard thing to make up stories to live by. We can only retell and live by the stories we have read or heard. We live our lives through texts. They may be read, or chanted, or experienced electronically, or come to us, like the murmurings of our mothers, telling us what conventions demand. Whatever their form or medium, these stories have formed us all; they are what we must use to make new fictions, new narratives.
>
> (p. 37)

Heilbrun helps us see temporality as intergenerational through the ways that language and storylines shape our relationships, our stories to live by, our identities. She calls us to see the ways these intergenerational narratives are not neutral but are handed down within familial, institutional, cultural and social narratives. In these ways they shape our present and future lives and experiences.

In *Black Sheep and Kissing Cousins*, Stone (1989) helps us see one way of understanding how intergenerational family stories shape us, stories that are told of us such as stories of who we are (the smart one, the pretty one) and who our ancestors were (aunts who eloped or ran away). These are the stories told within families that fit within contexts over time. Family stories impart a sense of belonging and of shared history as well as stories that help us to define ourselves. They are the stories that grant us access to our families. She points us to Robert Frost (1914), who writes, 'Home is where, when you have to go there, they have to take you in' (pp. 122–3). Stone also drew attention to the ways in which the 'particular human chain we're part of is central to our individual identity. Even if we loathe our families, in order to know ourselves, we seem to need to know about them, just as prologue. Not to know is to live with some of the disorientation and anxiety of the amnesiac' (p. 7). And this is one way in which we can understand the intergenerational temporality in narrative inquiry, this focus on the individual and the ways that family stories can shape individual identities and family identities.

Attending to Fragments: Composing Intergenerational Stories

While Stone and Heilbrun are helpful in understanding temporality over generations, we also see the more complex intricacies of the interwoven relations of temporality, people and place(s) that become apparent in Sean's story. Sean tells of learning, from viewing a documentary film and from meeting his grandfather, of some of *the pieces* of himself. He learns how others have storied his grandfather and how his grandfather has storied himself in relation to Sean. In the documentary, Sean sees people from his grandfather's community seeking his grandfather's help to find a lost child. His grandfather, storied as a *well-known guide in the area,* draws on his knowledge of the particular area, of the interconnections among plants and animals, of the relationships that composed this particular place, in order to seek the lost child and to offer comfort when he found him. This story of his grandfather, retold in the film, helps Sean begin to understand some of the family and community stories that have shaped his grandfather over time. These stories are not ones Sean knew as he was growing up but are ones that came to him later, as he met his grandfather, his mother, his sisters and brothers, and community members.

We see in Sean's account, stories that are *pieces of* Sean. What we mean by the idea of pieces of Sean are not disconnected fragments that are found and put together into certain and distinct patterns to compose

Sean. Rather these stories create an intergenerational web composed by the land, individual people, communities, places, and sentient and non-sentient beings, that storied Sean into being and that Sean now uses to compose stories of who he is and is becoming. As Sean learns stories of his grandfather, he knows that these stories of his grandfather shaped the stories that family and community tell of Sean, stories in which Sean was the young child who could not be kept because his grandfather was *too old* to keep him. These were stories that were kept alive by his community and his family even as Sean was in another home, another place, until he was seventeen years old. During Sean's childhood, he knew that he was brought to his adopted home and that he came from another place, although he imagines/does not imagine that there are stories of him that live within an intergenerational web of stories in another place, in other places. MacIntyre (1981) reminds us of the ways the stories of our lives are embedded in the communities

> from which I derive my identity. I am born with a past; and to try to cut myself off from that past, in individualist mode, is to deform my present relationships. The possession of an historical identity and the possession of a social identity coincide. [...] What I am, therefore, in key part what I inherit, a specific past that is present to some degree in my present. I find myself part of a history and that is generally to say, whether I like it or not, whether I recognise it or not, one of the bearers of a tradition.
>
> (pp. 205–6)

For Sean, he awakened to the ways that he was a bearer of the intergenerational stories of which he was a part.

As he watches the documentary film, Sean recollects an earlier time when he met his grandfather for the first time. He knows his grandfather spoke to him in the Cree language and that he also communicated to Sean via gestures and looks. Community and family members clustered together in the place where Sean first met his grandfather. There is a moment and physical place created in order to allow Sean to sit beside his grandfather. And in that moment, in Sean's telling of their meeting, Sean recollects the details of how his grandfather looked, and remembers his physical presence, a presence that allows Sean to recognize himself and to feel welcomed into his presence. Sean recollects details of the meeting: sitting beside him; his own long hair and the need to push it back from his face; his shirt and jeans; his hope that he *looked presentable to him*. Sean, too, remembered his grandfather holding his hand, and putting his hand on Sean's face. *No words were said between us. Tears began to well at the corners of my eyes; it was more difficult to breathe.* As they sat together, his grandfather, an old man, told Sean a story of how he was unable to keep Sean with him, with his family, as a young child. But he also lets Sean know that Sean is now home. And in that moment of meeting, we see Sean's stories of who he is, and is becoming, begin to intertwine with his grandfather's and his grandfather's community stories of who he is, who their community is and who Sean is in those stories. Sean both knows/does not know all the stories that live in that place. As Sean's grandfather welcomes Sean home, we understand the opening of questions about the interweaving of place, home and temporality across generations.

Pratt (2002), a pragmatist philosopher, writes of the logic of place and the logic of home. Pratt notes the logic of place 'made a case for cultural pluralism in places by adopting a way of understanding the relationship between people, culture, and home', which 'makes explicit the elements that sustain different cultures and interactions among them: history, people, practices, and land. The logic of home focuses on the complex relations that constitute the interaction of difference within culturally distinct communities' (pp. 228–9). And so we see the logic of home at work as Sean's grandfather welcomes him *home*, into the storied history of people, practices, and land interwoven.

Drawing on Child, Pratt (2002) shows the history of place 'is found in the "domestic detail," the particulars of the lives and relations that occurred in a particular location' (p. 235). We see this history of place in the lives of community members, in Sean's grandfather's life, and in Sean's sister's life. 'More than a story of place, then, meaning becomes a story of the domestic context where "domestic" is taken in its oldest sense of having to do with where one lives, one's home and relations' (p. 235). Sean recreates a sense of the domestic as he describes where his family, his grandfather, his sister live. It is *a place surrounded by trees and lakes, grasses and plants.* The meaning becomes a story of the domestic context that allows Sean to name *pieces of himself:* Woodland Cree, grandson, Kingfisher, Settee, brother, son, grandson. Notes from his oldest sister keep him wondering about these stories and places that shape him now, that have shaped him, over place, home, time and generations. She tells of the domestic details that allow him *to travel back to early memories of home and re-turning home after being disconnected from it.* Through her notes, she allows him to negotiate intergenerational ways home, ways lost over time, where the gaps and silences in family and community stories leave stark omissions and make it difficult to find familiarity.

Reverberating Forward: Intergenerational Temporality and Responsibility

As time stretches forward into present and future moments, bringing with it the past, it carries with it personal and social responsibilities that shape the lives of people, places, communities and relationships. Through temporality and interaction, we see reverberations. While in the following quotation Pratt (2002) draws our attention to interaction among people, we see more profound and complex ways in which temporality stretches across generations.

> It is only in the interaction between people that they can be known at all. Who they 'really' are, in a sense, is not relevant, at least to embodied life. What serves as the common ground among people, as implied by the principle of interaction, is rather what people do, the ways they act in the context of a community.
>
> (p. 269)

And interwoven with temporality, carried along in family, community, place and cultural stories, there is responsibility. As Sean writes, *Carrying them back each time I go home, they fill my body, caring for them in this way can be heavy.* There is a lingering sense of responsibility within Sean's words such as the heaviness of caring for these stories, a heaviness that fills his body as he carries them with him. Responsibility lives in Sean's body as he travels between places entering, leaving, re-turning and beginning again each time.

For Sean, there is more than a personal responsibility in those stories he carries. There is a broader sense of responsibility that does not leave, that remains both with him, as Sean, but also within the community. These broader community responsibilities that stretch over time are recognizable physically as Sean shares stories of returning home. As he is introduced, he is Sean but also acknowledged as 'Jim Settee's grandson' or 'Elder Jim's boy'. These acknowledgements carry responsibilities that Sean has to communities, responsibilities that stretch intergenerationally backward and forward, inward and outward, to multiple communities. The words that remind him of who he is in relation to his grandfather and who his grandfather was in various communities carry responsibilities rooted in narratives of home and place. While the words bring forward the past, they also point towards responsibilities that shape Sean's stories into the future. Responsibilities are in this way inherited over time, place and relationships.

In narrative inquiry, this sense of temporality that stretches backward and forward helps us understand that people, places, events, communities and artifacts all come from somewhere. They are always on their way. The experiences of each individual cannot be understood without what they are emerging out of, what they are still nested within. We cannot look at a moment in time as separate from all of the other moments that come before.

Language as Intergenerational Temporality

Speaking the way my mother and father taught me is important to me. My mom didn't speak English; she is from the old ways that are still in me. My mother was raised by her great grandmother who taught her a lot of spirituality about the land. When I went to school I was learning to read English mostly.

But the way we learned at home was through our ancestors. It was through nature. We were always outside learning.

We are survivors (as a people).

We go where the water is.

We go where the buffalo are (that is what we learned).

Our language is not a written language handed over. We must ask ourselves, 'Do we really believe that Wahkan (the Creator) gave us the language?' I believe the Creator is the language. We should always hear our mothers and their voices through the language. She, our mother, is the person who brought us into the world. She is life giving.

(Elder Isabelle Kootenay, personal conversation, 2018)

The words of Elder Isabelle Kootenay direct our attention, as narrative inquirers, to the ways that language is intergenerational and is imbued with temporality. Elder Isabelle reminds us that language embodies what has come before and carries within it a deep sense of the spiritual as she says, *We must ask ourselves, 'Do we really believe that Wahkan (the Creator) gave us the language?' I believe the Creator is the language. We should always hear our mothers and their voices through the language.* Elder Isabelle, and other Elders (Cruikshank, 1990), understand language as a way that one's ancestors, and their Creator, share important cultural knowledge over generations.

Language embodied in the words and expressions are shaped in protocols and it is within the actual spoken words and ceremonies around those words and concepts that we can understand the ripples forward into the lives and experiences of future generations. Elder Francis Whiskeyjack (in Lessard et al., 2020) also helps narrative inquirers be attentive to the ways that language shapes intergenerational temporality, as he speaks of teaching

> children about Kitsi, the roots. I ask them: who are you attached to? Who is your mother, grandmother, clan mother? It is in these relationships that you see the connections and the relationships. [...] I turn to the word Miyo, which speaks to how you move in that sacred circle in a beautiful way. When I talk about this, it is to help them understand the spiritual concepts that are part of moving in a good way. It is in our life path that we choose to connect our spirit, body, and mind. In these moments, new learnings are a gift from the creator.
>
> (p. 33)

Within narrative inquiry we understand Elder Francis's attention to language as intergenerational, particularly as he notes that language 'links the world around us and the people we meet. The Cree word *waskawewin* and *miyo waskawewin* call us to attend to a sense of movement, movement marked by moving in a beautiful way. [...] The language is so important because it carries who we are, and it is important to know the language' (Lessard et al., 2020, p. 33; italics in original text).

Both Elder Francis and Elder Isabelle point towards theoretical ideas around intergenerational temporality in narrative inquiry as they stress the importance of seeing language as intertwined with 'the roots of where we come from, and the roots of our knowing' (Lessard et al., 2020, p. 33). For Elder Francis, 'language has a way of connecting relationships' (Lessard et al., 2020, p. 33) and it is the relationships that hold knowledge. For Elder Isabelle, these connecting relationships also include the relationships she holds with nature. 'This close connection to nature was fostered by her mother, who helped her experience the importance of listening to plants. These teachings are connected to language, in as much as they are connected to silence. A silence that emphasised the importance of listening' (Lessard et al., 2020, p. 33).

For Elder Isabelle, knowing her language, learned from her mother, is something she carries with her into the present and she offers narrative inquirers a way to understand intergenerational temporality. While she highlights the importance of her personal experience, she draws attention to the social responsibilities for future generations. Young (2005) also writes of

> the intergenerational narrative reverberations we all carry in our bodies, in our memories, in our souls. Because of *Niin's* [a research participant] parents' experiences in the residential school system and *Niin's* father's experience in the seminary, *Niin* was not given the opportunity to learn her language. Her father did not want her to learn the language. This gap, this void, now impacts her son, Douglas.
>
> (p. 162; italics in original text)

Young draws on Bateson (2000) to show 'how *Aanung* [a research participant], *Niin,* and *I* have been shaped by [our] individual history and the history of our communities' (p. 227; italics in original text). Young draws on her experiences, and the experiences of Niin and Aanung to understand the ways lives have changed and the way this plays out intergenerationally as important to theoretical groundings in narrative inquiry.

Place as Intergenerational Temporality

Elder Isabelle is also helpful to conceptualizing how place embodies intergenerational temporality (Lessard et al., 2020). Elder Isabelle provides narrative inquirers with a theoretical grounding from which to think about the knowledge that people carry with them from other places and times, knowledge composed intergenerationally though familial and community processes. Elder Isabelle, in her story of Rock Island, a story shared across generations, animates the many ways in which she has been taught. She shares the story in order for us to understand intergenerational possibilities within the stories.

Bateson (2000), too, offers insight into how we understand temporality as stretching across generational places. She, like Elder Isabelle, offers us, as narrative inquirers, insights into personal and community stories that reappear into the future through reverberations across time.

> Hope for a sustainable future depends on reshaping the life cycle–not the individual life cycle alone but the overlapping and intersecting cycles of individuals and generations, reaffirming both the past and the future, not only in families but in the institutions we build and shape. [...] Full circles.

The wheel of life. The cycle of the seasons. From the myths and rituals of ancient peoples to the most modern nuclear physics, the circular recurs and becomes the cyclical as it moves through time.

(pp. 243–4)

In the story Elder Isabelle tells of Rock Island, the place itself is a character in the story. She tells the story to Jean, Vera and Sean, in part, so that we can come to understand the ways in which place is interwoven with temporality. We explore theoretical understandings of place in narrative inquiry in Chapter 7.

Summary

These understandings of intergenerational temporality interwoven within people, language, places and relationships provide theoretical grounding for narrative inquirers. As narrative inquirers we learn that these theoretical understandings live within the stories. The knowledge that the stories carry shape people's and communities' identities in the present and stretch into the future across many communities. While Hampl (1999) reminds us of the importance of a person's memory, Elder Isabelle reminds us of the importance of a community's memory across generations.

Section II

Methodological Notebook

This methodological notebook draws us to considerations of temporality within lives but also across lives, within storied memories, and the making of new memories. We also attend to temporality that stretches backwards but also forwards. In conceptualizing our research and in writing our grant application, we worked closely with Yvonne Chiu from the Multicultural Health Brokers (MCHB). Vera knew Yvonne and was aware of the MCHB's work. Working with Yvonne enabled us to situate our work within ongoing community work. Because we wanted to come alongside families in diverse community settings, working with Yvonne, and through ongoing programming, made sense. We were allowed to be alongside, mindful of the responsibilities and commitments to individuals and communities that are part of narrative inquiry. Shortly after Edmonton welcomed many Syrian refugees, the MCHB opened a gathering place for people from the Syrian community. At the Syrian Centre, diverse programming offered extensive supports such as an English language class for women on Friday mornings. Childcare for young children was provided at the same time.

The Syrian Centre was located on the second floor of a strip mall, above the stores, and spread across four rooms of different sizes. At the entrance there were multiple shoes, some neatly placed on the shelves, others strewn across the small entrance way. Each Friday morning for an entire school year, we spent our time together with women from Syria who were enrolled in English classes. While the women spent time in class, their young children were in the playroom with activities and supervision provided by women who could speak Arabic. Each Friday morning we, as a group of 3 to 5 researchers, arranged our time to be spent across the playroom and the classroom. Those of us who had young children brought them along. Our favourite time became a snack break where we gathered together with the women and children. It was in these breaks that we could see the importance the space held for creating social interactions, for connecting women from Syria with each other, and also with us. Their connections with us mattered to them.

In this methodological notebook we show, through story fragments, how some of our key theoretical ideas shape the ways we engage in our research.

In the Midst

I have always enjoyed my conversations with Yvonne; I walk away knowing I have learned something new, that I see things differently. Yvonne was key to COSI's work. It was through COSI that I was introduced to Niga Jalal. Niga and her parents, who had arrived many years ago as refugees, were active within the refugee community.

Niga led the efforts of the Syrian Centre and invited us to come to the Centre. In negotiating entry, we had several conversations about what our work could look like, and how we might contribute to the Centre and the lives of the refugee community more broadly. Working closely with Niga, we identified two women, Hanan Alhendi and Zamard Rajab de El Houch, who were interested in working alongside us as translators and cultural guides. We offered them formal positions as research assistants.

We wanted to meet potential participants slowly and for them to have an opportunity to meet us, so that we could negotiate their potential participation in the research study. In conversations with Niga, we identified that becoming part of the English language programming the Centre offered to women was most appropriate.

I am not sure we really understood what we were agreeing to initially, we were simply excited by the idea of being part of people's lives and being part of a community. Looking backwards, it was an incredible year we spent in the Center. Each week we were there for three to four hours, meeting people and participating in field trips whenever possible. Over time we negotiated ways of being useful. I remember how each week we played with children, helped prepare the coffee/tea and food for the breaks, participated in, and helped organize celebrations, as well as learned how to be useful in the language classes.

Early interactions were marked by ongoing negotiations on how to work within the community. We had a sense of being in the midst of unfolding events and lives; it was in these moments that we were grateful we worked alongside Yvonne, Niga, Hanan and Zamard.

I was nervous that first Friday morning, but when the English language instructor gathered the women at the large table, I began to feel at ease. This was a class and, as a teacher, I knew how to teach. However, I was not quite sure just who I was in this class. One woman, Farah, greeted me warmly when I arrived. She must have sensed my dis/ease as a newcomer to the group. She patted the chair alongside her at the table and I gratefully took it. Initially I sat back, allowing the teacher to set the tasks but Farah invited me in. 'Is this how you say it?' she asked? 'Can you say it so I can listen?'

Jean's arrival at the group a couple of weeks after the other researchers arrived was a time of dis/ease for her. Jean was sensitive to her arrival in the group within the midst of their meetings. Farah, one of the mothers, noticed her and was concerned with making her feel at ease. Farah knew Jean was a newcomer and wanted to help her belong; Farah was always so attentive to welcoming everyone. When we sat at the table for the English language instruction, she again wanted to help Jean fit in, to understand what was happening but she also very quickly began to subvert the class to one in which she was more actively involved.

I realized that the other women seated close by were listening to Farah and I. As I watched, women around Hiroko, another researcher, began to invite her into an active role in the lesson. The young instructor was hesitant, as she watched her control over the group begin to loosen, and as the women became more engaged with us and less attentive to what she had designed as turn-taking tasks around the table.

Jean wonders now whether Farah was aware that her efforts to help Jean belong by involving her in completing the instructional tasks would disrupt the class. As a result of our presence in class, the class became more interactive with more opportunities to speak English. A new rhythm of class instruction unfolded.

Thinking with Memory

Our research was marked by being in the midst of unfolding events in the Syrian Centre, in the lives of women and children, and in our own ongoing lives. While learning English remained a central focus, we were wakeful to how much the women, and we, enjoyed a sense of community. The multiplicity of our lives created possibilities to learn. After several weeks, we were beginning to connect with individual families and, slowly, we invited

people to become part of our study. Some participants approached us and
wondered if they, too, could engage in our study.

> *Our time at the Syrian Centre was more than a time of connecting with people.*
> *It was a time of creating memories – we often tell stories about the days we*
> *spent alongside the children, the celebrations we held, and the food we shared.*
> *Creating memories together enabled us to engage in different ways. I remember*
> *how the staff at the Centre invited everyone to plan a party with them in early*
> *December.*

The hard work of learning English was disrupted – the invitation to plan
a party brought forward memories of parties, but also opened up worlds
of everyday experiences. The sensory experiences of joy, happiness and
anticipation were called forth by memories of smells, sounds, touches and
feelings of home and belonging.

> *When we arrived at the Syrian Centre that Friday morning, there was a sense*
> *of anticipation. A veritable feast of food was laid out; a table was set aside*
> *for hand painting. Syrian music was playing loudly and women and their*
> *children were dressed for a party. Farah invited me to dance and I noticed*
> *other researchers were also invited. As the music and dancing continued, I*
> *saw there was some kind of ritual being acted out. When I asked, I learned*
> *they were playing out a marriage ceremony. I watched as many women and*
> *children had henna designs painted on their hands. Such joy and laughter*
> *filled the room.*

Memories, in this way, were critical to being alive, to remembering what
home was, and could be. The day of the party seemed almost less important
than the journey of remembering and sharing experiences past, and futures
yet to be imagined.

> *While the party brought much joy, I also remember when one woman said*
> *'I wish my sister could be here'. The sadness was palpable and the sense*
> *of loss profound. The tragedy of loss and sorrow lived close to experiences*
> *of happiness. Perhaps memories in that moment become a tragedy of*
> *happiness.*

Our thinking, and experiences with memory in this study, shaped many
team conversations. We were mindful that even memories of happier times
could call forth a sense of loss and trauma. Yet, we also were wakeful that
without a sense of where people came from, it might be difficult to imagine
a future, and even more challenging to live in the present.

Recognizing Intergenerationality

On an early May Saturday afternoon, just before Ramadan, we gathered, at our invitation, with the mothers at the Syrian Centre. We wanted to celebrate our year in the Friday morning sessions. As a group of researchers, we made preparations for a celebration, a space for looking back on our friendships. Our primary connections were the women and with some children. While we only invited women to the party, all of them brought their children along. Having their children present was important to them.

> *The day of the celebration finally arrived. Many women had come with their children and they were dressed for a party. Vera designed an activity where each of us would tell a story of our connections through our belly buttons. Twenty five of us gathered around the tired carpet, seated on the floor, leaning back against cushions, legs folded under us or stretched out and with children on mothers' knees or leaning against them.*

The belly button is usually the first scar that marks one's body, a reminder of close generational links.

> *Vera began with a belly button story that connected her back to her mother and Germany; it grounded her in many ways in both her familial and cultural stories. Vera had grounded her stories in the past. Vera turned to the person beside her and I noticed something began to shift. The mothers began to tell stories of umbilical cords that they buried in places that foreshadowed dreams for the child. Buried at schools to foreshadow an educated life, at hospitals to foreshadow medical training and so forth. Mothers who had given birth in Canada spoke of not being allowed to have their newborns' umbilical cords. And there, amidst laughter, they spoke of where they would bury their newborns' cords in Canada, in order to tell a forward looking story for their children in Canada, a story of their hopes and dreams for their children.*

The umbilical cord that marks the close relationship between mother and child carries with it many cultural and social meanings. Many mothers we were with that day pulled us into their forward looking stories. Yet, they also remembered their own mothers and grandmothers, who taught them about their customs, of why it mattered to recognize the importance of the umbilical cord. In this way, how one cares for their children's first scar became a matter of generational acts.

Section III

Living within and on Landscapes

In this section we take up ideas of place and community in narrative inquiry. In Chapter 7 we conceptualize place both in the sense of the concrete and topological, as well as in the more complex sense of place that acknowledges the interwoven nature of temporality, social relations, and material relations. Place, alongside time and sociality, is a dimension of the three-dimensional narrative inquiry space. Place, understood as the 'specific concrete physical and topological boundaries of place, or sequence of places where the inquiry and events take place' (Clandinin & Connelly, 2000, p. 49), is present in all experiences and is critical to understanding experiences lived and told, as well as experiences that remain silent.

Place is integral to each person's identity-making within thinking narratively. However, too often, this concept of place is taken up too narrowly without a consideration of the more complex aspects of place. We show how places and people are connected, and how places as geographical markers carry relations in embedded and embodied ways. Places also carry forward memories at the same time as they shape the agency and experiences of those who are within place. Places act on each of us and, through working on each of us, shape who we are and are becoming. In Chapter 8 we draw on diverse scholars to show how we understand community. In thinking about what pulls us into, as much as what pushes us away from, places of community, we realize there are many aspects that puzzle us in thinking narratively with, and about, place and community. Considerations of place make visible the challenges of staying with singular concepts, such as place, or identity or community.

7

Place

Abstract

In this chapter we take up understandings of place within narrative inquiry. Every story has a geography (Caine, 2007). From this we understand that every story has a place; every story, every memory, every experience, is placed. Drawing on theoretical insights from Dewey (1938), Ahmed (1999), Leslie Marmon Silko (1977, 1991) and Keith Basso (1996) we developed our understandings of place. Within narrative inquiry, place is understood ontologically; that is, we understand that place shapes each person's being at the same time as each person also shapes place. We are shaped by, and shaping, the places in which we live as well as understanding that place shapes individual and community identities.

Coming to Place in Narrative Inquiry

The first paper written about narrative inquiry, in which Connelly and Clandinin name narrative inquiry as such, was published in 1990 in the *Educational Researcher*. Four years later, in 1994, Clandinin and Connelly wrote of the links between Dewey's theory of experience and narrative inquiry. Dewey's theory of experience is specified by two criteria, interaction and continuity, as outlined in Chapter 1.

As they conceptualized narrative inquiry as the study of experience understood narratively, Clandinin and Connelly (1994) wrote of the methods they used as 'simultaneously focussed in four directions: inward and outward, backward and forward' (p. 417). By inward they meant the internal conditions of feelings, hopes, aesthetic reactions, moral dispositions and so on. By outward we meant existential conditions, that is the environment. […] By backward and forward we are referring to temporality, past, present and future. To experience an experience is to experience it simultaneously in these four ways and to ask questions pointing each way.

(p. 417)

Clandinin and Connelly did not mention place in their discussion of the four directions one moved in narrative inquiry, although place did find a mention. They wrote '[s]cene or place is where the action occurs, where characters are formed and live out their stories and where cultural and social context play constraining and enabling roles' (p. 416).

In part, place or scene pointed towards the places where participants lived or told their stories and to the kinds of field and research texts that were written in order to give a sense of context. Situation also assumed a place or places where people lived their lives. But place was not a central focus. It was somewhat hidden within the four directions of backward, forward, inward and outward.

This conceptual frame with its four directions, and with place assumed/ subsumed within the concept of situation, served Clandinin and Connelly well as they did their early studies and continued their work at Bay Street School and in other places. However, as more and more Indigenous students were drawn to narrative inquiry, they began to raise questions about place and spirituality. They shared ideas such as: Certain places are sacred. Places are living. Places shape people, as people shape places. Places are within people and within stories. Places are alive and act upon us. They are agential. Place in narrative inquiry was rapidly becoming much more complex with layered multiple meanings. Other scholars whose experiences in place were disrupted by social events, including migration, also called for more complex understandings of place.

Indigenous scholars such as Wayne Gorman and Young engaged in spirited conversations around narrative inquiry as we struggled with what we meant by place. They suggested we read Basso's (1996) book, *Wisdom Sits in Places*. It was in reading scholars such as Basso, Marmon Silko and Richard Wagamese and participating in conversations with Adrienne Wiebe, Duane Burton, Wayne Gorman and Young, that Clandinin and Connelly began to think again about place and introduced it as one of the narrative inquiry commonplaces in the late 1990s.

Turning to Experience

In the middle of the morgue was the open casket that contained my grandmother's body. Her body was surrounded by flower arrangements that, even now, I only recall through the photographs that have been passed on to me. At barely 10 years of age my parents thought it was important for me to attend my grandmother's funeral. I did not anticipate the open casket nor the grief that was overwhelming me when I first saw her body. The whiteness of her face, the stillness of her body, and the absence of her gentle eyes called forth streams of tears in me. Even now I can still feel the wetness of my cheeks as I cried for what seemed like hours – I could not leave the place that held her body. I experienced my grandmother's death, and my loss of her, in ways I did not understand at that age. My body was frozen, my eyes fixed on her still body – my eyes did not wander out of fear I would miss her catching her breath. I had buried dead birds and squirrels and killed spiders and flies, but never in the same way connected them to death - death had seemed a necessary part of life for the animals I had buried. The grief felt raw, unexpected, and overshadowed the relationship I had held with my grandmother while she was still alive. Covered in tears, I recall the repetitive chants of the rosary, the slow trek to the graveside, and the lowering of the casket that involved my grandmother's children, her neighbors, and friends. The graveyard became my grandmother's final place – a homecoming in a community that was marked by war, privilege, and traditions. Geographically her graveside was close to the place she was born and the place in which she had lived her life, the place in which she worried about her children, and where she would have come to know her grandchildren. This sense of place was significant to me and to those around me – it provided me then and continues to provide me with a geographic place that is most intimately linked to my history. Place is marked by and carries the history that has and continues to shape who I am.

Place Understood Ontologically

Looking backwards, the mortuary was the first time Vera had become attentive to place. For Vera this was followed by a long stretch of time, in which place was important, but a time during which she was not wakeful to it. Many years later it was Debra who turned Vera's attention back to place. By then Vera had immigrated to Canada and was engaged in a narrative inquiry study alongside Indigenous women living with HIV. Elsewhere, Vera (Caine, 2010) writes,

Drawing on the life stories of Debra, an [Indigenous] woman living with HIV, I reflect on the feeling of (dis)placement from a geographic landscape and cultural heritage that both Debra and I experienced, although in different ways. I explore how place is inscribed onto and into our bodies and how home can be understood as embodied. In this way I explore place as geographic position of home and as ontological.

(p. 1304)

Sitting in the living room of Debra's apartment, I recall our conversations about the precariousness of locating ourselves geographically. Each time Debra began to locate her life geographically her story became fragmented, it became filled with a sense of hopelessness that too had marked her early life. At the age of 11 Debra had lost any sense of permanency of home – instead her life was shaped by the rhythms of sleeping in the emergency room wards or in beds of men who wanted her body to be accessible to them. This lack of place shaped the geographical markers of her experiences – in each of our conversations she could hardly recall the names of the cities, neighborhoods, or streets that served for increasingly shorter duration as a shelter in her life. I struggled to attend to her experiences – recalling the death of my grandmother and the unexpected, impactful and haunting view of her still body surfaced in my conversations with Debra. Debra consistently took me home.

Debra pulled me into her life and called me to reflect on my understanding of geography, as well as my sense of location. Geography can and does position us, it too can freeze us. Yet, this sense of freezing can shift and change across time and social contexts. I thought of the places Debra showed me – the emergency room ward, the street corners, the shady hotels and motels, and the places in which she was seeking care.

After knowing Debra for several months, months during which she was homeless, I recall walking into Debra's apartment – an apartment that was rented by and paid for by her then boyfriend. A boyfriend whose love for Debra was overshadowed and driven by jealousy, brutality, and entitlement.

Torn up by jealousy the apartment became a prison to Debra – a prison she could neither leave, nor come home to. Debra would call me at times in the middle of the night filled with fear that the rage and jealousy would once again consume her life. She feared death and the absence of her friends, neighbors, and family chanting the rosary. She too feared the absence of her children at her funeral. At the same time, she feared that her children would know the places that were part of her life. I wondered then about the notion of place and geography in our lives. Places that mark our lives, but were not limited to or by the geographic markers that trace our lives in their particularity. These particularities I learned from Debra; particularities that are engraved into our bodies. For both Debra and I, places drew themselves onto our bodies and into our experiences.

It was Debra who helped Vera understand that 'there is a geography in all of our stories' (Caine, personal conversation cited in Lessard, 2010, p. 44). When Vera first shared this idea with us in this seemingly simple sentence fragment, it became a kind of entry way to our considerations of how place needed to be understood ontologically in narrative inquiry.

Understanding place as ontological challenges us to stay wakeful and not misconstrue place as only pointing towards a physical place. Understanding place as ontological draws our attention in two directions: to the ways that place shapes our being/living as people but also to the ways that people shape place(s). Marmon Silko (1997), a Laguna scholar, helps us see how place is carried in us and how places carry us. Too frequently, place or landscape is assumed to be separate from people, as if they could 'survey' a landscape that they stand upon. As Marmon Silko writes, '[t]his assumes the viewer is somehow outside or separate from the territory she or he surveys. Viewers are as much a part of the landscape as the boulders they stand on' (p. 27). This view of place from a relational ontology highlights the importance of understanding that our lived and told stories are always in place, shaped by place, and shaping place.

In the midst of living alongside Debra, there was a presence of death – moments marked by a sense of despair and hopelessness that was difficult for me to comprehend then and even now.

While Debra's experiences were shaped in, and by, places, there also was a sense of placelessness. In the moments when there was a strong sense of placelessness or displacement, memories surfaced for Vera at her grandmother's graveside. Gathering at the graveside in the years following Vera's grandmother's death has been important, and slowly, as her children have passed away, the graveyard has become filled with family stories – place holds memories, it eases the despair and it becomes the meeting place of generations that will meet their grandmother through the stories told, the places visited that shaped her life and that were shaped by her.

Debra often wondered what would happen if she died – a thought that was shaped by her experience of living with HIV and of her experiences with substance use. Her children long ago apprehended, the lost connections with her parents, the lovers and boyfriends who, much like the men before, cared more about the usefulness of her body, she asked often – who would remember her? Would the place where she would be buried, be marked in some way, or perhaps engraved with her name? Did anyone know what places were important to her?

There were times that Debra's experiences were shaped by the absence of place, the invisibility of the connections to places, landscapes or other topographical matters. Place too carried and marked extraordinarily difficult stories for Debra; they held experiences that were brutal, cruel and unfeeling.

In as much as place shapes and is shaped by our experiences, place also erases who we are – it holds our experiences silently, in ways that they are invisible to others. At the same time place understood ontologically draws attention to the complex relations among people, plants, animals, sentient and non-sentient beings. Place needs always to be seen as part of these complex interrelations, as shaping and being shaped by human and non human relations over time.

Place and Identity

Place is in us, as we are in places; we are shaped by, and shaping, the places within which we live. Place, as Basso (1996) argues, connects our identities to the landscapes that carry who we are and are becoming. As he wrote in his work with the Apache people, 'the landscape in which the people dwell can be said to dwell in them' (p. 102). And yet for many who are rooted in place, they live without a conscious awareness of place. Sometimes awareness of place, and who one is within place, 'is brief and unselfconscious, a fleeting moment (a flash of recognition, a trace of memory) that is swiftly replaced by awareness of something else' (Basso, 1996, p. 54). It is only when we pause within our everyday experiences that we may actively sense the ways that place shapes who we are, who we are becoming.

The landscapes, within which we live, shape and sustain who we are as people. Basso (1996) writes of the importance of place as sustaining when he describes place as akin to water. 'It's like water that never dries up. You need to drink water to stay alive, don't you? Well, you also need to drink from places' (p. 127). Basso is not alone in arguing for the intricate interrelationships between place and identity. For Lessard (2014), place shapes experiences moving forward and, in Lugones (1987) sense, allows us to travel from world to world.

In part, we know the depth of the interconnections of place with identity through our longing for place. Marmon Silko's longing for place was so intense when she was 'away from the Laguna country that the writing [of Ceremony] was my way of re-making the place, the Laguna country, for myself' (in Wright, 1986, pp. 27–8). As Marmon Silko suggested, we crave places that shaped our bodies, our identities. We strive to recreate them. Sandra Cisneros, in her book *The House on Mango Street* (1989), tells stories of Esperanza, a young 'girl who didn't want to belong' (p. 109). She writes of 'Mango Street, sad red house, the house I belong but do not belong to. I put it down on paper and then the ghost does not ache so much. I write it down and Mango says goodbye sometimes. [...] One day I will go away'. She describes how Esperanza leaves but, in the leaving, the neighbours 'will not know I have gone away to come back. For the ones I left behind. For the ones who cannot out' (p. 110). Cisneros shows us how a particular place shapes identity and in that intense shaping of a person, shows how identity and place are forever entwined, that even in the leaving, there is a longing for return to place. Marianna de Marco Torgovnick (1994) also shows how place is inextricably linked to identity as she writes, I am 'reminded of my own roots, of their simultaneously choking and nutritive power' (p. 11).

But sometimes we want to silence, erase places from our lives and work to reimagine place as otherwise. In Vera's story of her experiences alongside Debra, we learn that Debra knew that many places had shaped her life. Some of the places were places she wanted to erase, places she did not want her children to know *were part of her life*. Rather than celebrating the particularities of some of the places that shaped her life, they were places she wanted to keep secret from people she loved. As Vera writes, *For both Debra and I, places drew themselves onto our bodies and into our experiences.* For Debra, fearful of her own death in part because of how she might be storied as a person after her death, there were place(s) she wanted to erase or at least not make visible. Places that would tell a particular story, that in their telling would mark her.

Basso (1996) writes that our sense of place fuels who we are 'by sentiments of inclusion, belonging and connectedness to the past' (p. 145) noting that place 'roots individuals in the social and cultural soils from which they have sprung together, holding them in the grip of a shared identity, a localized version of selfhood' (pp. 145–6). It is in this sense of place as shaping identity that we see the link between place and personal and community identities that we explore in more detail in Chapter 8.

Place, Memory and Intergenerational Reverberations

We show how place and memory are deeply connected, and that our relationships with place evoke and return us to other times and places, that they are marked by intergenerational reverberations. While we can see the reverberations, we are also mindful that when we arrive as strangers to new places, questions arise. Questions such as,

> [h]ow to narrate a place and a time as stranger. How to manage the indexical seductions of the institutional archive and the metropolitan knowledge it fosters while remaining alive to the productive possibilities of the accident. […] How to be […] without recourse to the metaphors of colonial exploration, including of course the very idea of an empty landscape.
>
> (van Wyck, 2008, p. 188)

Debra knew that there was never an empty landscape, that the places she entered as a stranger would call forth not only unknown stories, but also would call forth stories that told stories of who she is. What became much harder for both Debra and Vera to understand and live by was the idea that 'I learned how history makes a place and how retelling the past makes new futures possible' (Pratt, 2002, p. ix). If retellings create new future possibilities, then intergenerational reverberations reach forward and backward, while also marking our presence. The landscape recognizes us, the concept of stranger, as the unknown, is no longer possible. Instead, it follows the original meanings of the word stranger, as 'one who has stopped visiting' (Online Etymological Dictionary, n.p.).

Basso, in his book *Wisdom Sits in Places,* pushes us to think of place in several distinct ways. He describes the knowledge holders within the community as being the physical markers and manifestations. The unique landscape within the community of the Western Apache where water and mountains, certain trees and pathways hold meaning for the community through their physical representations. The stories passed on orally and held by certain members within the community serve as intergenerational markers and moral teachers that reverberate in the careful sharing and protecting of the stories that continue to guide the community in the present. In Basso's work he travels alongside a community member who has the responsibility of taking care of the stories that have been passed down to him through generations. The reverberations of early experiences are especially noteworthy as the knowledge keeper physically travels through the familiar terrain, pointing out the specific markers and sharing the teachings that are specific to the place.

As both Debra and Vera enter places as strangers, as people who have stopped visiting, we think about who travels alongside us. The stories told by others, which return us to both the routes and roots of our lives, show the intergenerational reverberations of place. Young (2005) made visible the importance of the intergenerational reverberations of place, and how place stretches forward into the storied memories of children and grandchildren in both sustaining and potentially harmful ways. It is Debra who knew the harmful ways.

In her doctoral dissertation Vera (Caine, 2007) writes:

> My heart sings again the songs of my childhood and like Berger (1984) I slowly begin to see and understand home as an ontological place where my world can be found; '[h]ome is no longer a dwelling but the untold story of a life being lived' (p. 64). (p. 4)

> It is these places that I have left, but as Rushdie (1981) carries the sea by which he was born to every new place, so too do I carry the strawberry fields, the river, the hills and the stories with me always. Place holds memory and defines who I am and place invokes memory. And it is particular places that remind me of my shared memories with my mother and aunt most of all, and with my father and siblings, and my husband and son. It has become impossible to look at a map and not recount the stories, the happenings and past events and it is impossible to not think of place.
>
> (p. 41)

It was Vera's experiences alongside Debra that allowed Vera to see what Young refers to as the harmful ways of seeing place in sentimental ways. In recognizing this, Vera could understand the words of Ahmed (1999), who pointed out that

> [t]he assumption that to leave home, to migrate or to travel, is to suspend the boundaries in which identity comes to be liveable as such, conceals the complex and contingent social relationships of antagonism which grant some subjects the ability to move freely at the expense of others.
>
> (p. 338)

In this way we can see how place also grounds relationships, relationships past, present and future. Place becomes more complex and notions of visiting, of absence and presence, of boundaries and landscape shift. The intergenerational knowledge that rests deep within and that is protected, held close and sacred, can be recognized in places and in the physical movements, through the body within, and in, response to place.

Debra's experiences and her presence in Vera's life shifted Vera's understanding of place in relation to the body, but also in relation to strangeness and home. Vera began to understand place as being strange, while at the same time as holding memories of home.

> The association of home with familiarity which allows strangeness to be associated with migration (that is, to be located as beyond the walls of the home) is problematic. There is already strangeness and movement within the home itself. It is not simply a question then of those who stay at home, and those who leave, as if these two different trajectories simply lead people to different places. Rather, 'homes' always involve encounters between those who stay, those who arrive and those who leave. We can use Avtar Brah's notion of diasporic space here: there is always an intimate encounter at stake between natives and strangers (Brah, 1996: 181). Given the inevitability of such encounters, homes do not stay the same as the space which is simply the familiar. There is movement and dislocation within the very forming of homes as complex and contingent spaces of inhabitance.
>
> (Ahmed, 1999, p. 340)

And it is the feeling as Ahmed (1999) suggests that 'being at home is here a matter of how one feels or how one might fail to feel' (p. 341).

Summary

Place calls us to remake relationships and to form new communities, communities that are wakeful to the stories carried within place. And it is '[t]he community [that] comes to life through the collective act of remembering in the absence of a common terrain' (Ahmed, 1999, p. 344). We pick up on the close link between place and people's experiences in communities in Chapter 8. The longing, the searching for places that carry who we are, that carry aspects of the communities that shape and hold our identities, pull us into geographic considerations. Community becomes animate as we think narratively. We can understand experiences narratively only when we place them within places, both home places, community places and imagined places.

8

Community

Abstract

In this chapter we explore ways that place is not only in relation with individuals but in relation with communities. Drawing on Marilyn Friedman's (1989) distinction between found and chosen communities and Martin Buber's (1971) idea of communities of sameness and difference helps us to shape conceptions of community in narrative inquiry. While community holds notions of geography and home, it also pushes back against these notions, and, at times, outrightly defies these.

Turning to Experience

Living within a rural farming community in my childhood and youth, community was something that I took for granted. I rarely wondered about communities and about just what communities were. I gave little thought to the ways the word, community, was used to describe dances, a small school converted to a hall, and social events. The word 'community' frequently preceded events and happenings. In hindsight, my thought was that community was a word used to symbolize people who lived in a shared physical area.

I assumed my membership came from the fact that our family farm was in the geographical area. Sometimes, though, I wondered about the ways that some people fit into that rural community. I wondered for example about one neighbour who lived a few miles from our farm who did not come to the 'ladies' club' meetings my mother regularly went to and which she hosted when it was her 'turn'. I also wondered about the neighbours who had arrived in Canada just a couple of years before I was born. I now know they had left their European homeland after the Second World War and were described as displaced persons, a category that was given a derogatory title. I wondered about the ways family stories were composed within community stories and the ways that the stories told by those who lived in the community shaped the people who lived in the community. My mostly unquestioned assumptions about community were ones such as: communities are good, people are responsible for each other, communities are shaped by physical places. Because I was a member of the small rural community, I belonged. Nothing really made me think about the phenomenon of community. As I recollect my childhood there was nothing that disrupted my sense of a community as a good thing.

Interconnections among Place, People and Community

From Jean's story of her experience of growing up on a small farm in rural Alberta in the late 1940s and 1950s, it is clear that she understood community as synonymous with a simplistic notion of place as a physical area. A community was a shared or common place. A community was a group of people with common interests who lived in a particular area. There were some family stories that shaped how Jean was to live in her community (and in her family) that directed Jean to understand a sense of her responsibilities to living in her family and in her community. With little else to consider, communities were seen as something good. Jean understood that her parents were strong members of the community and that gave Jean a sense of needing to live up to her parents' story and the community story of her parents as strong community members. It is Hilde Lindemann Nelson's (1995) ideas drawing on Friedman (1989) that are helpful in considering, perhaps, Jean's unquestioned notions of community. A found community is a community in which a person finds themself, much as Jean found herself living in a rural farming community. Lindemann Nelson writes about chosen communities as different from found communities. Lindemann Nelson argues that within a chosen community there is a need for a

moral space within it where its members can come together to discern, construct, correct, and celebrate the community's story. The work that goes on within this space affords a nonauthoritarian and nonarbitrary means of allowing the community to define itself morally. Stories that are collectively and democratically self-defining provide the community with a certain coherence and integrity, especially when a particular kind of story is told – I will tell one – that allows its members to resist the temptation to dominate or to fear difference within the community.

(p. 24)

While in Jean's story there was no sense of her awareness of the possibilities of a chosen community, there was a sense that Jean was aware of community stories that held moral directions suggested by her awareness of the need for responsibilities that were part of the found community.

> *It was when I moved away from my rural home and began to attend courses in teacher education at an urban university that I began to consider community. The first author I read who turned my attention to more explicit considerations of community was Dewey. My first readings of his book Experience and Education (Dewey, 1938) were in the context of learning to teach. As someone learning to teach, I was interested in how he helped me think about democratic means to shape a community with students and among students in a classroom. I was intrigued by thinking about how 'the moving spirit of the whole group' establishes order [...] 'The control is social, but individuals are part of a community, not outside of it' (1938, p. 54). He affirmed some of what I had tacitly understood with thoughts about how 'the primary source of social control reside in the very nature of the work done as a social enterprise in which all individuals have an opportunity to contribute and to which all feel a responsibility [...] A genuine community life has its ground in this natural sociability' (p. 56). These ideas felt comfortable to me as they gave me a way to think of who I was going to be as a teacher, someone who was a leader but also a learner alongside children. What he wrote resonated with my idea of individuals as being 'part of a community, not outside it'. While this initial reading of Dewey helped me understand a bit more about community, I did not question the nature of different communities nor how an individual became part of a community and what belonging meant. Community was still a good thing. These mostly unquestioned ideas of community were ones that I carried with me as I began to teach.*

In retrospect, with a sense of the possibility of shaping democratic spaces within what would have been the found communities of classrooms Jean imagined herself teaching, Jean may have been considering the possibility that a classroom community could, with some work, become a chosen community. It seemed, as Jean imagined the future community she and students would build together, that she was wondering about how it could be a 'moral space' where the children and Jean could come 'together to discern, construct, correct, and celebrate the community's story' (Lindemann Nelson, 1995, p. 24). However, as Jean realized in hindsight, she was not very far into opening questions about the nature of different communities. Greene's (1995) work was not part of Jean's understandings as she was learning to teach but perhaps she gleaned, through her reading of Dewey, some sense of what Greene writes about as 'imagining a democratic community accessible to the young is to summon up the vision of the "conjoint experience", shared by meanings, common interests and endeavours described by John Dewey' (p. 33).

Communities as Animate: Thinking with Found and Chosen Communities

As I began to live in schools with children, families, other teachers, and administrators, puzzles about community began to emerge. As I worked with colleagues and families, we figured out how to create a space for a child in a wheelchair to attend his neighborhood school, how to meet as a group of teachers over lunch away from the staffroom in order to consider how we might shape more inclusive classrooms where children would not be pulled out for remedial instruction but to receive appropriate assistance within their classrooms, how to work with families to create an early childhood classroom, and how to create multi age groupings of children that would allow students to work in friendship groups. Questions about belonging and inclusion, oppression and exclusion, about how communities shaped individual identities, about how individual people shaped communities and for what ends or purposes they shaped them, began to emerge for me.

Again it was in hindsight that Jean began to see that she was attempting to shape chosen communities within the found community of the schools in which she worked. As she gathered with colleagues in one teacher's classroom at lunchtime, she and her colleagues were forming a kind of chosen community, a community in which they could work towards change in the school which would make the school a more inclusive space. These lunch time meetings became a space where the small group could plan to live

counterstories-narratives of resistance and insubordination that allow communities of choice to challenge and revise the paradigm stories of the 'found' communities in which they are embedded. The ability of counterstories to reconfigure dominant stories permits those who have been excluded or oppressed by a 'found' community to gain fuller access to the goods offered there.

(Lindemann Nelson, 1995, p. 24)

While Jean recalls these lunch time meetings as tacitly subversive, and she later wrote of them as places for secret stories within a professional knowledge landscape (Clandinin & Connelly, 1995), in hindsight, she can see them in the words that Lindemann Nelson describes as a chosen community for developing a counterstory. For Jean and her colleagues, this was a way to bring about change for more inclusive ways of living with children and families. Thinking of this as a chosen community developing counterstories became a way to think about experiences narratively.

My puzzles were often shaped by questions around how the schools in which I worked shaped families and their communities and by wonders around inclusion and exclusion within classrooms, schools, and out-of-school places. A bit vague and messy, I had no clearly formed questions. Some of my struggle is captured by Greene's wonders about the need to not allow children and families to 'be left to the realm of separateness and privacy that makes community so difficult to achieve and alienates the fortunate from those who remain tragically in need' (Greene, 1995, p. 34). It seemed that only within more inclusive communities in which all children and families belonged was it possible to change dominant stories of school where children and families were sorted into categories. As I worked on my master's thesis part time alongside my work in the schools, I was interested in the interplay between the social and the individual. My master's degree program seemed largely focussed on how to 'fix' individuals through one-on-one counselling, testing, sorting, and grading individuals within social milieux. There seemed, at least to me, no spaces for considerations of community and the tensions between individuals and community. I struggled with how we could shift or change the cultural and social narratives that shaped communities, and that were enacted in social policies and practices. I can, in hindsight, see these tensions as shaped and lived in the spaces between the individual and the social.

In reading, thinking, and living alongside many diverse children and families in school, Jean's notions of community began to be questioned. In her master's program, Jean recalls being most attracted to the work of Carl Rogers. In searching out the writing of Rogers, she read an article that contained a transcript of a conversation between Rogers and Martin Buber (1960). Buber, a philosopher, offered her ideas for thinking about the individual and the social, the person and community. It became a way to think about the nature of communities with more insight. The article opened up new ways for her to think about what she was doing in schools.

Communities of Sameness, Communities of Otherness

I sought out more of Buber's (1971) work when I left my work in schools and began doctoral studies. I read Friedman's (1993) book where he outlined what I saw as an idea of communities of sameness and difference. His ideas bumped against my confused and uncertain ideas of community as he outlined a more complex notion of community. Drawing upon Buber's metaphor of a 'narrow ridge' (in Friedman, 1993) within a community of otherness, Michael Connelly and I wrote

> 'Buber's concern was to conceptualize communities in which people with different points of view thrive. He imagined the community of otherness as located on a narrow ridge, a place of tension between two gulfs where there is 'no sureness of knowledge' but only a 'certainty of meeting'. From the ridge there is the possibility of response without the withholding of self. The ridge allows the possibility of 'overcoming otherness' in a lived unity that is the community'.

(Connelly & Clandinin, 1998, p. 247)

Buber and Friedman distinguished communities of affinity or likemindedness from genuine communities that affirmed otherness. Even at this early point in the development of narrative inquiry, Jean was aware of the importance of attending to the interplay of the individual and the social, to the ways that the social narratives, including institutional and cultural narratives, shaped the lives of individuals and families and the ways that individual and family narratives shaped social narratives. Buber's and Friedman's ideas were generative for conceptualizing community and offered an entry point into thinking narratively of the phenomenon of community. With their work providing an interruption that allowed for a more conceptual development of community, Jean began to think about communities of sameness or affinity and genuine communities which affirmed otherness as grounded temporally, as grounded in place, as well as grounded both socially and personally. People within different communities were shaped by the stories that lived in the community; similarly different communities shaped those who participated in them in different ways.

Different people could also shape their storied communities in different ways. Communities were always in context and shaped by those who lived within them. However, people could, as Friedman (1989) pointed out, 'form radically different communities based on voluntary association', 'rather than accept as binding the moral claims of the communities in which they find themselves' (p. 285).

While Buber's work opened up more complex concepts of community for us, and helped us identify key tensions in what we meant by place and community and the tensions between the person and community, with attention to the individual and the social, we began to think narratively about community with key authors such as Buber, Greene, Friedman, Maurice Friedman, Lindemann Nelson and Hannah Arendt. It was the ideas that these authors gave us, that were generative as we developed narrative conceptions of community.

Community as Integral to Thinking Narratively

One key idea in narrative inquiry is that we can only understand experience when it is situated temporally, socially and within place. We understand place and community as integrally connected in narrative inquiry. And yet community is not understood in the simplistic terms of being synonymous with geographic area. Drawing on Friedman (1993), and the key concepts of a community of otherness and a community of affinity or likemindedness, narrative inquirers acknowledge the false community within a community of affinity that is shaped for security and a sense of safety; these are communities that feel secure because members of such communities come together as they fear oppression and conflict. Friedman (1993) allows a way for narrative inquirers to draw on the concept of communities of otherness that speak more to acknowledging the complexities of narrative understandings of community where we recognize diversity, and are together because of shared common concerns, shared common situations. While they are common space, they are approached and responded to in different ways. Working with more complex understandings of community, narrative inquirers see the importance of recognizing diversity, power and oppression within communities, and, in so doing, resist romantic notions of community.

As Jean returns to reflect on her childhood experiences, she wonders now if the rural community in which she lived was a false community of affinity or likemindedness that perhaps provided safety and security for its members. She wonders, too, if there were communities of otherness within the larger community. Was the smaller community of women that her mother belonged to a community of affinity or was it a community of otherness that worked to welcome diversity or, perhaps, worked to counter the oppression of women within the community?

Possible and Multiple Communities

Within narrative inquiry, community is understood as in the present, but it is always something emerging from the past and with a sense of a forward direction. This sense of moving into the future contains within it, a sense of a 'possible community', a sense of 'envisaging what might be' (Greene, 1995, pp. 33–4). This sense of a moving community, not as something fixed and unchanging, is picked up by Friedman (1989) who wrote,

> communities of choice foster not so much the constitution of subjects but their reconstitution. They may be sought out as contexts in which people relocate the various constituents of their identities, as Adrienne Rich sought out the Jewish community in her college years. [...] The modern self may seek new communities whose norms and relationships stimulate and develop her identity and self-understanding more adequately than her unchosen community of origin, her original community of place.
>
> (p. 289)

What Friedman helps us understand is that each person within a chosen community is changing, or restorying oneself, but communities themselves are also in the making, always remaking themselves depending upon who and what are shaping a particular community of choice.

While it sometimes is easier to categorize or attend to experience as situated in only one community, within narrative inquiry we are always attending to the multiplicity of communities that are always at work within each person's experiences. We draw on Friedman (1989) who helps us see that

> [m]ost lives contain mixtures of relationships and communities, some given/ found/discovered and some chosen/created. Most people probably are, to

some extent, ineradicably constituted by their communities of place, the community defined by some or all of their family, neighborhood, school, or church. It is noteworthy that dependent children, elderly persons, and all other individuals whose lives and well-being are at great risk, need the support of communities whose other members do not or cannot choose arbitrarily to leave. Recent philosophical investigation into communities and relationships not founded or sustained by choice has brought out the importance of these social networks for the constitution of social life. But these insights should not obscure the additional need for communities of choice to counter oppressive and abusive relational structures in those nonvoluntary communities by providing models of alternative social relationships as well as standpoints for critical reflection on self and community.

(p. 290)

As Jean and her colleagues gathered in what became a kind of counterstory, a narrative of resistance, to the dominant stories of school around the lack of inclusion of children with physical disabilities and of children with different learning abilities, their intentions were to shift the dominant stories in their particular school enough to allow competing stories to take root. While they were still part of the found community of the school, they were also part of a community of choice, a way for them to not 'accept as binding the moral claims of the communities in which they find themselves' (Friedman, 1989, p. 285). They were able, by situating themselves within at least two communities, to counter oppressive structures through offering a different story of social relationships within the school.

Longing for and Resisting Community and Belonging

The idea that communities can be shaped by resistance as well as by a longing to belong, narrative inquirers draw on Lindemann Nelson (1995) and Friedman's (1989) ideas of found and chosen communities. We follow Lindemann Nelson's use of Friedman when she argues that the moral space within communities of choice 'can be used as a place to tell self-defining stories. But if persons can tell self-defining stories, so can the communities of which they are a part' (p. 28). Within chosen communities, the characteristics of the dominant group are not taken as the norm. The characteristics of the chosen community are not taken as deviant from the dominant group.

Drawing again on Lindemann Nelson (1995), a community of choice is

> a community that creates moral space in which narratives can be told, it has the resources to put faces on people, and so to deal with difference in a manner that is attentive to individuals. [...] through particular stories of humility that are their own act of strong moral self-definition, they offer resources for resisting the tendency to homogenize difference.
>
> (pp. 30–1)

Further Lindemann Nelson argues,

> when a community of choice tells stories that reconfigure the distorted and biased stories of 'found' communities, retrospective narrative is put to a task for which communities of choice are particularly well suited: the moral task of resistance and insubordination.
>
> (p. 33)

Thus, Lindemann Nelson offers narrative inquiry ways to conceptualize the work of chosen communities. Communities of choice

> are well suited to challenging the 'found' communities in which they are embedded. But it is important to notice just what the nature of the challenge is. In those 'found' communities reside not only our oppression but also our moral good: a considerable portion of the richness and variety of life lies in the given. The trouble has been that the goods of 'found' communities have been preferentially available to dominant members. To claim these goods for themselves, then, the marginalized members of the community must enter the story sideways, as it were, correcting for the biases and distortions of the dominant interpreters.
>
> (pp. 35–6)

As Jean reconsiders her work in schools, particularly the work she did alongside members of her chosen community, there is a sense that the teachers were claiming for children, who did not fit what was considered normal categories, the goods of 'found' communities that were not available to those outside those categories. For example, teachers within the chosen community worked to enable one child in a wheelchair to come to his neighbourhood school. As they worked together to create school stories which would not allow *children and families to 'be left to the realm of separateness and privacy' (Greene, 1995, p. 34), they saw themselves as reshaping schools by changing who belonged within the dominant stories of school.* They worked with one wheelchair-bound child and his family to allow the child to enter the story of school sideways in ways that corrected 'for the biases and distortions of the dominant interpreters' (Lindemann Nelson, 1995, pp. 35–6). They enabled the possibility of a counterstory to take root in the school, a counterstory that was lived and told 'for the specific purpose of resisting and undermining a dominant story' (p. 34). Their intent was that this particular child, and other children who also lived with physical differences, could eventually be able to enter the found community of school and be able to 'freely enjoy the goods to be had there' (p. 38). As their chosen community began to live and tell a story of who belonged within the stories of their school, they reconfigured 'the distorted and biased stories' (p. 33) of the found community within the school. It was, of course, part of a way of recomposing stories of school in ways that resisted dominant stories and allowed the counterstory to weave its way into the dominant story.

Home Places, Community Places, Imagined Places

As narrative inquirers we are always attentive to how communities shape us as they can prescribe identities on to people and then act upon these prescribed identities. In this ascription and assignment of identities with the subsequent actions upon those identities, possibilities may, or may not, be enabled.

Narrative inquirers understand, as does Lindemann Nelson, that 'our communities do more than guide us-they constitute us' (p. 28). Living by our communal allegiances, Lindemann Nelson (1995), drawing on Michael Sandel, notes,

> 'is inseparable from understanding ourselves as the particular persons we are-as members of this family or community or nation or people, as bearers of this history, as sons and daughters of that revolution, as citizens of this republic' (Sandel 1982, 179). Within these communities we belong to something larger than ourselves; 'found' communities place us within a particular tradition; they give us a language, a culture, an inheritance, a home.
>
> (p. 28)

However, we follow Lindemann Nelson (1995) who helps narrative inquirers see that community narratives are not 'fundamentally informed by one monolithic tradition [... in which] the traditions of the community are largely interpreted and transmitted by those who occupy positions of influence and authority [... that] discounts the particulars that do not fit its dominant patterns' (p. 28). In narrative inquiry, we see that communities, particularly found communities or communities of affinity, can be 'deaf to the stories of women and of the men who do not stand at the centre of their traditions' (p. 28).

In Jean's imagined stories of who she would be as a teacher as she studied Dewey in her teacher education classes and later in her lived stories of teaching, she awakened to stories of oppression and separateness that kept some children and families separated into communities of otherness, outside the communities that were within the dominant stories of school. As Jean wrote, she *struggled with how we could shift or change the cultural and social narratives that shaped communities, and that were enacted in social policies and practices.* She worked against those in positions of authority who created policies that kept children and families outside found communities. In doing so, they were able to attend to the stories of children and families who 'do not stand at the centre of their traditions' (Lindemann Nelson, 1995, p. 28).

Summary

While community holds notions of place, identity and home, it also pushes back against these notions, and, at times, outrightly defies these. McKenna and Pratt (2015) offer understandings about borderlands, drawing on Gloria Anzaldúa (1987), as demonstrating 'the importance and complexity of community, but do not undermine the importance of place' (pp. 375–6). McKenna and Pratt draw on the resistance traditions of American philosophy to situate 'the questions of identity and community'. For them borders and borderlands are 'ever-changing places that constitute who we are as individuals and members of communities. [...] these borderlands are a means of understanding difference and sameness and the possibilities of the future' (pp. 375–6).

Section III

Methodological Notebook

Memories of experiences were called up as we came alongside refugees whose lives are frequently shaped by earlier places, places that they fled – places that are remembered and recognized as being home – as well as places that offered temporary shelter (although time in the refugee camps can be measured in months and years) and, over time, places that become their host country. Understanding place as shaping family stories is particularly relevant in intergenerational reverberations of place. This frequently became visible within the field alongside participants. Through earlier studies in schools and within communities, we became more awake to multiple meanings within place and community.

In the study, individual members of the research team engaged in a series of face-to-face conversations with each of the eleven families. Each research team member met many times, over time, with families. We also organized a party and an outdoor BBQ where everyone could come together. We learned the families valued these gatherings.

As researchers, we attend carefully to place and community, in relation to time and social context. We wrote field notes on events as well as on recorded conversations and tape-recorded conversations where possible. As we analysed field texts, including field notes and conversation transcripts, we composed narrative accounts for each participant (Clandinin, 2013). In this methodological notebook, we draw forward fragments of narrative accounts relevant to place and community. What we offer here gives only a sense of the narrative accounts. In order to understand the complexity of participants' experiences of places and communities, it is necessary to read each participant's account.

Places Where We Met

Over two years alongside families, we met them in many places. We first met many of the eleven families in the Syrian Centre at Friday morning English classes. With the exception of one family, Hanan or Zamard accompanied us, as we met individually alongside families in their homes, and community places. Hiroko Kubota, one researcher, recalls when she first met a family at their home.

> Opening the door, Farah opened her arms and welcomed me with her bright and cheerful smile. Her one-year-old girl, Rose, and four-year-old girl, Soufi, also followed her to the entrance with curiosity. Yet, upon seeing a translator and me, Soufi quickly turned around and looked at us from a distance, with half her body hidden behind a pillar. I said, "Hello Soufi!" as I knew her from the Friday English class [...]. Farah often took Soufi and Rose with her to the class. Hearing my voice, Soufi completely hid her body and then quickly peeked at me behind the pillar with a shy smile.

We met all participants for some meetings in their homes. While many conversations at the Syrian Centre focused on practising English, when we met participants at their homes we developed a sense of their ordinary living. In the narrative account Hiroko writes:

> It was our first meeting and my first visit to Farah's house. Her house is located in a quiet neighborhood. In the living room, I saw one old woman sitting on a couch. Farah told me that she lives in the neighborhood and comes every week to visit her. Farah added she was expecting another neighbor to visit her tomorrow as well. The old woman sitting on the couch told me that their community takes good care of the family and they had held a welcoming party and a baby shower for Farah when they just moved here in 2016.

In places participants called home, we began to see their ordinary lives, met people important to them, and learned how their lives were embedded within, or bumped against, larger communities.

Places They Left

Place and memory are deeply connected, and our relationships with place often return us to other times and places. Memories of experiences are written on bodies. Often, as we came alongside the families, we saw that their memories, written on their bodies, are shaped by earlier places. Sometimes, in our conversations, the women and other family members took us back to places they had left. Sometimes these were stories of long ago. Gillian Vigneau, a graduate student researcher, wrote of the stories she heard from Gamila and Nadim of their journey from Syria to Lebanon to Canada.

> During their third year in Lebanon, Gamila and Nadim realized that they, who had refugee status, would not be returning to their beloved home. While Lebanon had provided refuge from the rebels in Syria, they found it was a difficult place to live. They lived in an old office condo made of cement with few windows. Because their home had burned, they had no possessions. Living in Lebanon with almost nothing was devastating. Nadim worked in construction, but was not always paid. Nadim and Gamila felt the people of Lebanon did not respect them. The children recounted school experiences where they often felt scared. They hated school in Lebanon and remembered being disciplined by being hit and yelled at. The children experienced racism in schools and Nadim experienced racism in the workplace. Their experiences in Lebanon contributed to their decision to find refuge in another country, somewhere far away from their beloved Syria, their family, and friends.

Stories of places families had left were told to us often. Sometimes participants chose not to tell the hard stories; sometimes, they told of good memories before the civil unrest. Stories of place were intertwined with stories of relationships over temporal spans of many years. Young (2005) made visible the importance of what she called the intergenerational reverberations of place, how place stretches forward into the storied memories of participants and, we imagine, into the stories of their children. Stories of place shape their family stories, even as their experiences of these places became more temporally distant.

Places They Took Us

Engaging with participants in their homes was marked with a sense of joy. As researchers, we experienced generosity and welcoming. We were always offered tea, coffee and treats; sometimes, we were invited to family dinners. Sometimes, we, Hanan and Zamard, were asked to help navigate challenges they encountered. They asked for our help to make telephone calls to government agencies and schools, places that were marked by privilege and power. Sometimes we went with families to these places; sometimes they invited us while, at other times, we offered to come with them. Gillian accompanied Nadim and Gamila on visits to schools.

> As Nadim was trying to figure out how to re-register the children in Bell School [school names are pseudonyms], I offered to go with him. My intention was to ensure that there were not any misunderstandings between Nadim and the schools. First, Nadim called Bell School and made an appointment for both he and I to attend a meeting. During that meeting, the assistant principal said that before he could approve the transfer for the children, he would have to get approval from Evergreen School. As we sat in the office, he called Evergreen and was told that we needed to meet with Evergreen staff first. Nadim called and made an appointment for us to go to Evergreen School. When I met Nadim the following day to go to the meeting at Evergreen, his body was tense and he was more nervous than he was at Bell.

The experiences at the schools were complex. In this fragment of a narrative account, we make visible that coming alongside participants in different places offers new understandings of their experiences. On the school visits, power dynamics and experiences of institutional racism became visible. While Gillian, a teacher, was comfortable being in school places, this experience, alongside participants, shifted her understanding of who she is, and is becoming, as a teacher. This shift was shaped by going to places alongside participants.

Situating Relationships in Communities

In Chapters 7 and 8, we showed how place and community are intertwined. Meeting participants in places significant in their lives, as well as exploring places they once were part of, helps us situate relationships in community. Farah often took Hiroko back to early experiences.

> Farah's families live close to each other in the same neighborhood. Her hometown is a small village where about 3,500 people lived. The village is located in the south of Syria, not far from the Jordan border. In her neighborhood, there are several small food stores where Farah walked to buy fresh vegetables and fruits every day. [...] Farah [...] recalled that people used to call her family a loving family, as her family members always showed love and care for each other. In summer, they often ate supper together as a big family on a deck on the roof

of the house, while feeling the breeze and looking at the moon and stars right above their heads.

As Farah shared her stories, we see her community was shaped by strong familial relationships, and a love for what she referred to as a *simple life*. It was important to gain a sense of Farah's past experiences in places and within communities, as it shaped our understanding of her and her families' experience in Canada. We saw how important it was for Farah to have neighbours join her on a weekly basis, to hold celebrations that involved others.

In Hiroko's work alongside Maria and her daughter, Elham, the connection between past and present experiences of place and community also became visible.

I invited Elham to join us and asked 'Are you happy living in Canada?'. She quietly shook her head. When I asked, 'Oh you don't like living in Canada?', she shook her head with certainty. Elham revealed that she misses her cousin, Jazzid, who lives in Jordan. Maria showed me pictures on her phone. Elham wore a white dress and Jazzid wore a tuxedo. Many sparkling hearts surrounded the photo and they looked very happy as they leaned on each other. [Elham] told me she really wants to see him in person and prays every day that he will come to Canada. From her voice, I felt her sorrow planted deep in her heart, as her close relationship was disrupted and as she embraced the memories of time spent with her beloved cousin.

Elham had never attended school in Syria and Jordan. Kindergarten in Canada is her first schooling experience. I wondered how she builds new relationships amidst these transitions in her life and in a new school, and how her relationship-building continues or discontinues her prior patterns of building relationships.

We share Hiroko's wonders around the connection of time with place and community. Forward-looking stories are important as Elham composes new stories to live by.

Yearning for Communities to Belong in Canada

Composing forward-looking stories was shaped by a yearning for communities to belong to in Canada.

On a warm September Saturday afternoon, friends gathered in a colleague's back yard in suburban Edmonton. There were streamers and flowers with tables laden with potluck desserts and brightly wrapped gifts guests brought. Friends gathered to welcome Hiroko's new baby. I recognized, among the 25 to 30 guests, members of our research team. I made my way to Hiroko and gratefully took her baby daughter, found a comfortable chair and cuddled the baby. As gifts were opened and food eaten, new guests arrived. It was Farah and her young daughters. 'How lovely', I thought, as she laid her food offerings on the table. She greeted Hiroko and her baby and then began to give her money. 'Oh no.' Hiroko said. 'I do not want money, your presence is what I want'. But Farah insisted. 'No, please, you must. We do this in my home country when a baby is born'.

This moment showed Farah's desire to honour her friendship with Hiroko, a friendship built over time in a research relationship. It also shows Farah's openness to accepting Hiroko's invitation to the shower, an invitation to join one of Hiroko's communities in Edmonton. Farah, who did not live in the suburban community, drove some distance in order to participate. While Farah wanted to be with this new community, she wanted to belong in ways that were narratively coherent with what she knew in Syria. Blessing a new baby with a gift of money is what she knew. In this she reminded us of Buber's sense of an authentic community in which otherness is overcome in the spirit of friendship.

Section IV

Imagination, Inquiry, Wonder and Playfulness: Opening into Liminality and Uncertainty

Imagination and wonder have long preoccupied our thoughts, not only as they provide openings into understanding the liminality and uncertainty of our lives, but also as they are central in creating new and endless possibilities. Imagination disrupts a linear view of experience, and allows for the possibility of retelling and reliving experiences. This, in turn, allows us to continuously compose and recompose our lives in relation. It allows us to acknowledge experiences past and present, and experiences yet to be had. In Chapter 9 we explore more closely notions of imagination, while in Chapters 10 and 11 we explore what might be seen as processes of igniting our imagination, such as wonder and inquiry, as well as the uncertainty and liminality linked to our understanding of imagination. In Chapter 12 we explore the ways playfulness allows us to connect with imagination and uncertainty.

9

Imagination

Abstract

Imagination has a long history in philosophical thought, as well as in the arts. In this chapter we trace the ideas of imagination in ways that are most relevant to narrative inquiry. This means that we situate imagination within a relational context. We see that we sustain close connection to others through imagination (Caine & Steeves, 2009). Theodore Sarbin (1998, 2004) reminds us that our imaginings are emplotted narratives and critical to these emplotted narratives is our believed-in imaginings. For Arendt (1958) it is imagination that allows us to ask new questions, as well as create the ground of becoming.

Turning to Experience

$1234.62 was the amount on my monthly cheque stub as a youth worker at an outreach school named the Main Street Program. I open up my filing cabinet from time to time to go back to these early experiences. I kept every cheque stub from this time period. The stubs are held together by a paper clip in a manila folder, with hurried words written marking the dates and months. The colour is starting to fade, worn out over time. Paper memory markers filed safely away.

The Main Street Program was located just off Broadway Street in Saskatoon, Saskatchewan, in a little brick storefront; it was a school program for young people (grade 9) who struggled with the mainstream school system.

I recall memories of my initial interview: the door opening slowly; meeting a middle-aged woman named Laurel; her warm welcome. She was the program coordinator. I introduced myself and scanned my surroundings. There was a green 1970's vintage couch, a little stove, a kitchenette, and posters with positive messaging covering the walls. These images stayed with me.

During that first meeting Laurel and I talked with ease for over an hour. We sat on the couch talking about summer travels and how we thought about working with youth. As I think about this now, we didn't discuss school in a formal sense. Before I left that day, she offered me my first job in a school. This was a formative beginning of learning how to work with youth in a different way. I was 19 years old.

Midway through my second year at the Main Street Program, Laurel called me in for a 1:1 meeting and evaluation. She told me she wanted me to go back to school and formally become a teacher. She said, 'you can't stay, you must keep going'. My initial thoughts were filled with resistance but also with doubts about not being smart enough. No one in my family had ever gone to university.

As I write, I awaken to recognizing Laurel as a teacher in my early experiences, someone who saw something different within me, something that I could not see within myself at this time. What I saw was limited by my imagination of what was possible.

Laurel offered me ways to be more at ease in worlds where I had no confidence or experience. Through small purposeful experiences that only now I see as important, she was teaching me. She was teaching me by showing me possibilities along the way. She took me to coffee shops to discuss a local play and to introduce me to books and authors I did not know. A small walk through the university campus to get registration forms had purpose. She shared stories of her own university experiences as she took me for an initial visit to the university library. She used her credit card to help me with registration and to officially get the paperwork in on time. I was eventually accepted to the Indian Teacher Education Program.

This was a shifting story in many ways. I started university in the fall semester. I felt as if I had been there before. While I recognized places when unfamiliarity crept over me, I also recognized I had walked in these spaces alongside Laurel. I had been to the library. I had listened to music in this way before. I had read some of the authors I learned about in my first year of studies.

$1234.62.

I feel the edges of those paper memory markers as I think of one of my first teachers.

Imagination as Coming to 'Otherwise'

As we read Sean's story of coming to his first position in the Main Street Program, and from there into a teacher education program, we see how it was Laurel, through watching and working alongside him, who helped him imagine himself as 'otherwise' (Greene, 1995). Slowly and carefully Laurel shifted the stories Sean had of himself in ways that drew on imagination as Greene defines it. For Greene (1994) imagination enables us to move through the barriers of the taken-for granted and summon up alternative possibilities for living, for being in the world. It permits us to set aside (at least for a while) the stiflingly familiar and the banal. It opens us to visions of the possible rather than the predictable; it permits us, if we choose to give our imaginations free play, to look at things as if they could be otherwise.

(pp. 494–5)

Greene's conception of imagination is a powerful one in narrative inquiry. It highlights the possibility for change that awakens us to 'alternative possibilities for living' at the same time as it draws attention to what might be possible rather than to what is already known and what might be seen as predictable. In Sean's story of applying for the position and coming to the Main Street Program for the first time, it is the physical building and its internal decor that first challenges his taken-for-granted view of schools and what it means to be a teacher and a student. Sitting with Laurel and talking about many things, but not what Sean recognized as a discussion about *school*, also challenge what he knows about what matters when one works with youth in schools. Sean's expectations are disrupted in ways that lay the ground for new possibilities.

When Laurel walks alongside him, and carefully scaffolds who he might be in the world, we see Sean beginning to develop the capacity to disrupt what he knew and to begin to imagine himself as otherwise, as *smart enough* to go to university, as the *first one from his family to attend university*. Later, as he struggles with the unfamiliarity of studying at a university, he calls on his imagination, carefully shaped by Laurel, to sustain him. As Sean writes now of his experience, he attends to 'the wonder of multiple perspectives' (Greene, 2001, p. 187); at this time, it was the wonder of multiple perspectives on who he is and is becoming. These multiple perspectives were shaped by the possibilities Laurel had offered him. He was beginning to think about what happened to him and what might be possible if he could imagine himself otherwise. This notion of imagining otherwise has been critical to our work in narrative inquiry as we work alongside participants.

Sean describes two interruptions in his stories of himself: the first interruption is his conversation with Laurel in which he first questions what it means to work with youth in school: the second challenge comes later when Laurel says, *you can't stay, you must keep going*. With those words, Laurel sharply interrupts Sean's telling of his story as someone who works with youth but not as a university-educated teacher. With that interruption,

Laurel opens up another possibility for Sean; that is, he could attend university and become educated as a teacher. Slowly Sean begins to shift his stories of who he is and slowly begins to see something else. 'It [became] possible to abandon one-dimensional viewing, to look from many vantage points and, in doing so, construct meanings scarcely suspected before' (Greene, 2001, p. 187). For Sean, perhaps his story of himself was a 'one-dimensional viewing' of what he could be as he worked alongside youth in the Main Street Program. He was someone who could work with youth but initially he could not imagine himself as someone who held knowledge (see Chapter 2) nor could he imagine himself as someone able to study at a university.

We wonder if, as Greene points out, this process of opening up possibilities was also marked by surprise for Sean. For narrative inquirers, it is important to continue to draw on imagination to open up spaces within stories for otherwise, knowing that it is our capacity to be open to otherwise that also opens the possibility of surprise. Greene (1994) helps us conceptualize this understanding as narrative inquirers understand identity making as an ongoing process in which there can be surprises.

> The surprise comes along with becoming different – consciously different as one finds ways of acting on envisaged possibility. It comes along with hearing different words and music, seeing from unaccustomed angles, realizing that the world perceived from one place is not the world.
>
> (p. 20)

We see this in Sean's story as he is surprised by his initial experiences as a student in the university. He was surprised when he *felt as if I had been there before and when I recognized I had walked in these spaces alongside Laurel. I had been to the library. I had listened to music in this way before. I had read some of the authors I learned about in my first year of studies.* While we hear his surprise we also know that he has now acted on the possibilities of otherwise that Laurel imagined alongside him. He realized that the world he had earlier perceived as one place with him in it, was not the world he was now inhabiting.

Imagination Embedded in the Relational

In Sean's story, he tells of opening himself to new possibilities, because Laurel was able to imagine different stories for him to live by. Greene (2001) elaborates this sense of opening ourselves and how that opening is possible when she writes,

> [o]pening ourselves, putting one-dimensionality aside and shallow conventions, we can nurture a desire or *communitas* by means of art experiences while preserving differences. We need to affirm ourselves and touch our own horizons as we work to fuse with others, as we offer more and more pathways out of the fixed and the ordinary pathways toward what might be. (p. 190) [...] None of this signifies that you are required to like these works or that you are bound to discover openings within them. I am pointing to, suggesting to you the possibilities opened by imagination – possibilities that something may happen in your experience, that something may open to a new way of seeing or feeling or coping with the world.
>
> (p. 188; italics in original text)

Thinking with Greene shaped how narrative inquirers understand imagination, not as an individual effort, but as something that happens in relation. Greene points out that the desire for *communitas* is significant. Caine and Steeves (2009) argue that our 'imagination is inextricably intertwined within our lives and our relationships' (p. 1). While we have been thinking alongside Laurel and Sean and their relationship, it is also important to understand that the relationships they each hold are also part of a larger community. Laurel opened up worlds by connecting Sean with local plays, authors and books that were unfamiliar to him. In these ways she opened up possibilities for others to come to know Sean. In doing so Laurel reflects Greene's sense of horizons fusing in her actions, which are filled with care and concern for others, for *communitas*.

Narrative inquirers work with an understanding of imagination that offers the possibility of 'hearing different words and music' (Greene, 1994, p. 28), seeing from different angles and recognizing the multiplicity of the world and the multiplicity of the communities we are part of, those we live on the edge of and those from which we are excluded (see Chapter 8). Our connections to and within the worlds that shape our lives fuel our imagination. These connections call us to closely attend to our own and others' lives; they too call us to imagine 'as if'.

And while much of our work as narrative inquirers is marked by listening to people tell and retell their experiences, we, too, are interested in the living (Clandinin & Connelly, 2000). It is in the living that we see most clearly that we are not simply observers, but that we shape the worlds we are in – that we offer at times an unaccustomed angle, that we shape possibilities to act differently. In working closely with people, we or those we work alongside, 'may open to a new way of seeing or feeling or coping with the world' (Greene, 2001, p. 188). Sean, by retelling his story alongside Laurel, helps us see what we are doing and that imagination is a necessity of coming to be otherwise.

Stories to live by, a narrative term for identity, are composed within relational spaces; spaces that are in-between, that are marked by tensions and attention to being otherwise. The 'in-between' spaces are spaces where we ask one another 'who' and not 'what' we are (Arendt, 1958). They are places of loving perception (Lugones, 1987) and we wonder if it is the 'loving perception that breathes life into our relationship so that we can feel the wind, and on it travel to each other's worlds lovingly and playfully, to believe in and to imagine' (Caine & Steeves, 2009, p. 8). These in-between spaces speak to, and about, the relational, yet they, too, make visible how we are embedded within larger communities which shaped our lives and the possibility to look 'at things as if they could be otherwise' (Greene, 1994, p. 495).

Imagination as Thinking Metaphorically: Thinking 'as If'

There is a need to stimulate and release the imagination – to engage in play with notions of 'as if'. There is a deep sense of awakening, awakening to new possibilities, to new stories to live. Thinking with Sean's experience of entering university, we can see that Sean holds memories of moments with Laurel, moments in which he looks at himself and remembers as if he could be a teacher. In the moment of remembering the 'as if' story, he also starts to act as if he is a teacher. He begins to create a story that will sustain himself as he goes to university. As Sean starts to take up these 'as if' stories, he has to defy the story of being Indigenous – he has to defy stories of who he should be, defy a sense of judgement of what is possible. Sean chooses to enter the Indian Teacher Education program, which helps him to find a space for himself – a space that supports his 'as if' stories and defies the narrow scripts composed for him of having lived on a farm, of being poor, of being displaced from his birth family or of being Indigenous.

Cynthia Ozik (1989) writes

> [t]hrough metaphor, the past has the capacity to imagine us, and we it. Through metaphorical concentration, doctors can imagine what it is to be

their patients. Those who have no pain can imagine those who suffer. Those at the centre can imagine what it is to be outside. The strong can imagine the weak. Illuminated lives can imagine the dark. Poets in their twilight can imagine the familiar heart of strangers.

(p. 283)

And yet we are lost so many times in the wonders that are raised by the question of what if. Lost in a sense of imagination that is limited by our ability to see otherwise, to see how the contexts and contours of our life could be changed. Yet, what happens if we cannot imagine what it is like to be our students, to be our patients, to be our sons and daughters, to be our lovers. Or when we cannot imagine ourselves in response to the question of what if. In these moments, perhaps, our sense of being lost changes who we are, as it shifts the ground beneath our feet. Letting ourselves be lost creates a sense of vulnerability while raising questions of what if. And in this moment of feeling lost, Ozik (1989) reminds us that

[w]ithout the metaphor of memory and history, we cannot imagine the life of the Other. We cannot imagine what it is to be someone else. Metaphor is the reciprocal agent, the universalizing force: it makes possible the power to envision the stranger's heart.

(p. 279)

In times of loss, it is significant to reach out to our memory and our history; it is an opportunity to 'attend to one another, [... to] attend from [within our] changing landscapes, and [...] embodied knowing' (Caine & Steeves, 2009, p. 3). To understand 'imagining as a form of perceptual and embodied knowing (Sarbin, 1998, 2004; Greene 1995) and an essential way of being (Merleau-Ponty, 1962), and as a way to attend from our experiences (Polanyi, 1969) such that we attend in particular ways' (Caine & Steeves, 2009, p. 3) sustains us. It is imagination that grounds our what if. It is imagination that allows us to explore self and others, an exploration that engages others in play.

Embedded in this is a sense of humanness, a sense of the other, whose breath grounds their body, grounds who they are. Caine and Steeves (2009) write, 'our believed-in imaginings are dialogic, reverberating through the relationships we have within ourselves, our histories, present lives and future, our relationships with one another and within the stories we live' (p. 8). As we contemplate questions of what if, our imagination takes flight and we begin to create new ground for becoming.

Imagination as Fused with Memory

As narrative inquirers we attend closely to the ways that imagination and memory are deeply entwined processes. As Kerby (1991) reminds us,

> [i]magination is difficult to separate from memory because it shares a similar phenomenal structure. [...] Imagination very often presents us with a past that we wish we had lived, or with the past as we now wish we had lived it. We might say [...] that imagination augments recollection and the values of the memories recollected.
>
> (p. 25)

Kerby is directing us to the ways that our imagination fills in, or augments our memories. In narrative inquiry we do not see memory as something like what we obtain through video recording or audio recording events. In narrative inquiry we understand memory, much like Kerby does, as fused with imagination for 'memories are thereby knit into the fabric of our world, and they attain their status as memory largely through connectedness with other events known and recollected' (p. 27).

Aiden Downey and Clandinin (2010) play with Bruner's (2002) notion of narrative as subjuntivizing experience as a way to think about the ways that narrative inquirers see memory and imagination as connected. Bruner helps us understand that

> [t]hrough narrative, we construct, reconstruct, and in some ways reinvent yesterday and tomorrow. Memory and imagination fuse in the process. Even when we create the possible worlds of fiction, we do not desert the familiar but subjuntivize it into what might have been and what might be. The human mind, however cultivated its memory or refined its recording systems, can never fully and faithfully recapture the past, but neither can it escape it. Memory and imagination supply and consume each other's wares.
>
> (p. 93)

As Sean writes his story in the present, we see the ways that he described the room where he met Laurel, part imagined, part memory record of details. As he remembers the moment and place of the meeting, it is both remembered and imagined, but subjuntivized 'into what might have been and what might be' (p. 93).

In narrative inquiry, this process of weaving together imagination and memory, we see as also entwined with our experiential knowledge (see Chapter 2). In other words our experiential knowledge is grounded both in memory and in imagination. Caine and Steeves (2009) note

> [w]e travel through time in our memories shifting our imaginings backwards, expanding out our life stories, enabling multiple possible resonances that may connect our storied worlds to others (Hale Hankins, 1998). Connecting through imaginings with others we can feel our relationships evolving, creating a possibility to discover what is unknown, what is different, what connects us to others and others to us.
>
> (p. 6)

They draw on the German expression 'Spuren im Gedächtnis' to help us see that remembering is a process that is often triggered by the relationships we find ourselves in. In this way the fusion of imagination and memory is expanded by being in relation. This sense of remembering creates the possibility to access our memory, to call forth events and happenings and connections that may have been forgotten. In narrative inquiry we understand that imagination and memory are fused in ways that leave gaps and silences, that can erase events and happenings, that allow us to reinvent what we remember, while lamenting the loss of what we once knew. It is here that we turn towards the believed-in imaginings.

Emplotted Narratives as Believed-in Imaginings

Sarbin (1998, 2004) reminds narrative inquirers that our imaginings are emplotted narratives and critical to these are our believed-in imaginings. In 1998 Sarbin wrote 'human actions we call believings have no independent status outside of imaginings. I also make the claim that assigning credibility to an imagining is an action in the service of sense making to meet the demand for a consistent self-narrative' (p. 17).

For believed-in imaginings to take hold they require a relational space, and an attentiveness to an unfolding life. It is within this space that people can compose and recompose their lives in ways that create narrative coherence (Carr, 1986), and a space where 'narrative-inspired imaginings can influence belief and action' (Sarbin, 2004, p. 6). The emplotted narratives in this way create ways to make sense of the continuities and discontinuities, the gaps and silences that are part of all of our lives. Yet, it does more. It creates the possibility to shift a life.

As we think with Sarbin's ideas, we return to Laurel, who created an emplotted narrative in relation to Sean that was shaped by believed-in imaginings. Laurel saw new possibilities and placed a high degree of value on Sean's ability to be a teacher. This is interesting, as it is Sarbin (2004) who points out that narratives can not only shape actions, but influence identity development in profound ways.

> $1234.62.
>
> *I feel the edges of those paper memory markers as I think of one of my first teachers.*

The memory markers take Sean back to Laurel, but also to times where he imagined his life unfolding in different ways. It is through engaging with Laurel that new stories become possible and new imaginings unfold. It is Sarbin (1998) who makes the case 'that the contents of those human actions we call believings have no independent status outside of imaginings' (p. 17).

Laurel's believed-in imaginings lead to particular actions, she interrupts the stories Sean has of himself. As a result of these interactions, Sean's life changes in profound ways. In many ways she makes 'moral issues central to a particular plot' (Sarbin, 2004, p. 18). Sean can no longer think of himself as not smart enough to go to university. Her believed-in imaginings help Sean create a different story of who he is and is becoming. Caine and Steeves (2009) write that

> [t]his resonates with us as narrative inquirers, as we understand that the 'classrooms, halls, grounds, and community – become memory boxes in which people and events of today are re-told and written into the research texts of tomorrow' (Clandinin & Connelly, 2000, p. 66) and are lived in the stories people live and tell of their lives.

> (p. 6)

Imagination as Creating New Ground for Becoming

For Arendt (1958) it is imagination that allows us to ask new questions, as well as to create the ground of becoming. Sarbin (2004), in his conceptualization of imagination, also highlights the ground of becoming, the contextual, in ways that create the possibility of making new ground or new contexts for becoming. Sarbin helps narrative inquirers work from a view of people as living in 'story-shaped' worlds, one which highlights a distinction between 'narrative as a mode of representation and narrative as an ontological form' (Smith, 2008, p. 112). For Arendt, and for Sarbin, imagination allows us to create new grounds of becoming.

As Sean worked in the Main Street Program, we imagine he might have begun to ask himself new questions about who he might become alongside youth who, like himself, had not imagined themselves in other ways or with other possible life trajectories. And it was Laurel who, through asking Sean questions, began to encourage Sean to imagine the possibility of going to university and becoming a teacher. These were emplotted narratives she was composing with/for him.

Years later, when Sean begins to teach, we see him working alongside youth who resisted or did not 'fit' the dominant structures and systems of school. We see him creating new ground for becoming with youth in the ways that Laurel had taught him. Sean described in his doctoral work establishing what he called a powwow school, a summer school for Indigenous youth that was offered in their home community. He was imagining a new ground of becoming that would allow youth to attend summer school, at home, and subsequently allow them to graduate. He began creating that new ground by asking questions of them, trying to learn why they were not completing their graduation requirements. Composing this summer school and stepping into this new 'ground of becoming' represented a different world to Sean as he began to imagine a different life and different possible stories of himself and the youth he was working with.

As Arendt (1958) indicates, imagination can set the ground for the questions we are able to ask. Greene points out that

> [i]magination seeks meaning and widening perceptions; but it also gives rise to glimpses of possibility, to what is not yet, to what ought to be. It is beyond prediction. Imagination opens windows in the actual, releases people from the coercion so characteristic of this media-dominated time. Saying that, however, I think we have to always remember that imagination opens not only to visions of the beneficent and the decent, but it can also lead to terrible things.
>
> (Greene in conversation with Ayers, 1995, pp. 321–2)

It, too, sets the possibilities to travel 'to each other's worlds and to do so in loving ways, setting the ground for becoming together in the in-between space in narrative inquiry' (Caine & Steeves, 2009, p. 9). Yet, we also know that while we can shape the ground of becoming, we must attend to issues of positioning, power and equity.

As Greene (in conversation with Ayers, 1995) points out, the moral is always interwoven with these new grounds of becoming.

> We think constantly, for example, of what it signifies to be in a world becoming increasingly diverse and multiplex, rich with contending values and competing ways of life. It takes an enormous act of imagination to attend to the lived reality of so many different persons without subsuming them in groups and categories. It takes an enormous act of imagination to grasp a world that is pluralist, relativist, perspectival, and, at once, yearning towards community. There is no chart for this. We are living through new beginnings; we require imagination to light the slow fuse of possibility.
>
> (p. 322)

Greene connects us back to Caine and Steeves and the importance of how the ground is shaped in ways that allow each person; and the contexts in which they live, to be attentive to the moral ground we each walk on.

Summary

In this chapter we laid out ideas of imagination that are significant to narrative inquiry. We show the importance of becoming otherwise to our unfolding lives. This sense of otherwise is marked by surprise and of play with notions of 'as if'. We show the criticality of imagination as embedded in relationships and as connected to memory. In the next chapter we turn towards inquiry and wonder and their links to experience.

10

Inquiry and Wonder

Abstract

In this Chapter we show how wide-awakeness and awakening are central to sustaining our inquiries and wonders and allow us to sustain ourselves in uncertain situations without shutting down inquiry and wonder. It is important in narrative thinking that we are attentive to questions of who we are within relational contexts. Drawing attention to what is unimaginable allows us to stay open to the unrecognizability of others. Kearney (1988) talks about 'the ethical demand to imagine otherwise' (p. 364). We cannot respond to this ethical demand without a sense of inquiry or a sense of wonder. It is to inquiry and wonder as key concepts, that we turn our attention in this chapter. For us this sense of wonder is part of a curiosity that asks 'who are you?' and not 'what are you'? (Arendt, 1958), as well as who we are amidst ongoing lives and relationships.

Townhouse Moment One: Familiarity Tricks Us into Being at Ease

As Azima and I sat together in the family's rented townhouse, I thought about how this new place is shaping her. The townhouse living room is filled with an overstuffed sectional sofa; with tables that are familiar to me in size, shape, and style. It is a physical place that looks like many townhouses I have lived in, and visited, over the years. The ease with which Azima greets me in English adds to my sense of familiarity.

In these first conversations I asked about what she has left behind in her journeys from Syria to Lebanon to Western Canada. I wonder though, even as I ask, if she wants to remember. Does she want to 'remember everything [...] remember what happened [...] long ago. [To] think about it and keep on thinking about it' (Basso, 1996, p. 70). Who am I here as I open conversations about these places she has left, places her grandparents and great grandparents did not leave and that she has now left? Does she want to help me travel to her worlds, worlds she has left and can only return to in memory? I wonder if it is easier for her to talk about what is happening in this new place.

I look around the room, searching for what appears out of place to me, things that do not trick me into being at ease. I spot a coffee pot that fits my idea of a coffee server she might have grown up with in her family home in Syria. I look at her seated carefully on the sofa and I notice a plate of fruit prepared for me in front of me. She is working to make me at ease, and I think about what she might had prepared for me if I had met her years ago in Syria.

I look out her living room window to the large park and hill behind the townhouse, a hill that is covered with snow. I ask whether the children slide on the hill and whether they like playing on the hill. I am reminded of my son when we lived in a similar townhouse with a sliding hill much like this one. I think about how this northern snow and cold are new for her and for her children. I wonder about how Azima's new place, many degrees of latitude and longitude away from what she knew as home, is shaping her life.

Inquiry into Experience

As has been clear throughout this book, it is in Dewey's ideas about experience that we first grounded our theoretical ideas about narrative inquiry (see Chapter 1). His ideas of experience are foundational with their focus on the unfolding, enfolding nature of experience, each experience being taken up into future experiences. Dewey developed his understanding of experience over time. In 1916 he wrote of experience in the following way: 'When we experience something we act upon it, we do something with it; then we undergo and suffer the consequences. We do something to the thing and then it does something to us in return: such is the peculiar combination' (p. 139).

As Downey and Clandinin (2010) wrote,

[f]or Dewey, doing can lead to undoing in the sense that our actions in a world act on us, with the result being an irrevocable alteration in both 'it' and us. Dewey understood 'us' and 'it' not as distinct entities but rather as parts or aspects of an experiential whole, a point he struggled to make in a language prone to dichotomies.

(p. 384)

In this way we see that an experience 'occurs in the relationship between what we do in the world and what this does to us, the relationship between actions and reactions' (Downey & Clandinin, 2010, p. 384). Dewey (1938) outlined two criteria of experience: continuity and interaction. By continuity he means 'every experience both takes up something from those which have gone before and modifies in some way the quality of those which come after' (p. 35). For Dewey an emerging vantage point was created by the unfolding of experience. Each subsequent situation

offers a new perspective to look back on the experiences leading up to, and out of, an experience, making 'growth' provisional and emergent rather than fixed and found. For Dewey this retrospection is always prospective, a looking backwards in the service of looking, and ultimately moving, forward.
(Downey & Clandinin, 2010, p. 384)

Dewey's (1938) second criterion of experience, interaction, involves the interplay between 'objective' and 'internal' conditions. Dewey highlighted that

we each live in, and on, our own experiential middle grounds, always somewhat stuck in the mud of trying to get from here to there, from is to ought, and that this muddling around was something we should work on, as doing so would prepare us for the inevitable muddling that comes with the unknown of the future.
(Downey & Clandinin, 2010, p. 384)

As Jean walked into Azima's home, she found herself drawn back to memories of many other townhouses, townhouses she had lived in, and those of friends she visited. Jean found not only the familiar townhouse layout but also familiar stuffed leather furniture, and chairs and tables arranged in familiar ways. Familiar experiences were called forward as Azima greeted Jean in English and welcomed her inside. It would have been easy to be tricked into a sense of the familiar, of the known, of the feeling of having been here before. But Jean came with a sense of wonder, of knowing that she was not meeting someone who had lived in Edmonton, in Canada, for years but of someone who had just arrived, and had arrived from another country, and who had arrived as a refugee.

The Importance of Wide-Awakeness

Working with these Deweyan ideas of experience to understand phenomena narratively, inquiry becomes a part of life. We are always engaged in inquiry, in figuring out the moment by moment living of our lives, as we undergo experiences, taking up what came before into new experiences. Anticipating what might be. This ongoing inquiry that is life can, of course, become habituated in ways that mean we are no longer awake to what we are in the midst of living. Greene (1995) points out the importance of wide-awakeness, that sense of skin tingling awareness to all that is in the world. Greene uses the term wide-awakeness to highlight that '[w]ithout the ability to think about yourself, to reflect on your life, there's really no awareness, no consciousness. Consciousness doesn't come automatically' (p. 35). For Greene, the concept of wide-awakeness is an 'awareness of what it is to be in the world' (p. 35). She highlights the ways wide-awakeness calls us to think about phenomena narratively through being wakeful and attentive to the life-making and meaning-making of each person engaged in the living of their life. Greene provided conceptual depth to how narrative inquiry takes up wide-awakeness, that is, as a call to be active, to be engaged, to be attentive to experiences, both our own and others. She describes wide-awakeness as linked to the ongoingness of life inquiry, that is as coming through 'being alive, awake, curious, and often furious' (p. 35).

While Greene (1995) draws attention to wide-awakeness as an ability, or a state, which is linked to curiosity and inquiry, narrative inquiry also works with a concept of awakening. These processes of waking up to the complexities that live within each experience are significant. As lives come together, we attend to the complexities of lives in relation.

Greene and Dewey draw attention to aesthetic dimensions of experience. Greene startles us awake by pointing out that anaesthetic is the opposite of aesthetic (Greene, 2007). The anaesthetic numbs us and closes down the possibility of wonder and inquiry. At first the physical space and furniture threatened to create a familiarity that made Jean feel at ease, threatening to dull her into a lack of wonder, a kind of anaesthetic. As she sat in the room noticing the familiarity that threatened to dull the awe, Jean attended carefully to the strange, the out-of-place, rather than the in-place.

Wonder became an early and key concept in theoretical understandings of narrative inquiry. Wonder, according to the Oxford English and Spanish Dictionary, means a 'feeling of amazement and admiration, caused by something beautiful, remarkable, or unfamiliar' (Oxford Lexico, nd). As narrative inquirers we were first drawn to the idea of wonder by our sense that we needed to enter new situations with a sense of awe and with a sense of the unknown. Annie Dillard (1974) wrote of wonder in a way that resonated with Greene's (1995) idea of wide-awakeness. Dillard writes of seeing trees catching sunlight as 'less like seeing than like being for the first time seen, knocked breathless by a powerful glance' (p. 33). It is this sense of wonder that became a kind of metaphor for what is so central to narrative inquiry. Dillard helped us see the importance of wonder, of puzzles that arise when we are open to the truly remarkable, beautiful and unfamiliar.

Bateson (1989) offers us insight into the importance of wonder as a key concept in narrative inquiry as she offered us ways of conceptualizing wonder that forefronted our not knowing as we moved into new situations. In order to understand experience as a narrative phenomena, we attend with a sense that we are always in the midst of an unfamiliar phenomenon. In order to understand experience narratively, we linger in uncertainty, unfamiliarity, without assumptions. In this way, thinking narratively allows us to be open to attending to the relational within each situation. This notion of wonder as a way of being was often critiqued by those who felt it did not clearly establish our standpoint but, for us, it was the openness to possibility that was central to coming alongside in order to understand experience as a narrative phenomena.

Cultivating a way of seeing with wonder is nested within a Deweyan view of experience. It requires that we do not allow ourselves to, as Greene (1995) so eloquently stated, fall asleep but to stay open to what lives outside our usual ways of seeing, to be open to Bateson's (1989) 'possibility of delicious surprise' (p. 4).

Townhouse Moment Two: Crossing the Threshold through Wonder

Three white dresses, three little girls standing in front of their mother, greet me at the door on my first meeting with them. This is a memory that stays with me, in part because the three girls are similar in age to my own girls. They proudly welcome me into their home, a third story apartment on the north side of the city. Hanan, a translator who is part of our research team, brought me to meet this family. For my first visit, I carried a yellow bag filled with some basic supplies, the consent forms, and a brief summary of the study. In the bag were coloured markers and construction paper, the items that eventually became most important on this first meeting day.

I remember my trepidation during the first knock on the door. I was unfamiliar with the experiences of being a refugee family. Uncertainty surrounded me, there were language differences, cultural and gender differences, protocols that are unknown and a stark unfamiliarity with their geographic homeland and the political and social history of the place they had come from. I worried for a while before this first visit and wondered: How do I begin? What do I wear? What are the right steps? I remember saying to myself 'just go slow. I will only stay for a short time during this first visit, maybe a half an hour'.

Three white dresses, three little girls standing in front of their mother greet me at the door. The oldest reaches out to shake my hand, and tells me her name in English. She introduces her sisters and mother. In her introduction, she shifted back and forth between English and Arabic. I was not used to the sound of Arabic – I was not sure what I was expecting. I looked to Hanan for guidance. I am waiting to meet the father of the family and find myself searching for a cue as to what to do next. Too late, the youngest one has me by the hand and brings me into the apartment, crossing the border from hallway carpet to laminate apartment floor. As I step across the border, I notice that I still have my jacket and outdoor shoes on.

I enter into a living room that has a glass door that leads to a little balcony overlooking the street. There is no couch, only a white plastic patio set with a few chairs. As I stand in the middle of the living room, yellow university bag in hand, I feel like I am taking up space. The girls are asking questions, the youngest one connected to my leg. I am awkward and uncomfortable. I look to Hanan and their mother and they both laugh. Hanan asks me if I would like tea but, before I reply, the oldest girls have already answered for me. I ask Hanan to ask their mom if I can give the girls the markers and paper to play with. Hanan assures me that I can, this is o.k. We spread paper on the floor. They all want the most colorful papers and they begin to draw. I join them on the floor and we're all drawing with the many colours available.

I am still waiting to meet their father and I find myself thinking that time is getting away from me. The sound of keys jingling and the creak of the door. Their dad is home now. The girls jump up immediately. I know this feeling but now I am seeing it from the other side. I am usually the dad coming home, not someone with the children greeting the dad. I am nervous as I sit on the floor with markers surrounded by paper creations. Hanan and his wife drink tea while sitting at the plastic picnic table. They do not move and continue their conversation. I wonder what he will make of me. I wonder what I should say, how do I introduce myself in the right way.

I hear the girls calling out to their dad 'meet our new friend Sean.' They tug him into the room the same way they pulled me in earlier. I look up from the floor to see a gentle smile greeting me. I pull myself up and we shake hands, introducing ourselves in English. Speaking the same language is a connecting point that meets my need to be comfortable. 'Stay for supper,' he says. I look at my watch, thinking I need to go home to my family, but I can't say 'no'. I am confused. I know it is the middle of Ramadan and he will not be eating yet. I look to Hanan. She nods and indicates that it's alright, they asked you to stay. You should stay.

Staying Awake to Who I Am

In townhouse moment two we see again the key concepts of inquiry and wonder; we see again how experience is understood as an ongoing inquiry process. This is made visible as Sean tells of his coming to a new place – a place in which a refugee family agreed to become part of a research study. Experience is, as was visible in townhouse moment one, understood as unfolding and enfolding over time, in diverse places and social contexts.

We return to wonder, a feeling of amazement and admiration, caused by experiencing something as beautiful, remarkable or unfamiliar. Bateson (2000) wrote of how a friend advised her to 'stop sounding like a little girl just wondering about things' (p. 236). Bateson, in resistance to her friend's advice, continued to see wonder as more powerful than explicit conclusions. We, like Bateson, see wonder as a way to think about phenomena narratively, a way to acknowledge each new experience as something unfamiliar or remarkable.

As Sean arrives at the family's apartment, he acknowledges his sense of wonder, of knowing that he is in a liminal space. As the apartment door opened, he searched for resonances, for the familiar, for something to help him feel comfortable. He knows what his daughters like to do and he immediately wonders if the three girls in white dresses are like his daughters. He wonders: 'Who am I in this new place?' He stands on the doorway threshold, hovers, looking for a father who is clearly not present. He is awake to knowing he, as a male stranger, is entering a home inhabited in this moment only by a woman and her three daughters. He knows that he is with Hanan, who he turns to frequently for guidance. But he is wakeful to being a man in a Muslim home and wonders if his presence in the apartment bumps up against gendered social and cultural narratives. He is caught in his wonders and searches for an inquiry edge, a way to wonder himself into the apartment. As he wonders about who he is in the unfolding events, the girls act, pulling him forward into the apartment.

As in Townhouse Moment One, we see how important it is to enter into situations with a sense of staying open to the unfamiliar, to not foreclose situations with labels and certainty, erasing the unfamiliar in an attempt to make ourselves comfortable. Doing so could erase others and shut down any possibility of wonder. We see again the importance of lingering in uncertainty, lingering with a sense of dis/ease, of dis/comfort. This way of living with ongoing inquiry and wonder, so key to understanding the phenomena of experience narratively, allows an openness to what we can imagine and what we cannot imagine, what we can recognize and what we cannot yet recognize.

Another key idea linked to understanding experience narratively through wonder and inquiry is the importance of a sense of dis/ease and uncertainty. Not turning away to seek comfort and ease is central to narrative inquiry. This living in uncertainty allows us to continually be in a space of vulnerability, of not knowing, for it is within this space that we are most awake to the experiences of those we are coming alongside.

Townhouse Moment Three: Attending to Invisibility and Vulnerability

It was amidst the spaces that were created when we were meeting each Friday morning at the Syrian Centre that we found participants for our research. It is here that I met Jaan. Jaan was very quiet and, with few English skills, she often smiled at people, but rarely engaged in conversations. I was intrigued by her quietness and calm presence. Her two children were different in demeanor than Jaan in how they engaged in social relations – like Jaan they often smiled, but they also sought out opportunities to play.

It took several months to come to know Jaan better. We engaged in visits and conversations at her house, always in the presence of a translator. When Jaan became pregnant she isolated herself and started to attend English classes less often and eventually left the program. During my visits and conversations with her, I frequently wondered about how her life and days were structured. As someone who had come as an immigrant to Canada and who had wondered about my own happiness, I wondered if she was happy. As I wondered about her happiness, new questions started to arise for me. What is happiness? How do we determine someone's happiness? Why did I think about happiness in relation to Jaan?

As Jaan's experiences brought forward questions about happiness for me, I wondered: Why does happiness matter to me? is happiness a promise (Ahmed, 2010)? and I wondered if the promise of Canadian citizenship, also had been a promise of happiness (Ahmed, 2010).

There are moments when I looked at Jaan and felt a sense of sadness, a sense that she has had few opportunities 'to become someone' (Swanson, 2019). Yet, the more I watched Jaan, the more I wondered about my failure to recognize her. I too wondered about the failure of the Canadian government, and perhaps my failure, to give happiness in return for becoming Canadian (Ahmed, 2010). Ahmed (2010) asks me to consider if happiness recedes from where one is; she states that the loss of the 'whatever' is also the loss of a 'wherever'. Often I left Jaan's home feeling as if she was estranged from happiness – I wondered if this was indeed her experience.

Considering the Unimaginable

In order to understand Vera and Jaan's experiences as narrative phenomena, we turn to theoretical notions of wonder and inquiry by contemplating the unimaginable (Ahmed, 2010) and strangeness. We, too, wonder about who we are amidst our own and others' ongoing experiences.

As we unpack Vera's encounter with Jaan, we see how complicated and complicating their relationship is and that the ability for Vera to raise wonders at times disappears, or is erased. Embedded in the moments of disappearance and/or erasure is the unimaginable. It is the unimaginable and the subsequent inability to recognize, or to misrecognize, Jaan, which shapes Vera's sense of who Jaan is and that forecloses a sense of wonder and inquiry. It is in these moments that we take note of the significant impact the unimaginable holds. We cannot describe or explain the unimaginable. In naming the unimaginable, it becomes imaginable and shapes our wonders and inquiries in different ways. While it is difficult to wonder amidst experiences we cannot name, it is important to stay with the unimaginable, to resist the search for familiarity.

Often the unimaginable is reflective of a social suffering lived in silence, where wonders do not surface, and where differences are emphasized. It is in the moments where words fail us, moments where we are unable to imagine, that we have to work carefully to continue to understand experience as a narrative phenomenon. While often we rely on recognizing the other as a way of relating, it is here that we need to find other ways of relating to differences. The unimaginable pushes us in unfamiliar ways.

The unimaginable might also live in stories that are too difficult to hear. It raises wonders and questions. Returning to Vera and Jaan's experience alongside each other, we can see that the unimaginable complicates understandings of happiness, as well as notions of what home, and perhaps more so 'being at home', means. In thinking with home and belonging, something that was called forth for Vera in Jaan's experiences, we turn towards Ahmed. For Ahmed (1999) the

> relation between being, home and world is partially reconfigured from the perspective of those who have left home. This reconfiguration does not take place through the heroic act of an individual (the migrant), but through the forming of communities that create multiple identifications through collective acts of remembering in the absence of a shared knowledge or a familiar terrain.
>
> (p. 329)

It is Ahmed, who calls us to turn to communities and, in so doing, stretches our sense of wonder and inquiry. In our turn towards communities, we recognize that it matters who people are.

For us, wonder is part of a curiosity that asks 'who are you?' and not 'what are you'? (Arendt, 1958), as well as who we are amidst the ongoing experiences of our own and others. For Arendt the question of 'who are you?' is connected to her concept of natality, which is an affirmation of life. It is Arendt who forges a connection between natality and politics, whereby actors appear before each other. Natality is actualized in the spaces of appearance, it provides the space to think differently and act otherwise. It is here that we can do something new and ask with a sense of wonder and inquiry: 'Who are you?' (Arendt, 1958, p. 179).

It is Arendt (1958) who points out that

> each [person] is unique, so that with each birth something uniquely new comes into the world. [...] If action as beginning corresponds to the fact of birth, if it is the actualization of the human condition of natality, then speech corresponds to the fact of distinctness and is the actualization of the

human condition of plurality, that is, of living as a distinct and unique being among equals.

(p. 178)

This sense of natality calls us to situate our sense of wonder and inquiry amidst relational spaces and a space in which we travel with loving perceptions to worlds other than our own (Lugones, 1987); spaces in which we and others appear (Dewart et al., 2019).

Situated within this context new wonders are called forward and it is imperative to inquire. Questions arise about what it means to wonder, or inquire into contexts that are unfamiliar and unimaginable. If we do not recognize the other, how do we ask questions about the context, history, future and places that shape experiences. How do we raise wonders that would help us understand happiness within the context of Jaan's life and within the context of Vera's relationship with her. It begs the question of how – if we take the idea of world travelling (Lugones, 1987) seriously, and consider Arendt's writing around engaging in public spaces in a way that asks 'who are you?' – we create spaces within narrative inquiry for making visible the vulnerabilities and social suffering in ways that leave possibilities of imagining otherwise.

In thinking with Vera's experiences, we can see assumptions embedded in what it means to be a migrant. Notions of happiness are tied up in particular understandings – Vera has to work hard to allow for Jaan to appear. Arendt draws a connection between invisibility and vulnerability – something we must consider seriously as narrative inquirers. If sustained by a sense of world traveling and playfulness (Lugones, 1987), inquiry and wonder are possible in ways that create and do not erase spaces of appearance, and honour the unimaginable.

Summary

In this chapter we showed how inquiry and wonder are key theoretical concepts in narrative inquiry. We nested this chapter within the section on imagination and uncertainty for imagination, wonder and uncertainty disrupt a linear view of experience. It allows us to acknowledge experiences, past and present, and experiences yet to be had. Wonder and inquiry are processes which ignite imagination and disrupt familiarity and the unimaginable. In the next chapter we turn to the uncertainty and liminality and the ways in which they shape imagination and inquiry.

11

Uncertainty and Liminality

Abstract

One key concept in narrative inquiry is the importance of wakefulness to the uncertainty that lives within lives and within the worlds in which we live. Worlds we often do not know. We first turned to the importance of uncertainty as central to narrative inquiry through Dewey's attention to uncertainty as part of people's everyday experiences in, and with, their worlds. For Dewey, uncertainty was part of our lives and part of what it meant to live a life. Uncertainty is integral to the worlds within which we each live. Liminality, which offers us the possibility to be otherwise, becomes visible in the moments where we, according to Heilbrun (1999), stand at thresholds.

Turning to Experience

The fall of 1996 was the first time I went to the Northwest Territories, one of the most populous of the three territories located in Canada's North. Maggie and I, both senior Nursing undergraduate students, were excited to engage in our last clinical placement in a small community in the North. Initially we were placed for two weeks in the emergency room of the Yellowknife Hospital to allow us to better understand where people from the small communities came when they needed tertiary care. From there we were heading for our two month placements in the small communities. Being in the hospital emergency room provided us with the contexts of the nurses and physicians we would phone when our own experiences were limited, when our knowledge was not enough to provide the care required for people in the community.

Even now, I recall the busy-ness of the emergency room. The emergency room was filled with people whose experiences were foreign to me. In some moments I wondered why I had come north; in most other moments I was busy learning necessary skills to be used in the small community. I remember we spent one day with the medical evacuation team – a team that provided flights between the small communities and, depending on the severity of a patient's condition, the hospitals in either Yellowknife or Edmonton. Stories of despair were told, of times when planes could not land for days in the small communities due to weather conditions. At other times, stories of resourcefulness and happenstance were told, where people worked together to ensure access to care was created. There never was a simple storyline.

I began to realize how different my nursing practice would be. Much of my practice would depend on being able to work in collaborative ways with community members, and on the relationships I was part of. The impact of my work would not be measured by the skills I could perform, but by the relationships and attentiveness to the processes in which I engaged. I quickly began to see that, while what I learned over the past three years was important, I needed to learn to be at ease with the uncertainty I would experience in these new places, and alongside people I did not know.

Living and Learning in the Midst of Uncertainty

As we showed in Chapter 1, within Dewey's (1916) concept of experience, people are always working to make connections between what they do and what the situation does to them. Experience is understood as transactional between the person and the environment.

> To 'learn from experience' is to make a backward and forward connection between what we do to things and what we enjoy or suffer from things in consequence. Under such conditions, doing becomes trying; an experiment with the world to find out what it is like; the undergoing becomes instruction – discovery of the connection of things.
>
> (p. 140)

As Downey and Clandinin (2010) wrote

> [f]or Dewey learning from experience is less a connecting of the dots of our doing to what it does to us than a reconsideration of the dots themselves. Most profoundly, this makes education an ongoing 'reconstruction' of experience in the service of enhancing its meaning and one's ability to 'direct the course of subsequent experiences.' (Dewey, 1916, p. 40)
>
> (p. 384)

As Dewey argued, learning begins when certainty ends. Learning 'involves a state of doubt, hesitation, perplexity, mental difficulty in which thinking originates; and an act of searching, hunting, inquiring, to find material that will resolve the doubt, settle and dispose of the perplexity' (Dewey, 1933, p. 12). While uncertainty and perplexity are part of situations, there is a quest for certainty at the end of each situation.

In Dewey's 1910 book *How We Think,* he draws heavily on the scientific method, which he believed served as the best model for learning from experience. The scientific model is one in which uncertainty was the impetus for inquiry. Dewey was 'aware of the problems associated with transporting the scientific method into the uncontrollable uncertainty of everyday life' (Downey & Clandinin, 2010, p. 388). For Dewey, the starting point of learning from experience acknowledged that understanding starts in puzzling about concrete situations with an intention that this puzzling will lead to change in the understanding of a situation.

In Chapter 1, we wrote that Dewey considered living in the world to be living in a 'series of situations,' filled with unexpectedness that produced uncertainty. For Dewey, education is a process of putting unexpectedness to work for, and ultimately on, us in ways that foster growth and shape and direct future experience. Within a Deweyan view, as Downey and Clandinin (2010) wrote, it is through these processes of working through uncertainty that 'we bring an order to the situation and ourselves, banishing unexpectedness into the future to be met again and again' (p.89). For Dewey, uncertainty creates unexpected puzzles and, as we learn from experience, we focus both on the puzzling situation and on possible solutions that would lead to action and resolution. As Downey and Clandinin (2010) show, the two concepts of living every day within an uncertain world, and recognizing that we leave one condition of uncertainty for another, are linked in narrative inquiry.

In Vera's story we have a sense that, as she flies into the northern community of Yellowknife and contemplates learning to care within the context of remote northern communities, she understands she is facing the unexpected, entering into uncertain situations, as Dewey would have it. She notes that even though the emergency room was familiar, it was *filled with people whose lives were foreign to me.* She knows that she is moving into an uncertain situation but, even in her puzzling, we see her focus on *learning necessary skills to be used in the small community.* The uncertainty was still approached through the quest for learning all she could to make the situation more certain at that time.

But within narrative inquiry there were hints that Dewey's notion of uncertainty would not take us far enough to attend to what Vera was describing as her need *to learn to be at ease with the uncertainty I would experience in these new places, and alongside people I did not know.* She was beginning to show that in her experience of uncertainty, perhaps she could not find certainty, that certainty could not be the end goal.

> *Days later, Maggie travelled along the gravel road to a community within the Tłįchǫ Territory as I waited for a flight to WhaTi. I remember sitting in a lobby at the Yellowknife airport. As I quietly watched and waited, the lobby filled with people who knew each other. I was glad when it was time to board the plane. A sense of unease, mixed with feelings of responsibility and doubt, filled my body. What did I actually know about the place I was going to? Who was I and who would I be in this new place? How would I be able to make sense in the absence of familiarity?*

Vera (Caine, 2002) wrote in her master's thesis:

> Sitting in a small airplane flying further north and west than I had ever been, I asked myself: What would it be like? … why was I doing this?
>
> Luckily I met Johnny on the airplane 'Yah, we heard about you' … and then silence … 'look some caribou' … 'oh, I missed them' I said, my eyes were not yet trained to distinguish between the different autumn browns and yellows and those of caribou – my eyes were too accustomed to the grays of the city where I had been living for the last few years. That was the extent of our conversation – what did I expect him to say? I began to realize things were going to be different from now on.
>
> (p. 5)

Considering Liminality

While Dewey drew our attention to uncertainty in living, it was Heilbrun who directed us to considerations of liminality, a related concept in narrative inquiry. Heilbrun (1999) wrote that '[t]he word limen means threshold. To be in a state of liminality is to be poised upon uncertain ground, on the brink of leaving one condition or country or self to enter upon another' (p. 3). Uncertainty is part of liminality. It is grounded both outside and inside the person. Liminality is 'to be leaving one condition [...] and entering upon another' (p. 3). This sense of liminality helps us see uncertainty as always unfolding.

As Heilbrun (1999) unpacks her concept of liminality within women's lives, particularly as women are portrayed in literature, she writes that

> the reason why these old structures so appeal to some people is precisely that they can, in following them, avoid liminality, avoid hovering on the threshold, avoid having to take brave decisions and then having to live with the anxiety and uncertainty those decisions inevitably produce. It is easier to do what is expected of you than to live in 'intensity and suspense'.
>
> (p. 90)

For Heilbrun, these old structures are the plotlines or storylines that set out a course or a way of composing or writing a woman's life. These structures let women locate themselves in stories so they know the outcomes; stories that are written for them. These are the storylines that have shaped women's lives with closure: "'If he notices me, if I marry him, if I get into college, if I get this work accepted, if I get that job" – there always seems to loom the possibility of something being over, settled, sweeping clear the way for contentment' (Heilbrun, 1988, p. 130). Each one of these 'if' statements that leads towards a settlement, a certainty, carries within it an old structure, something that takes away the uncertainty and precludes liminality. Heilbrun (1999) notes that '[t]he threshold [...] is the place where as women and as creators of literature, we write our own lines and, eventually, our own plays' (p. 102). merle Kennedy (2001), a narrative inquirer who draws on Van Gennep (1960), describes a liminal space as

> an in-between space, the space between what was and what might be, where one engages with future possibilities. Its apparent lack of structure is both its strength and its weakness, a strength because of what it offers to those who engage with it and its weakness because, in the structured society in which we live, there is a fear of the chaotic.
>
> (p. 130)

The tensions between the stories that are composed for people and the possibility to be otherwise became more visible to us as we considered ideas of liminality.

We see Vera struggling with the familiar as she is *glad when it was time to board the plane.* Boarding a plane is a familiar story for Vera. Yet, longing for something familiar does not preclude her feelings that this plane ride provides only a temporary place of certainty. She knows that this plane ride is a threshold place, one that will take her to uncertain ground, to a place where she must live with intensity and suspense. She is open to the possibility of living within the threshold as she describes how *a sense of unease, mixed with feelings of responsibility and doubt, filled my body. What did I actually know about this place I was going to? Who was I and who would I be in this new place?* And in her time on the plane she begins to ask those questions of what she knows of this place, perhaps what she knows will help her to be more at ease with the uncertainty. She knows though that this place will ask her to be open to intensity and suspense, to not knowing, to unfamiliar structures or storylines.

And it was Johnny, who sat beside her on the plane, who began to awaken her to what she did not, could not, know. While she learned that she was already a storied character in Johnny's community, *Yah, we heard about you,* she did not learn what stories were told of her. Knowing she was a storied character already, may have created a bit of a sense of certainty but this was quickly taken away by the reminder that she did not know the landscape, that her eyes, her body were used to the landscapes and sights of a different place. Despite Johnny's brevity in words, he was beginning to become a character in Vera's stories. Johnny helped Vera acknowledge that she must accept the unexpected, the uncertainty and liminality that lived around her in the place she was going to. *What did I expect him to say?*

Vera could not get inside Johnny's skin, even though she sat close beside him on the plane. In the 45-minute plane ride, Vera wondered if she would be able to come to a place where the uncertainty felt less daunting and more like new possibilities. What are the conditions that shift the ground? Ahmed and Stacey (2001) write

> [w]hile the nearness of others is always 'felt' on the skin, that nearness also involves distance, or the impossibility of getting inside the other's skin. [...] embodied empathy. Inter-embodiment is hence a way of thinking through the nearness of others, but a nearness which involves distanciation and difference. [...] Thinking through the skin is a thinking that attends not only to the sensuality of being-with-others, but also to the ethical implications of the impossibility of inhabiting the other's skin.
>
> (p. 7)

As the plane carried Vera closer to the community of WhaTi, she struggled to continue to inhabit her own skin, knowing that things were already otherwise.

In her body, Vera carried the knowledge that she is going to a threshold place, a place not 'designed for permanent occupation, however, and those of us who occupy thresholds, hover in doorways, and knock upon doors, know that we are in between destinies. But this is where we choose to be, and must be, at this time, among the alternatives that present themselves' (Heilbrun, 1999, p. 102). Knowing that the threshold was not designed as a permanent place, Vera wondered what would carry her through the next two months. She wondered if she would be able to engage in relationships with those who called WhaTi home, or would she remain a stranger, suspended in the threshold for the duration of her stay.

Living on Landscapes Experienced as Liminal

In 1993 Adrienne Rich ended her poem entitled *Diving into the Wreck* with

We are, I am, you are
by cowardice or courage
the one who find our way
back to this scene
carrying a knife, a camera
a book of myths
in which
our names do not appear.

As Vera sat on the plane, going from here to there, she wondered who she was. In a way she learned from Johnny, as Rich notes, that her name was already written in the storied landscape of the community of WhaTi. Yet, Vera does not know what is written about her. Who was she in the storied landscape? What was written by her name that would allow her to begin to compose a life in this new place?

Linda, the nurse in charge at WhaTi, was waiting for my flight to land. She waited in the local truck owned by the First Nations Band. The Tłı̨chǫ community of WhaTi is located on Lac La Martre and stretches along a short stretch of the eastern shores. As I landed, I was struck by the beauty of the lake. As my time in the community passed, I came to know that the lake also holds the stories of people who disappeared. Sometimes the lake gave up those who died in the lake, but this could not be taken for granted. I learned in those moments how closely the connection was between the land and those travelled on the land.

Linda took me to the nursing station located in the middle of the community, next to the school and across from the Band office. The small local grocery store was located within 100 meters, next to the Catholic church. Even though I had spent my childhood in a rural community in northern Germany, I knew I could not count on my experiences to help me understand this new place.

As the darkness settled on that first evening in WhaTi, silences sounded across the vastness of the lake and the land. An uncertainty settled in my body. A sense of ambiguity and disorientation became part of my experiences; a threshold place opened up possibilities.

Kennedy (2001) offers us the possibility of inhabiting the threshold, of staying with liminality rather than moving off the threshold into a new space. She describes liminality as presenting

a story that is chaotic and non-linear. It is a story that begins without language because it is a story written on the body and experienced in physical and emotional dimensions. We may or may not put words around the experience. If we do, the words may be few and descriptive in nature so that the listener becomes aware of the physical/emotional/spiritual/moral dimensions of the experience.

(p. 141)

As Vera looked around the small community, she recognized some familiar landmarks: a beautiful lake, a Catholic church, a grocery store, a school, mixed with the laughter of people and the sounds of conversations. At the same time she senses the liminality inherent in this new place and knows that her body does not carry embodied knowing of this place, of WhaTi. The lake is beautiful but carries secrets and bodies in ways that are unfamiliar. The familiar landmarks do not carry the same meaning as they had in the German small town of her childhood; they, for now, were unfamiliar. As she writes, *I could not count on my experiences to help me understand this new place,* she acknowledges that she has entered a liminal space, a space where she needs to read what might be familiar, as unfamiliar, as unstoried, as chaotic. She experiences stepping off the threshold into what Kennedy (2001) called the abyss, a place of liminality. Kennedy developed a view of liminality using a notion of an abyss. Kennedy, a white teacher, conducted her research within school classrooms situated within Indigenous communities, which she conceptualized as 'liminal spaces' which

provides an opportunity for students and teachers to hear one another to the depths of the raced abyss. The chaos and confusion that might arise in such a place would be just that, chaos and confusion. It would not be a marker of the students' behaviour, nor would it be a marker of the teacher's ability to deliver curriculum, nor a marker of her classroom management techniques. Sometimes baffled and frightened, we could write our own lines and eventually our own plays, imagining new possibilities for life in a classroom and, indeed, for life.

(p. 143)

As Vera remembered the small settlement and told her story from a temporal distance of more than twenty years, she felt the chaos and confusion in the situation and in herself. She could not count on her knowledge. What she grasped in those first moments after stepping off the plane were fragments, a sense of trying to catch her breath, a distant and imagined story line to hold on to. Perhaps the story Johnny had heard about her, could be a story to hold on to. Yet, what she experienced was silence and *an uncertainty settled in my body. A sense of ambiguity and disorientation became part of my experiences.*

What she experienced as she gazed at the lake, a lake filled with beauty but death and secrets, did not fit the story structures she knew. Kennedy (2001) wrote that being in such a liminal space is to be in a space which

is fragmented and inconclusive, one that we are unaccustomed to hearing. Because it does not fit the story structures to which we are accustomed we usually do not 'hear' the individual who is telling the story or we superimpose stories to create a sense of familiarity and therefore avoid the pain of the story.

(p. 141)

As I got up each day, I arose with a sense of wonder that took me to walk the path to the lake, to seek out people, both young and old, Elders and others who had stories grounded in this place. My actions were shaped by a desire to move out of a nursing station and to somewhat be grounded in the community, to sit by the lake, to walk alongside people, hearing stories and learning to hear others' stories as I learned to live amidst the uncertainty.

Why Uncertainty and Liminality Matter in Narrative Inquiry

In narrative inquiry, unexpectedness is what awakens us to uncertainty and puzzles and guides us towards being open to liminality in our lives and in the lives of others. We cannot think narratively if we cannot see each situation is lived, 'replete with situations nested, tangled up in and woven into the complexities of the lives of many others. To inquire narratively is to focus on experience as stories lived and told with an understanding that uncertainty lives in and between the situations of lived and told stories' (Downey & Clandinin, 2010, p. 390).

As narrative inquiry calls us to live our lives open to uncertainty and liminality, we must also see that others are living their lives with those possibilities. We need to follow where our lived and told stories take us and where the lived and told stories of others take them; and where our stories intersect and possibilities of living alongside open up. As Downey and Clandinin (2010) wrote

> [i]n narrative inquiry there is no certainty in what future stories will be lived and told, even in the near future. There is no plan that can be implemented in action. People, places, other events, emotions, moral judgments and aesthetic responses continually shift and change the array of possible plotlines open to each person. As narrative inquirers we can map out possible plotlines, hint at that array of possibilities but all we can say is that this is how, inquirers and participants, are living and telling the stories for now. We follow one possible trajectory and move forward into other possible uncertainties.
>
> (p. 394)

Trin Min Ha (1989) helps us see these uncertain spaces, not within discrete borders or boundaries but as spaces where conditions and categories leak, or bleed, into one another. Homi Bhabha (1994) named these spaces or conditions as in-between spaces; it is amidst these spaces that personal and cultural identities are formed, and our values and interests are negotiated. These in-between spaces are filled with uncertainty and indeterminacy; they are places of liminality. And we sense that as Vera looks back now from a temporal distance on who she is and is becoming, she recognizes that she has been forever shaped by her experiences in those liminal spaces, spaces she opened herself up to. It is these spaces, spaces that at times are reminders of the abyss, that allowed Vera to negotiate and renegotiate who she was and was becoming.

Within narrative inquiry we attend carefully to the uncertainty we find in liminal spaces; in these in-between spaces around borders, we find – what Audre Lorde (1984) calls – borderlands. These are the spaces where we see the possibilities for otherwise, spaces which are not threatening, but spaces that can be sparks for our and others' creativity. Anzaldúa (1987) writes of a borderland as a vague and undetermined place created by the emotional residue of an unnatural boundary […] a constant state of transition. Los atravesados live here […] those who cross over, pass over, or go through the confines of the 'normal'.

(p. 3)

It is in the borderlands that Anzaldúa (1987) locates the possibility for resistance. And as Vera looks back on who she has become and continues to become, she locates some of her possibility for resistance within the stories she now tells of her experiences in WhaTi. It is this resistance that resonates across her life and in her practices as a nurse – a resistance shaped by uncertainty and liminality.

Summary

In this chapter, we described our understandings of uncertainty and liminality. Our understandings of liminality are influenced particularly by Heilbrun (1999) and her notion of threshold and Kennedy's (2001) notion of the abyss. In Chapter 12, we turn towards playfulness as a way to engage experience.

12

Playfulness

Abstract

While in previous chapters we have begun to show how we take up Lugones' ideas of playfulness, it is Paley (1993) who first helped us understand playfulness in relation to possibilities. Paley's work is situated within preschool classroom contexts and her work as a teacher. She contemplates her ongoing experiences alongside children, other teachers and imaginary stories – such as stories of magpie. While play is often seen in opposition to work, this take is not reflected in how we, or those whose work we draw on, have taken up this idea. In this chapter we highlight some of the attributes of play, unpack the complexities of play and contemplate how we sustain play and how we might think with playfulness across worlds.

Coming to Playfulness

The magpie's cawing startles me out of my fantasy and I laugh aloud. Suddenly I am in rhythm with the trees and the people and the buildings. I come upon a statue of Winston Churchill, and I feel the sting of tears. 'Have you been here all along, Sir Winston?' My spirit continues to soar as I shower, breakfast and, once again, mount a platform. Several hundred people are waiting with happy faces and immediately I tell them the magpie story – there seems no way for me not to tell it – beginning with my feelings of the previous night. Someone in the audience gasps, pointing to the window in back of me, and I turn to see a magpie flying by. 'So this is what it's like,' I say. 'This is how Angelo feels when he is a Ninja Turtle, in rhythm with the other turtles. He enters the classroom, into a land of strangers, and waits until he is caught up in a fantasy before he can see our smiles and smile back.'

But then, someone tells him he can't play […].

(Paley, 1993, p. 6–7)

Memories surface about times when we, too, were told that we 'can't play' both as children and as adults. The notions of play are different across our lives, but always there is a recognition that play is critical. Life is impossible for us without play.

The Attributes of Playfulness

Paley (1990) has written for several years about the importance of play and pointed out that '[t]here is so much to learn about play when you don't come to it easily' (p. 64). Play, in this way of understanding, is not a given; it is something that we have to work at and be wakeful to. Learning to be playful is a necessity, as much of what we do is impacted by a quest for logic, by rule-governed social systems, processes and structures that often underlie the notions of 'you can't play'. Paley (1986) writes,

> I think, rather, that the children and I are learning to ask questions about the crucial issues in a preschool classroom. We are not concerned about how the color green is made. But we do need to find the logic by which private fantasies are turned into social play, and social play into a rule-governed society of children and teachers. These matters are endlessly debateable, particularly when four-and five-year-olds sit in judgement, and the process of determining how the play goes is often more important than the play itself. […] Contentment lies in uncovering – not dismantling – the plot. It is clear to me that when I comment less on disruption and spend more time helping children talk about the characters and plot, the quality of the play advances.
>
> (p. 17)

Paley's writing is rich with descriptions of children's experiences and her reflections as a teacher. She is mindful of the interplay between children and adults, between child and teacher, and between children. Through a process of careful and ongoing inquiry, she realizes the significance to

> [p]ut your play into formal narratives, and I will help you and your classmates listen to one another. In this way you will build a literature of images and themes, of beginnings and endings, of references and allusions. You must invent your own literature if you are to connect your ideas to the ideas of others.
>
> (p. 18)

In as much as the focus is on the children's sense of playfulness, Paley contemplates play in her life and opens up detailed and intricate worlds that help us think about, and with, play. We recognize that teaching without contemplating play, as we read Paley, is an impossibility.

While Paley raises ongoing and significant questions about play within a preschool and teaching context, Lugones' (1987) theoretical idea of world-travelling helps us situate playfulness within a research context. In 2018, drawing on Lugones (1987), we wrote,

> "[t]hose of us who are 'world'-travellers have the distinct experience of being different in 'different' worlds and of having the capacity to remember other 'worlds' and ourselves in them" (p. 11). Yet this concept challenges [us] in the living when it is more difficult to 'world-travel' and, at other times, seemingly impossible [. .] times when [we] turn away from the challenges in relationships, the struggles in committing to understanding more fully the experiences.
>
> (Clandinin et al., 2018, p. 194)

Lugones, thinking about world-travelling and playfulness, is deeply shaped by her experiences as a woman of colour. These experiences have drawn her to think in relation to oppression and resistance, both of which shape her possibilities. Lugones situates playfulness amidst a complex world of interdependence and false linearities and quarrels. For Lugones (2003)

> playfulness in me, for me, is not a frivolous, disposable quality in me or in my loving. It is at the crux of liberation, both as a process and as something to achieve. I think there is something important in the relation between playfulness and tenderness. I attempt to unravel the connection arguing for a sense of playfulness that is tied to risk: we risk our ground as we prepare our ground, as we stand on a ground that is a crossing.
>
> (Lugones, 2003, pp. 32–3)

In her work, Lugones thinks about playfulness as an attribute. However, it is not a fixed attribute. She shows she both has, and does not have, this attribute; she creates a double image as she inquires into her understanding of playfulness. Lugones (2003) links the understanding of playfulness to her ideas of worlds. She recognizes that 'Okay, maybe what's happening here is that there is an attribute that I do have but there are certain 'worlds' in which I am not at ease and it is because I'm not at ease in those 'worlds' that I don't have that attribute in those 'worlds'" (p. 87). Yet, as soon as she offers us this line of thinking about being at ease in certain worlds, she writes

I was worried both about what I meant by 'worlds' when I said 'in some 'worlds' I do not have the attribute' and what I meant by saying that lack of ease was what led me not to be playful in those 'worlds'. Because, you see, if it was just a matter of lack of ease, I could work on it.

(p. 87)

In reading and re-reading her work, we can see how Lugones shapes different notions of playfulness, of what it means to be at ease in the worlds we inhabit, but also as we walk on shifting grounds.

While Paley and Lugones have shaped much of our understanding about playfulness, our understandings are also shaped by Arendt's distinction between 'who' and 'what' somebody is. Arendt helps us see Lugones' sense of playfulness as important to the living, to the ordinary and everyday worlds we live within. For Arendt (1958)

[t]his disclosure of "who" in contradistinction of "what" somebody is – his qualities, gifts, talents, and shortcomings, which he may display or hide – is implicit in everything somebody says and does. It can be hidden only in complete silence and perfect passivity, but its disclosure can almost never be achieved as a wilful purpose, as though one possessed and could dispose of this "who" in the same manner he has and can dispose of his qualities. (p. 179) [….] The moment we want to say *who* somebody is; we get entangled in a description of qualities he necessarily shares with others like him; we begin to describe a type or a "character" in the old meaning of the word, with the result that his specific uniqueness escapes us.

(p. 181; italics in original text)

In this way playfulness can be seen as linked to questions of identity, to 'who' we are. In the moments then where we are told 'you can't play' we are also told that we cannot be who we are. Attending to playfulness then calls us to attend to the details, possibilities of the other – it calls us, as Lugones helps us see, to world-travel always.

Resisting Playfulness

As Paley points out, we have much to learn about play and part of that learning is in finding ways to be playful and to world-travel. Through dialogue and in response communities we have realized that we, too, resist being playful at times in our own lives and across different worlds we inhabit. At times we resist playfulness, so we can protect who we are; at other times we live within oppressive structures that silence our playfulness. Resistance to playfulness is in these moments shaped by notions of otherwise.

As we contemplate our resistance, we return to Paley (1990) to understand ways and processes at stake within preschool classrooms. In her experiences alongside Jason, she notes: 'Jason knows the importance of disguises. Before he used Simon's name, he called him "that squirrel someone." It is often easier to reach out in a fantasy role than in barefaced, confusing, adult-centered reality' (p. 39). Later on she writes,

> The children pick up an idea and play with it, improvising until it makes sense, which is to say, takes on the aspect of a story. It is almost impossible to explain something effectively to a child without using an image that has come from the child. If the paper 'eats draw', then that is where to begin.
>
> (p. 43)

There are many 'eats draw' in our lives, and our work, as researchers. Often we have wondered if attention to these 'eats draw' can pull us into the worlds where we can be playful, that is, into worlds that do not resist the uncertainty and liminality necessary to wonder.

The Complexities of Playfulness

The ideas of playfulness that are central to conceptual understandings of narrative inquiry are shaped by Lugones (1987) who wrote of playfulness in world-travel. For Lugones,

> [t]he playfulness that gives meaning to our activity includes uncertainty, but in this case the uncertainty is the openness to surprise. [...] We are not self-important, we are not fixed in particular constructions of ourselves, which is part of saying we are open to self-construction. We may not have rules, and when we do have rules, there are no rules that are to us sacred. We are not worried about competence [...] playfulness is, in part, an openness to being a fool, which is a combination of not worrying about competence, not being self-important, not taking norms as sacred and finding ambiguity and double edges a source of wisdom and delight.
>
> (pp. 16–17)

Playfulness, openness to playing the fool and not worrying about competence, self-importance or being seen as scholarly, does not fit easily within the dominant stories of research. Abandoning particular constructions of ourselves as researchers allows us to see new possibilities. This playfulness is not marked by winning, or losing, or competition, rather it creates a sense of community where we become increasingly attentive to what we do not know, where we can gain a sense of 'wisdom and delight' (Lugones, 1987, p. 17). It is within this understanding of playfulness that we can see the complex interplay of imagination, wonder, uncertainty and liminality.

Imagination and Playfulness

In Chapter 9 we call forward how Greene has shaped our understanding of imagination in profound ways. Greene (1995) talks about the social imagination, in which she refers to

> the capacity to invent visions of what should be and what might be in our deficient society, on the streets where we live, in our schools. As I write of social imagination, I am reminded of Jean-Paul Sartre's declaration that 'it is on the day that we can conceive of a different state of affairs that a new light falls on our troubles and our suffering and that we decide that these are unbearable'.
>
> (p. 5)

Through imagination Greene responds to the immediate troubles of the world. Imagination allows us to come to a place of knowing that also calls forth action. Like Greene, Paley too, believes that imagination is critical. Paley (1984) shows us alongside the play of children her understanding of imagination.

> Even as I speak, I realize my distinctions are shaky. Is there a difference between 'Pretend our parents are dead' and 'Pretend I'm killing you'? The children know it is all magical play. The same magic destroys and resurrects, creates an orphan or a mother – or the Green Slime. The ability to imagine something is the magic; putting it into action is the play; playing it out is the safe way to discharge the idea.
>
> (p. 80)

In Paley's (2010) more recent works, we see the close link she draws between imagination, play and possibilities to be otherwise.

> Let me get back to the idea of creative kindness. Finding a new way of being a friend is the supreme act of kindness. It is important to keep the door open.

[…] It is hard work. She keeps dropping the picture, picking it up, pushing the block, and dropping the picture again. Finally she reaches the boy's side and sits next to him, on the block. "I made you a picture," she says. "You can hold it." The boy shakes his head and turns away. A few more minutes go by and then the little girl asks, "Do you want to be Batman?" A flicker of a smile appears. "I'm Robin, "he tells her. "You can be Wonder Woman." Instantly, everything about these two children has changed. You can see the relief on their faces. "Pretend I'm trying to find you, "the boy says, "and I don't know you're in the Batmobile." Softly he starts up the motor of the Batmobile and the two children leave the classroom behind. Is this not a love story?

(pp. 59–60)

This sense of otherwise can, if done carefully, help us imagine ways to be playful that dismantle privileged ignorance. It is imagination that helps us understand the necessity and possibilities of building coalitions across worlds.

Wonder and Playfulness

Yet, imagination is not possible without a sense of wonder; wonder that is also central to playfulness. Both imagination and wonder are necessary to disrupt the colonial and imperialist journeys that do not involve 'risking one's ground' (Lugones, 2003, p. 96). For Lugones (2003), 'play holds an attitude marked by an openness to surprise [which] inclines us to 'world'-travel in the direction of coalition' (p. 98). Lugones further writes that

[s]o, positively, the playful attitude involves openness to surprise, openness to being a fool, openness to self-construction or reconstruction and to construction or reconstruction of the 'worlds' we inhabit playfully, and this openness to risk the ground that constructs us as oppressors or as oppressed or as collaborating or colluding with oppression. Negatively, playfulness is characterized by uncertainty, lack of self-importance, absence of rules or not taking rules as sacred, not worrying about competence, and lack of abandonment to a particular construction of oneself, others, and one's relation to them. In attempting to take a hold of oneself and of one's relation to others in a particular 'world,' one may study, examine, and come to understand oneself. One may then see what the possibilities for play are for the being one is in that 'world'. One may even decide to inhabit that self fully to understand it better and find its creative possibilities.

(p. 96)

It is this turn to creative possibilities that helps us as narrative inquirers to link back to Greene's notion of social imagination. As we revisit the philosophical underpinnings of our work, as we re-read people's work that has shaped us, we, like Paley, recognize that '[t]he poetry and prose of the best children's books enter our minds when we are young and sing back to us all our lives' (Paley, 1990, p. 44). It is our sense of wonder that has been shaped by the books and stories of our childhood.

Uncertainty and Liminality and Playfulness

In Chapter 11 we trace our understanding of uncertainty and liminality to Heilbrun's work and also to how these ideas have been taken up by Kennedy. It is, however, Lugones (1987) who helps us see the link between uncertainty and liminality and playfulness.

> We keep on crashing stones for hours, anxious to see the beautiful new colours. We are playing. The playfulness of our activity does not presuppose that there is something like 'crashing stones' that is a particular form of play with its own rules. Instead, *the attitude that carries us through the activity, a playful attitude, turns the activity into play.* Our activity has no rules, though it is certainly intentional activity and we both understand what we are doing. The playfulness that gives meaning to our activity includes uncertainty, but in this case the uncertainty is an *openness to surprise.*
>
> (Lugones, 2003, pp. 95–96; italics in original text)

There is a close and multidirectional relationship between liminality, uncertainty and playfulness that is made visible by Lugones. Neither happens in the absence of the other – we can't engage in playfulness without a deep embrace of uncertainty. And we cannot be playful if we seek grounds that are fixed and frozen, that do not allow us to be open to the thresholds embraced by the living.

Sustaining Playfulness and Being Playful

While Paley and Lugones have helped us see and understand playfulness, as linked to imagination, wonder, uncertainty and liminality, it is Joy

Ruth Mickelson who helped us think further about what it means to be playful and to sustain playfulness. Joy Ruth was a well-known Edmonton social worker and psychologist who came to the Centre for Research for Teacher Education and Development in the early 1990s as part of her doctoral research. She undertook her doctoral study with Jean when she was close to retirement age. When she completed her doctoral dissertation (published as a book 2000 and entitled *Our Sons Were Labelled Behaviour Disordered: Here Is the Story of Our Lives),* she joined the Centre for Research for Teacher Education and Development as a postdoctoral fellow and subsequently as an Adjunct Assistant Professor. Her latest book *Facing the Shards* is a memoir published in 2015. For many years Joy Ruth attended the weekly Research Issues group in the Centre as she continued to engage in narrative inquiry on various research projects alongside Jean, Vera and Sean. As an experienced narrative inquirer she was an inspirational guide for many. Since 2010 she was less able to attend each week, but when she did she often shared her poetry and creative nonfiction writing. The laughter, imagination and sense of possibility Joy Ruth lived are evident in her work as an inquirer and as a poet. Joy Ruth passed away in 2017. After Joy Ruth's passing we started to write down her tape-recorded poems, including the poem *Once Lived.*

Once Lived

I once lived in a chicken coop
for 3 weeks
brushed feathers nightly from my brow
friend climbed through hexagonal wire
needing shelter from rain
food for bellies
coop a small isosceles triangle
hid our silhouettes bundled in sleeping bags
we nestled our nights, waking our days to follow our years of
dreaming of William
Shakespeare spirit twirls high in the sky
low on the earth
rests on the soft flowing river
the Avon, its tributaries and streams,
his life astonished us as did his words of brilliance
and never to be forgotten plots and plays

we came to celebrate the long ago nuptials of Ann and William
a play that out lasted words
we came as friends to welcome
a way to make us better friends
more known
so we'll live and pray and sing and tell old tales
and laugh at gilded butterflies
the last fraeulein of Shakespeare

As I reread the poem and listen to the sound of Joy Ruth's voice, memories surface and my heart begins to sing again. On Tuesdays we gathered at the table at the Centre for Research on Teacher Education and Development and each Tuesday I was already anticipating Joy Ruth's presence. For several years, as a graduate student, I shared a writing place with Joy Ruth that was adjacent to the Centre. While her poems have challenged me to be playful in my writing, it was her physical presence, her ability to embrace the liminality of her own life, that helped me think about my life and work as a researcher. Joy Ruth lived with a generosity and kindness that invited me and others to be playful alongside her. Joy Ruth's life was not always easy, as she recounted in her book Facing the Shards (2015). The abstract of her book reads,

When Hitler threatened to bomb London, the government arranged for schoolchildren to be evacuated to the English countryside. Joy Ruth and her older sister Vivienne leave their beloved parents. Being Jewish, they experience the kindness and unkindness of foster-parents. Set in a time of war, this coming-of-age memoir demonstrates that fear, loss, and love are the shards that cut and bind us together.

(Mickelson, 2015, back cover)

Joy Ruth's work reflects some of Paley's ideas that play is also connected to life-making. In 1990, Paley wrote,

[t]his is nearly always the way. Problems are not meant to be solved. They are ours to own, to explore the possibilities with, to help us study cause and effect. Important issues can't be solved with one grand plan – or in one school year. Some are worked at for a lifetime, returning in different disguises, requiring fresh insights. Play itself is the practicing of problems, a fact demonstrated by even the most casual attention to the passing dialogue. 'The monster is coming! He is almost here!'

(p. 48)

We can see that even at the end of her life, Joy Ruth continued in the kind of play that helps us to gain fresh insights.

Joy Ruth would have laughed at the sentences 'The monster is coming! He is almost here!' I miss Joy Ruth, the warm embrace of her laughter and the gentle touch of her hands on mine, are still something I can hear and feel. Joy Ruth would have encouraged me to play with the monster … to think with, and about, what might be around the corner. She too would have asked me to live with her in the chicken coop, even though I am afraid of rats. She would have encouraged me to ask questions, to go over things again, to explore possible misunderstandings, to carefully consider the words, and to listen for the uncertainties, the wonders, and possibilities monsters hold.

The kind of playfulness Joy Ruth lived was marked by a presence in the world that is filled with kindness and wonder that challenges, much like Lugones (2003) did, the understanding of Gadamer and Huizinga's notion of play.

Challenging Agonistic Play

In her work Lugones (2003) carefully considered diverse notions of play and writes,

> I discovered, to my amazement, that what I thought about play and playfulness, if they [Gadamer and Huizinga] were right, was absolutely wrong. Though I will not provide the arguments for this interpretation of Gadamer and Huizinga here, I understood that both of them have an agonistic sense of play. Play and playfulness have – in their use – ultimately, to do with context, with winning, losing, battling. The sense of play that I have in mind has nothing to do with agon. [...] An agonistic sense of playfulness is one in which *competence* is central. You'd better know the rules of the game. In agonistic play, there is risk, there is *uncertainty*, but the uncertainty is about who is going to win and who is going to lose. There are rules that inspire hostility. The attitude of *playfulness is conceived as secondary to or derivative from play*. Since play is agon, then the only conceivable playful attitude is an agonistic one: the attitude does not turn an activity into play, but rather presupposes an activity that is play. [...] The agonistic traveler is a conqueror, an imperialist. Agonistic playfulness leads those who attempt to travel to another 'world' with this attitude to failure. Agonistic travelers cannot attempt to travel in this sense. [It] is not a healthy, loving attitude to have in traveling across 'worlds'.
>
> (p. 9; italics in original text)

We see the turn away from agonistic play in Lugones' work, and in Joy Ruth's ways of being in the world. As we think about agonistic play, we see that our ideas of playfulness have been strongly shaped by Lugones and the link she makes of playfulness to world-travelling and loving perception. For Lugones, play is not situated in an agonistic way; instead it is situated within ideas of surprise and being open to being a fool. Her work disrupts common notions of playfulness and allows us to enter into relationships with participants in playful ways. When Joy Ruth worked alongside Lynn, a research participant in a narrative inquiry study about the experiences of youth who left school early (Clandinin et al., 2013), she recognized how different her life was from Lynn's. These differences called Joy Ruth to be attentive to world-travelling and to be playful. Her poem *Aware My Tense Is Ever Present* shows some of this.

> [...]
> Faces matter, color matters, places matter
> it's hard to choose the one that fits your comfort.
> we walk, we walk, we walk,
> at last we find,
> black face, white face, red face
> we seat ourselves
> eat pizza, words spring to lips
> kalamata olives shaped in circles stick to melted cheese.
> wind chill extreme freezes outside faces barely seen
> bodies brace and stumble, angles sliced.
> here we sit and eat, uncertain it's the place for conversation
> a private conversation for all the world to hear.
> the place is loaded, party group, singles, and we two.
> [...]
> We talk. You tell the ins and outs of contexts and of time
> of ups and downs, advances and retreats, of wonders and dismays
> and more. I listen. and listen.
> Respond then talk too much
> have I destroyed momentum and your flow of telling
> my search for threads too tautly strung

(pp. 174–5)

Arrogant Perceptions

What becomes evident both through the words and in-between the lines of the poem is that Joy Ruth pushed against arrogant perceptions that she might have held and that she carefully and playfully lived alongside Lynn as a researcher and person. We imagined what Joy Ruth might have said. Perhaps it would have echoed Lugones (1987) words,

> I want to point to the possibility of coming to appreciate this playfulness. Here, I exercise this playful practice. The appreciation of my playfulness and its meaning may be realized when the possibility of becoming playful in this way has been collectively realized, when it has become realized by us. It is here to be appreciated or missed and both the appreciation and the missing are significant. The more fully this playfulness is appreciated, the less broken I am to you, the more dimensional I am to you. But I want to exercise my multidimensionality even if you do not appreciate it. To do otherwise would be to engage in self-mutilation, to come to be just the person that you see. To play in this way is then an act of resistance as well as an act of self-affirmation.
>
> (p. 41, footnote)

This act of resistance is, in different ways, described by Paley (1984) as requiring courage. Courage to be self-critical, to understand that 'play is life' (Paley, 1990, p. 19), and that neither our life nor play has clearly drawn maps we can follow. We do not always know how to act, much like Joy Ruth did not know how to act alongside Lynn. Yet, we must always try to be playful across the worlds we, and the worlds others who join us, inhabit.

Summary

Mickelson reminds us to be playful with words and ideas, and to connect our lives to our work. She helps us see being playful as a practice. And it is Lugones (2003), who so clearly points out that the practice of being playful is part of world-travelling and part of building coalitions across difference. Perhaps the depth of playfulness is best understood through the words of Paley (1990) '[w]e are taught to say that play is the work of children. But, watching and listening to them, I saw that play was nothing less than Truth and Life' (p. 17). Thinking, with playfulness across worlds, allows us to hold open spaces of uncertainty, wonder, liminality and inquiry about truth and life in narrative inquiry.

Section IV

Methodological Notebook

In this methodological notebook, we turn our attention to the ways that narrative inquirers work within a relational ontology that shapes methodological considerations and particular research methods. Holding a relational ontology at the centre of narrative inquiry means that, as researchers, we do not study the other but study the spaces that live between researcher and participant. Narrative inquiry is the study of experience, and experience is a matter of people in relation contextually and temporally. 'Participants are in relation, and we as researchers are in relation to participants. Narrative inquiry is an experience of the experience. It is people in relation studying with people in relation' (Clandinin & Connelly, 2000, p. 189). In the spaces between researcher and participant we can most clearly see the ways that imagination, wonder and inquiry, liminality and uncertainty, and playfulness are at work. Drawing on fragments of field texts and narrative accounts we make visible how these theoretical ideas are lived out in a study.

Meeting Azima: Beginning in Wonder

Sitting in a local chain coffee shop and drinking a strawberry smoothie across the table from a beautiful young woman wearing a hijab, I wonder about how this place in a local strip mall on a hot summer day might feel so different from any places she has known. We are meeting for the first time. I know that circumstances made it difficult for her to stay in Syria, her homeland, or in Lebanon, a place that provided initial refuge for her and her family. I sense her yearning to be in a place where she feels at ease, but perhaps I am wrong. It is too early to ask her the many questions that are swirling in my mind. They will have to wait until we come to know each other more, until her stories in our conversations begin to make what Arendt (1958) calls a 'space of appearance', within our relationship.

In this fragment from a narrative account, we see Jean meeting Azima, a participant in the study. Jean is filled with questions and wonders but holds herself back from putting into words the questions that swirl in her head. She senses the space between her and Azima cannot be filled with her questions. Allowing herself to wonder, but not fill the space with her wonders, Jean knows she needs first to hear Azima's stories, not Azima's answers to her questions. As narrative inquirers we are mindful that our interactions are marked by an openness and curiosity so that we do not narrow the possible stories and silences that may fill the space. If we come only asking questions, we write ourselves out of the relationship and out of the possibility to know what matters to those we are coming alongside. We must, as narrative inquirers, begin in wonder and continue to live in wonder alongside participants.

Wondering Inward: Engaging in Inquiry along the Way

Jean also realizes that it is important that she inquire into her own experiences, to begin, through inquiry, to unpack the stories that she lives by. As narrative inquirers this self-facing is part of the reflexive and reflective work that marks each inquiry from beginning and throughout. We know that as narrative inquirers, 'we try to understand the stories under or on the edges of stories lived and told, as no story stands on its own but rather in relation to many others – including the stories of the narrative inquirer' (Downey & Clandinin 2010, p. 387). As Jean turns inward to inquire into her own experiences, she begins to make visible to herself stories she brings to co-composing a relational inquiry space with Azima. These processes of self-facing make it possible for Jean to hold open spaces for inquiry, for wonder, as she came alongside Azima. When she first met Azima, Jean was in the midst of moving from one place in Canada to another and it is the experience of her move that she begins to try to discern and to stay wakeful to assumptions she might have about Azima's experiences.

This place I have known as home cannot be separated from people who matter to me, schools which have welcomed me, a small office crammed with books, familiar hallways, a Centre which has been an academic gathering place. This leaving process is a gradual one, as I struggle to tear up roots grounded in this place. I struggle to leave the big sky with its seemingly endless reach, the sun shining brightly within a blue expanse, the air which sucks the moisture from my face and frequently makes my skin hurt with dryness and freezing cold. This is the place my body recognizes as home. I know how this place feels, smells, and looks. As I slowly move books and objects into my new home, I feel the tug of the familiar, the place of home. I unpack in my new home. I notice that the air feels different on my skin, the sky is much closer and is frequently covered with clouds which prevent me from seeing the sun, the smells that fill the air are of flowers, cedars and fir trees. And in this strange new place I search for familiar reminders of home.

As Jean attends to her experiences of place and relationships, she knows Azima may be experiencing something similar as she comes to her new place in Edmonton. But Jean also knows that she cannot assume her experience is like Azima's experience. Jean is awake to the privilege of her carefully planned move, one which she has chosen, and one that she can undertake with the ease that money affords her. Jean knows she is not being forced to leave one country for another where she will live without resources, without a familiar language. Without careful inquiry, with close attention to the ways that memory and imagination are interwoven, Jean's work alongside Azima could be marked by arrogant perception (Lugones, 1987).

Beginning to Inquire alongside Azima

Jean is with Azima again, visiting her at her townhouse in Edmonton, the place her sponsors found for her and her family when she arrived. Jean returned to Edmonton from her new west coast home for this conversation.

As I meet Azima in her townhouse, I think of how difficult my move has been for me, a move into strangeness, into a place that is not yet home, and how this new place is shaping me in unfamiliar ways. And yet, for me, the language has not changed, my house is filled with familiar belongings and books, I have the resources to set up my home, my car to help me establish myself. My new place is only a few degrees of longitude away and, while in a new provincial context, it is still Canada.

I think then of Azima as I sit with her in her new townhouse filled with the overstuffed sectional sofa, tables that are familiar to me in size, shape, and style but perhaps not to her. I look at her seated carefully on the sofa, with the plate of fruit prepared for me. She is working to make me comfortable, and I think about what she might have prepared for me if I had met her in Syria.

Jean is mindful of Azima's townhouse and awake to her own experience of moving away from what was her homeplace for many years, a move that Jean chose for herself. Jean wonders about whether these experiences of moving from one place to another, about whether the experience of being a migrant connects her and Azima in some way. Is it, as Ahmed (1999) suggests, their 'uncommon estrangement' as migrants that might allow Jean, in this time and place, to begin to make visible what they might have in common? But Jean knows that this is uncertain ground; she knows Azima's context was not one where she could stay; she became a refugee, a migrant within a political context. In narrative inquiry there are many inquiry starting points, and we return again and again to wonders that shaped the inquiry and reappear again in new ways. Only through accepting the liminality with which Azima lives and the liminality of being a narrative inquirer alongside Azima, can Jean find inquiry starting places.

Entering Liminal Spaces in Our Experience

I wonder about what she has left behind in her journeys from Syria to Lebanon to Western Canada. I wonder if she wants to remember. Does she want to 'remember everything about them. You must learn their names. You must remember what happened to them long ago. You must think about it and keep on thinking about it' (Basso, 1996). Who am I here now as I open this space for a conversation about these places she has left, places her grandparents and great grandparents had called home and places that she has now left.

In their conversation, Jean tries to stay open to the otherwise of imagination, as Azima tells her stories of what has happened since the civil unrest in Syria changed so much about her life. As narrative inquirers we understand memory and imagination as interwoven. Our work as narrative inquirers is, then, both memory work and the work of imagination. As we wrote in Chapter 9, it is imagination that allows us to ask new questions, as well as to create the ground of becoming. As Jean works to imagine Azima's experiences as Azima tells her stories of leaving home, Jean knows that she must world-travel with loving perception (Lugones, 1987) alongside Azima. As Jean listens, trying to let Azima tell her stories without asking questions, she knows that Azima may choose to silence stories, perhaps erase places from her life, and work to reimagine herself as otherwise.

Playfully Imagining a Past Home in a New Place

It is almost two years later and Jean is back with Azima. Jean and Azima have shared many stories over these months, and today Jean is bringing back what is the start of a narrative account. As Jean rings the doorbell of the house Azima and her family have purchased, she knows Azima and her family are trying to settle in their new country. As Jean enters, she enters to the sounds of Arabic music.

> *Azima was playing some Arabic music on her cd player for me, the music that she loves to listen to at home. She also made Turkish coffee for me, brewing it carefully on the stove in a small pot and pouring it into two small cups at the table. She had spoken earlier of coffee as making her happy and of reminding her of what once was. 'When I smell coffee smell, ohh! Especially in the morning, especially in the morning. Turkish coffee'. She described how she likes her mornings, the way she learned to live them when she was at home in Aleppo. She described how it was 'Smells. Smells. I think smells is powerful more than looking to the sun or looking to the moon or just thinking. Smells can take you during the second to many years'. As she invites me to sit at the table, I see that she has carefully laid out sweet treats that she would have served in her home in Syria. I am transported to the home Azima has left through the smells, sounds, and tastes of her home in Syria reimagined in a new place.*

Jean thinks about what Azima has done this morning when she senses that it might be her last meeting with Jean for a while. They both know that they will continue to be in touch, a sense of a narrative thread that links them together through friendship. For Jean's visit, Azima has playfully created a world using the smells and sounds of her home in Aleppo, Syria to invite Jean to travel to the world she has left. She is also showing Jean how she is reimagining her new home, one that will be filled with the smells, sounds and tastes that she carries with her from her home in Syria. In Chapter 9 we wrote of touching 'our own horizons as we work to fuse with others, as we offer more and more pathways [...] toward what might be' (Greene, 1994, p. 190). Narrative inquiry is a messy iterative process in which we work to keep wonder, liminality, imagination and playfulness alive.

Section V

Relationality

The idea of relationality is central to narrative inquiry. The ontological and epistemological underpinnings of narrative inquiry have their roots in the pragmatic philosophy of educational philosopher Dewey (1934, 1938). Drawing on Dewey, we developed the argument that experience is 'the fundamental ontological category from which all inquiry – narrative or otherwise – proceeds' (Clandinin & Rosiek, 2007, p. 39). Narrative inquiry works from a relational ontology; that is, experience itself is viewed narratively and necessitates considerations of relational knowing and being. A narrative inquiry proceeds from an ontological position, a curiosity about how people are living and the constituents of their experience. A narrative ontology implies that experiences are continuously interactive, resulting in changes in both people and the contexts in which they interact (Dewey, 1938, 1981). A narrative ontology calls researchers to enter into what Dewey (1934) termed 'ordinary experience', both theirs and their participants' – that is, to enter in ways that allow us to understand lives lived in relation. In Chapter 13 we show the theoretical underpinnings of the ways the political and social are shaped by a relational ontology in narrative inquiry. In Chapter 14 we take up ways that thinking narratively involves an ontological commitment that calls forth responsibilities.

13

Political and Social Landscapes

Abstract

In this chapter, we open questions about the relation between the personal within social and political contexts. Drawing on authors such as Coles, Neumann and Addams, we show that the political and social contexts are always at work in narrative inquiry but are not the starting point for inquiry. Lives are centred and are understood in context. We highlight the ways relational ethics are at the heart of understanding the personal and social as intertwined.

Blurring the Lines

> Jean recalls all of the moments when, looking up from her bookshelves, she has said, 'I know I have that book. I finished reading it only a short time ago.' It was in reflecting on moments such as these that she realized that many of these 'lost' books were on her home bookshelves. In realizing this, she understood that she could no longer draw a line between her personal and professional reading materials.
>
> (Clandinin & Connelly, 2000, pp. 163–4)

The inability to draw lines between personal and professional readings is a reminder that we cannot fragment our lives. Sitting in Jean's office at her home makes visible the depth and breadth of her reading. Reading materials that also include children's books, books spanning diverse historical periods and geographic places. Yet, it is not an eclectic sense of reading materials.

Many of the texts begin with the personal. There are texts that can be seen as memoirs and autobiographies; while others are theoretical texts that still are grounded in a sense of the personal. It is in reading the personal that we have learned to understand and make sense of the social and political landscapes that shape, and are shaped by, people's lives. When stepping back, we can see that we can read these texts in multiple ways and that they point us to ways in which we theorize the political and social while always beginning with the personal within narrative inquiry. Perhaps it is one way to understand the words '[l]ife has marked us with its slow stain' (Addams, 1930, p. 6). Sarbin helped narrative inquirers understand the importance of the distinction between narrative understood as representational and narrative understood as ontological. As narrative inquirers, while we are interested in narrative as representational, we understand narrative inquiry as centrally ontological. As Sarbin pointed out in an interview with Hevern (1999), neither he nor Bruner (1985) initially made the distinction between narrative as a mode of representation and narrative as an ontological form. For both, their interest was shaped more by narrative as representational. However, narrative inquirers see, as Sarbin did in later work, humans as always within cultural, social, institutional and temporal stories. Stories are always personal and, at the same time, they are embedded within contextual narratives.

As Vera turns to her bookshelves, she resonates with the inability to draw lines between her personal and professional texts. She, too, is drawn to the autobiographical, as she seeks to understand the social and political landscapes. Questions of who one is, grounds so much of what one does. She is often drawn back to poetry and plays, works that are marked by a sense of the imaginary – works that she began to read during her late childhood and youth.

> VLADIMIR: I'm beginning to come round to that opinion. All my life I've tried to put it from me, saying Vladimir, be reasonable, you haven't yet tried everything. And I resumed the struggle. (*He broods, musing on the struggle. Turning to Estragon.*) So there you are again.
>
> (Beckett, 1953, n.p.)

It is Vladimir who connects for Vera, a sense of commitment to life, and a sense of care for people and the landscapes they live within, landscapes that hold suffering. A commitment and care that are grounded across time, place and social context. In this chapter we show the idea that narrative inquiry is situated in political and social landscapes – landscapes that are shaped by and understood in relation to experience. Those who engage in narrative inquiry are part of the landscapes under study and acknowledge that they are complicit in the experiences they study, that is, that they help make the worlds in which they live. Within narrative inquiry, inquirers do not stand metaphorically outside of, but are part of, the phenomenon under study. We always need to acknowledge that '[w]e are in the parade we presume to study' (Clandinin & Connelly, 2000, p. 81).

Turning to Experience

As a youth, Vera spent time out of school and working in settings away from schools and outside the dominant narratives of youth within the institutional narratives of schools (see Chapter 1). Vera often bumped up against the institutional narratives of school that were marked by elitism and that silenced difference. She was in Grade 12 when she told her parents she had spent enough time fitting into a school system that made so little sense to her and was leaving school. After long arguments with her parents and discussions of Vera's future possibilities, she left school. Her parents insisted that she find work. She found work in a psychiatric institution.

> *Working in a psychiatric institution seemed fitting – I imagined the work being meaningful and most of all interesting. It would allow me to move to the city and slowly think about the life I imagined … moving seemed to hold possibilities. My parents' friends and neighbors wondered out loud about my choice of working in a psychiatric institution. I noticed the palpable tensions that began to surface as I bumped up against dominant stories.*
>
> *I wish you could have met Anna. She was exuberant, confident and stylish in her own way – she wore the most colourful, ill-matching clothing you can ever imagine. Her short dark hair was tucked back with various styles and colours of hair clips and elastics. She always wore multiple necklaces, and vivid lanyards long before they became popular. Anna was flamboyant.*
>
> *Anna's fingers were brown from constant cigarette smoking. Her nails, brightly coloured, never did match the stains on her fingers. It did not matter to Anna. Anna was not afraid to draw attention, nor was she afraid of calling people out. It was somehow easy for me to fall in love with Anna.*

Years after Vera first met Anna, she came across the writings of Coles (1989) who reflects on his turn towards narrative as shaped early in his career through his interactions with Dr. Ludwig, one of his supervisors in his education as a psychiatrist. 'What ought to be interesting, Dr Ludwig kept insisting, is the unfolding of a lived life rather than the confirmation such a chronicle provides for some theory' (p. 22). Coles drew her attention to her experiences of learning from life, and also to the ethical responsibility involved in narrative, noting that 'their story, yours, mine – it's what we all carry with us on this trip we take, and we owe it to each other to respect our stories and learn from them' (p. 31).

Reading Coles' work as a psychiatric resident triggered memories for Vera of the year she worked at the psychiatric institution where she completed a voluntary year with the Red Cross. The pay was minimal and she lived on site at the institution. In Germany at that time psychiatric institutions were often set up as little towns that provided locked and open units, forensic units mixed with units for people with disabilities, places where those unable to fit into the dominant narratives of normalcy were shut away. A cafeteria provided meals for staff and the adjacent bar provided evening entertainment for patients, yet without access to alcohol.

Anna was a patient. She had spent most of her life on a psychiatric ward and her lifelong struggles were marked by significant and debilitating mental health issues. Anna was in her early 50s when I met her. There were no visits from extended family. I became close to Anna, although I can not say that Anna ever became close to me. One of the highlights for me was a trip I took with Anna to the North Sea. I was 17 at the time and somehow thought that it would be great for Anna to see the world. I somehow convinced those working with Anna that it would not only be good for Anna, but also important for her to see the world. The small villages on the islands located in the North Sea in Germany were familiar to me. I knew that unlike the large urban centers, I would have an easier time keeping track of Anna if she decided to venture off. Of course neither Anna, nor I, had any money and the small salary I received, and the state income Anna received, only allowed us to stay at a local hostel. I still remember the day we arrived – a beautiful sunny and warm day. Anna had never been to the ocean and the set of new and unfamiliar experiences had created a sense of manicness for her.

I remember the check in at the hostel – high tables, surrounded by children and youth, who clearly were on a school trip. Anna immediately caught the children's eyes – in all of her flamboyance she was so clearly different. She stood by the table with the children, chain smoking and offering her cigarette butts to the children. Well, we were off to a great start … within 15 minutes of arriving at the youth hostel, we had created a storyline. Anna loved drinking soda pop, something that was difficult to access at the Psychiatric Institution. She noticed some of the children and youth drinking pop and, after offering them her cigarette butts, asked if she could have their pop … a bartering system that made sense to Anna.

Starting with the Personal

May Sarton (1980, 1987) in her journals helps us see that, as narrative inquirers, we begin with the personal but see within it the larger contextual narratives. Our starting point, as was Sarton's, is always the personal and, as we inquire into the stories, we see the ways that the social and political landscapes have shaped the personal. It is only through careful attention to the personal that we can understand those larger narratives. As Sarton writes of her days, she describes visits with friends, meals made and eaten, gardens planted and harvested – all intensively personal. However, she also shows, to careful readers, issues of privilege that she has in contrast to some friends, shows how age marks people as different in our social narratives, shows how sexual orientation shapes her life, and takes us to race and racism that shape the contours of American society. She does all this with stories of her daily life, that is, that position her in the midst of making her own life.

We see something similar in Vera's story as she begins with her own story, a story in which Anna becomes a central character. Vera tells of her own youthful search for meaning, as she *imagined the work* as *meaningful and most of all interesting. Her* work at the hospital *would allow me to move to the city and slowly think about the life I imagined … moving seemed to hold possibilities.* And she describes Anna as *exuberant, confident and stylish in her own way* and her relationship with Anna as one in which she felt close to Anna, although she does not know if Anna felt close to her.

As Vera tells her story, she makes visible the social and political landscapes that have shaped both her own and Anna's personal stories. It is through attending to the personal of each of their lives and the personal that lived between them that we can sense the shape of those larger narratives. We see Vera as a privileged youth with agency who experienced the constraints of school narratives and saw possibilities for leaving school early to find something more meaningful around which to shape her life. Vera composed her early life within a familial narrative in which there were sufficient resources for summer vacations to North Sea islands. She chooses to leave the institutional narrative of schooling and her family home to enter another institutional narrative, the one that shaped psychiatric hospitals in Germany at the time. Within the institutional narrative Vera becomes a poorly paid worker, albeit within a narrative of a Red Cross volunteer. For Vera there was always the possibility of returning after the year as these were social and institutional landscapes which were chosen by Vera.

Anna lives in the psychiatric institution embedded within different social and institutional landscapes: she has lived within this landscape for *most of her life*. The psychiatric institution has a script for people who have significant mental health issues and Anna would remain for her lifetime within that script, a script that holds her within the abnormal. Both Vera and Anna compose their relationship within the narrative of a psychiatric institution, which is a self-contained institutional place, both inside and outside urban centres in Germany at the time. When Vera comes to know Anna, Vera composes a different story for Anna, one which *would not only be good for Anna, but also important for her to see the world*. At this point, Vera again exercises her agency within the social and institutional landscapes and interrupts both her and Anna's stories. As they spend time in the hostel, other dominant social and political narratives become evident for children and youth: they are not to have cigarettes and are not to barter with strangers.

Vera reminds us that, as narrative inquirers think with, and about, the social and political landscapes in narrative inquiry – we must recall our own lives. Embedded in this is the recognition that we learn early on that our lives are not just our own, but that they are marked and scribed by others. We are learning from our lives (Neumann & Peterson, 1997). As we think with this notion of learning from our lives, there is a sense of finding our way home. It is Anna Neumann (1997) who writes,

> what I learned from that writing, for my self and for my work, is that how I now relate to others, seen in the conduct of my professional work, notably my research – how I listen for the knowing of persons whom I interview, how I imagine their lives, how I sense the limits of their words to convey what they feel and know, how I sense my own inability to comprehend what they know and learn even as they speak – reflects what I learned through my father's efforts to tell his stories years back.

> (p. 91)

Later Neumannn writes, 'at another level it pointed at what I could never hope to learn of a life apart from my own, no matter how hard I tried' (p. 91). Our work as narrative inquirers is to understand experience as something that is part of our own lives, and, as such, is important to the social and political significance of our work. A sense of finding our way home is marked by the necessity of attending closely to the details of stories lived, relived, told and retold and the silences, gaps and disruptions that occur within the living and telling. Close attention helps us see, and name, the social and political landscapes of people's lives.

Thinking with Silences

We are not always thinking of untold stories, that is, of the stories and experiences that have shaped us so deeply that we have yet to find words for them. Often it is the social and political contexts that come into shaping these experiences. It is here that we are unsure if we should pursue these untold or silenced stories (Neuman, 1997). The silences often embrace the socially inscribed challenges people face, the stigma, the horrors, the injustices and unfairness lives hold – can, and should, we open these? What good will come of it? As narrative inquirers think with silences, Neumann (1997) reminds us that 'I learned from my mother's life that even in the silence of a story that lives without words, there exists a text to know and to tell, though its telling may occur in unexpected ways' (p. 92).

Social and political landscapes that shape experiences and silences often reflect the impact of social conditions as well as political implications of happenings and events across time and place. Silences are an integral part of narrative inquiry, as 'we live with, and within, silences, and [...] our told and untold stories of experiences are shaped by silences and, in turn, also shape silences' (Blix, Caine, Clandinin & Berendonk, 2021). In recent work, Bodil Blix, Caine, Clandinin and Charlotte Berendonk (2021) explored intergenerational experiences of a Sami family, with particular attention to silences. While they explore notions of being silenced, they also recognize that silence signals 'a quietness or stillness that allows us to turn inward. In this way, silence holds the possibility of a different kind of presence, a presence of possibility that we know from what lives temporally alongside what we understand as stillness' (p. 583).

While silence may signify stillness and quietness, Kerby (1991) reminds us that shame and a lack of respect can magnify silence. When shame and disrespect shape silence, ethical questions marked by desire, recognition and responsibility become visible. While in the experience of silence in Blix's family, who are Sami, silence is marked by the experiences of colonization, including residential schools. Shame has manifested profound silences within her family stories, including the silencing of her family's identity as Sami. Often silences are difficult to disrupt as they act as ways to protect the family, individuals, or relationships. molly Andrews (2010) helps us see that,

> [s]ilence always and only exists in relation to that which surrounds it. It is the blank spaces between words, and as such it helps to frame not only the

meaning of what is said but that which can be said, a refuge for both the unsaid and the unsayable.

(p. 161)

Silence as a space of refuge makes visible how strongly social and political landscapes shape lives.

Vera turns once more to Anna and their time together, as she thinks about the connection between silence and social and political landscapes, and the relational aspect of experiencing silences. Sitting alongside Anna was the first time Vera was forced to think about abandonment or banishment. Anna, who lived all of her life in an institutional setting, had composed her life in relation to narrow structures and relationships that never came with a promise of permanency or a deep sense of love. There were many silences in Anna's life, silences that were visible in the absences of family photographs, of items that might have been significant in her childhood, or of items that represented memories of friendships or extended family relationships. Anna raised wonders for Vera about family stability, and of taken for granted notions of love and affection. Only retrospectively did Vera wonder about the impact of the visit to the island for Anna. Did the experience create further silences for Anna? Did it make visible, for Anna, the social and political landscapes of her life and the lives of others who lived in psychiatric institutions? What part did Vera play in furthering silences created by her own privilege?

Turning to Feminist Pragmatism

I think of Anna often, our time by the beach, the train ride with its sense of adventure, and the times we sat together at the beach as I wondered how each of us ended up there. I wonder now what Anna wondered as we sat together on the beach. The experiences with Anna led me to larger questions of social responsibilities as well as tensions between paternalism and what I saw as the never-experienced freedom and joy for people within psychiatric institutions. Who got to decide who was normal? Whose rules were we all living by and with?

As we think with Vera and Anna's experiences, we are reminded that our work as narrative inquirers resonates with, and is informed by, the work of feminist pragmatists, like Addams. In particular we are informed by the ways Addams undertakes her work at Hull House. Hull House was a settlement house, co-founded by Addams in 1889, in a poor and working-class, primarily immigrant, neighbourhood. While it served men and women initially, it later became focused on providing care to women. In her work at Hull House, Addams builds clear connections between listening, participation, leadership and activism. Addams made explicit the necessity of listening and engaging with experience in order to understand social issues and plurality, as well as to further a moral commitment to community. Addams (1916) writes about her experience at Hull House,

> [w]e are constantly impressed with the uniform kindness and courtesy we received. Perhaps these first days laid the simple human foundations which are certainly essential for continuous living among the poor: first, genuine preference for residence in an industrial quarter to any other part of the city, because it is interesting and makes the human appeal; and second the conviction [...] that the things which make men alike are finer and better than the things that keep them apart, and that these basic likenesses, if they are properly accentuated, easily transcend the less essential differences of race, language, creed and tradition.
>
> (Chapter 5, n.p.)

As Vera returns to think with her experiences alongside Anna, and others within the psychiatric institution, she awakens to how these experiences and her inquiry into them have shaped her in profound ways. Through her inquiry into her experiences, Vera raised questions about power, institutions and social norms, that is, about the social and political landscapes of people's lives. While Vera's early departure from school signalled a break with expected narratives of, and for, her, her early school leaving and her work in the psychiatric institution, with its highly structured and normative environment, set in motion her curiosity and interest in people's lives as key to understanding the social and political worlds we live within. It was in seeking otherwise, in listening and participating in others' lives, that Vera learned how important it was to imagine different possibilities. Addams' (2002) words resonate with Vera,

> [w]e have learned as common knowledge that much of the insensibility and hardness of the world is due to the lack of imagination which prevents a realization of the experiences of other people. Already there is a conviction that we are under a moral obligation in choosing our experiences, since the results of those experiences must ultimately determine our understanding of life. We know instinctively that if we grow contemptuous of our fellows, and consciously limit our intercourse to certain kinds of people whom we have

previously decided to respect, we not only tremendously circumscribe our range of life, but limit the scope of our ethics.

(p. 8)

Reading of Addams' work at Hull House made evident that she not only saw this as a place of work, but that this was her life. Addams' approach made visible the moral necessity of social experience. Addams, a prolific writer, took up philosophical ideas and thoughts that shaped many (although she was not always given credit for them). Haddock Seigfried (1996) observed that it was Addams, 'who took [Dewey's] argument one step further by adopting the radical position that scholars ought to be or become members of communities plagued by the problems their theories are supposed to solve' (p. 58). Addams helps narrative inquirers name the importance of pragmatist thinking to life and the necessity to inquire into the common ground of human experience.

The Social and Political as a Question of Ethics and Action

Maurice Hamington (2004) links Addams' work to a notion of care ethics. For her '[t]o make the case for Addams as a care ethicist who implicitly understood the moral significance of human embodiment, I will examine her notion of sympathetic knowledge, her relational approach to morality, and her valorization of context' (p. 99). She goes on to state,

> care denotes an approach to personal and social morality that shifts ethical considerations to context, relationships, and affective knowledge in a manner that can only be fully understood if care's embodied dimension is recognized. Care is committed to flourishing and growth of individuals, yet acknowledges our interconnectedness and interdependence.
>
> (p. 3)

This sense of growth, interconnectedness and interdependence that is so visible in Addams' work is central to narrative inquiry. Connelly and Clandinin (1998) describe 'living an educated life as an ongoing process. People's lives are composed over time: biographies or life stories are lived and told, retold and relived. For us, education is interwoven with living and with the possibility of retelling our life stories' (pp. 246–7).

Within narrative inquiry, we see ethics as interwoven with living lives and as negotiated in the ongoing processes of being together. Ethics is situated in close relationship with scholarship that happens both within, and outside of, academic institutions. What, then, gets raised as ethical within a narrative inquiry view? Talpade Mohanty (1993) writes in defining home, that home is not

> a comfortable, stable, inherited and familiar space, but instead is an imaginative, politically-charged space where the familiarity and sense of affection and commitment lay in shared collective analysis of social injustice as well as a vision for radical transformation.
>
> (p. 53)

Thinking with Relational Ethics

We see the link between the ethical and political and, in that way, see our focus on experience is a possible site of activism and of struggle. As we wrote in *The Relational Ethics of Narrative Inquiry* (Clandinin et al., 2018),

> [w]orking within this particular view of experience, with attentiveness to the practical consequences of life making, shapes the ways we live out relational ethics. Making visible our philosophical stance as grounded in pragmatist views of experience is particularly important to understanding how we come to consider relational ethics. Clandinin and Rosiek (2007) describe narrative inquiry as beginning with a 'respect for ordinary lived experience' (p. 42) as it explores both individuals' experience as well as 'the social, cultural, and institutional narratives within which individuals' experiences were constituted, shaped, expressed and enacted'.
>
> (p. 42)

In 2018 we laid out our understanding of relational ethics as marked by five key dimensions. We described the dimensions as the necessity of engaging in world-traveling with imagination, improvization and playfulness; the necessity of moving slowly in ways that allow for listening and living; the necessity of ethical understandings as always in process, in the making, with wakefulness to the ongoingness of experience; the necessity of always engaging with a sense of uncertainty and not knowing that acknowledges living ethically as living within liminal spaces that position us in places of dis/ease; and the necessity of understanding that ethical relations are always lived embodiments that ask us to be still and to attend carefully to, and with, silence and contemplation. While the key features outline ethical ways of being in relation, it is important to consider Addams' (2002) words: 'action is indeed the sole medium of expression for ethics [...] that a situation does not become moral until confronted with the question of what shall be done in a concrete case and are obliged to act upon our theory' (p. 119).

In Chapter 8, we discussed the ways that we understand community in narrative inquiry and used the work of Lindemann Nelson (1995) to show how 'counterstories-narratives of resistance and insubordination-allowed communities of choice to challenge and revise the paradigm stories of the "found" communities in which they are embedded' (p. 24). Lindemann Nelson also reminds us that '[r]esistance and insubordination are of course an ongoing process, as will be the storytelling that fuels it, but if a counterstory is to be effective, its telling will have to achieve a temporary stopping-point that permits the community to act' (p. 37). It is important to see our actions as interlinked with the community. While we can read Vera's engagement alongside Anna as taking a form of action, it is not until Vera considers and engages in action within the context of community that it holds significant consequences.

In Chapter 8 we also drew on Friedman (1989) to show the necessity of alternative social relationships, or communities of choice. In thinking with Friedman's words, we contemplated the role of imagination, something we took up in Chapter 9, in relation with our notions of ethics and actions. We also show, in this chapter, that imagination is taken up by Addams. Bateson (1997) notes that,

> [i]t is a cliche that experience is the best teacher, yet experience is a teacher from whom many fail to learn. What does it take to look at the familiar and discern the assumptions and power relationships that maintain it, to go on to say, this is not the only possible way, this is not how it has to be?
>
> (p. viii)

Following Bateson's argument, we recognize that we are implicated as we imagine new ways, recognizing that because we are implicated, we cannot walk away unchanged. In this way we understand any change in social and political landscapes is also a change of the personal. This does not come without a sense of personal risk and, as Hamington notes, 'acting is risky. [Yet,] Addams is willing to embrace that risk as part of the democratic spirit' (p. 119). Within narrative inquiry, action is a necessary part of the inquiry.

While we have shown in this chapter how we understand the political and social landscapes in relation to experience and, in turn, to relational ethics, we cannot lose sight of the importance to act. It is Vladmir, in Beckett's (1953) work, who not only shows us the connections, but also explicates the urgency for us to act.

> VLADIMIR: Let us not waste our time in idle discourse! (Pause. Vehemently.) Let us do something, while we have the chance! It is not every day that we are needed. Not indeed that we personally are needed. Others would meet the case equally well if not better. To all mankind they were addressed, those cries for help still ringing in our ears! But at this place, at this moment of time, all mankind is us, whether we like it or not. Let us make the most of it, before it is too late! Let us represent worthily for once the foul brood to which a cruel fate consigned us! What do you say? (Estragon says nothing.) It is true that when with folded arms we weigh the pros and cons we are no less a credit to our species. The tiger bounds to the help of his congeners without the least reflection, or else he slinks away into the depths of the thickets. But that is not the question. What are we doing here, that is the question.
>
> (n.p.)

Summary

In this chapter, we showed how we understand social and political contexts in narrative inquiry through a starting point in personal experience. Drawing on Sarbin, we show experience is always situated within social, cultural and institutional stories. Theorists, such as Neumann and Addams, are used to develop our view that the social and political are always entwined in relational ethics and action in narrative inquiry. In Chapter 14, we turn towards the importance of commitment, responsibility and obligations in narrative inquiry.

14

Commitment, Responsibility and Obligations

Abstract

In this chapter, we show the theoretical resources that shaped the relational ontology of narrative inquiry as it draws forth commitments, responsibilities and obligations. We ground ideas of responsibility in the work of pragmatist scholars such as Addams (2002) who showed, in her writing and in her work with Hull House, the need for those in positions of privilege to live in ways that are marked by social justice. Working from a pragmatist view, relationality draws forth responsibilities, commitments and obligations for living lives.

As we consider responsibility within a pragmatist view we draw on the meaning of responsibility from its Latin root word, *respondere*, with its meaning of to, 'respond, answer to, promise in return' (np). The word 'responsibility' retains the sense of obligation in the Latin root word. The word turns our attention to the need to answer to those with whom we are in relation, to be responsive to others, and to the communities of which we are part. The sense of a promise in return draws us to think about how our responsibilities are closely tied to our obligations, to those to whom we are in relation, and to our commitments to our forward-looking stories. In these forward-looking stories, we recognize that we need to shape our actions with a sense of a future – a sense that what we do or not do will continue to reverberate into the stories yet to be lived and told. We also draw on Arendt (1958) who argued that action and speech create appearances of individuals at the same time as their lives call forth action in relation to others and to the world.

Turning to Experience

In early 1990 I responded to an invitation to apply for a position at the University of Alberta. The advertisement was for an Associate Professor in the Department of Elementary Education with regular professorial duties with the addition of the requirement to frame a proposal for a research centre in teacher education. There was a tacit message that the centre was to be a place where qualitative research was to be welcomed, a kind of balance to an already existing centre on measurement and evaluation that had a strong quantitative research orientation. The centre was to be approved by the various departments, the faculty, and the university. There was little that framed just what a research centre should be.

In the summer of 1990, I was hired by the University of Alberta to fill that position. I was in my seventh year of being an academic and was entering a new institution. I had spent a great deal of time until then composing and living out counter stories of teacher education programs at another university. These programs had, at their heart, collaborative ways of working together across institutions, and across disciplines and subject matter areas. In the planning meetings for these programs, faculty members, teachers, and pre-service teachers spoke often about responsibilities to children, families, other teachers and professionals, and to the kind of world we wanted to create through education.

But a research centre? In teacher education? Without a definite model or plan that I was to live up to, or to live out, and surrounded by a community of playful colleagues/friends, I was open to being playful, to not being seen as competent, to not knowing, to the surprise of what might be possible. I suppose I did not quite know what 'being competent' looked like. At this point in my life, and in my academic career, I wanted to shape a space for a different way of thinking about a research centre and about what counted as teacher education. While there was already a measurement and evaluation research centre, writing a counter story for a different kind of centre was an opportunity to explore other possibilities. It was through playfulness that it seemed possible to imagine otherwise. Without much experience of playfulness within institutional narratives, I turned to my community of friends to open my mind to imagining otherwise, as Maxine Greene said.

A table, we definitely need a table.

It needs to be a big table. A table where anyone can come and talk.

We need to make commitments to sit at the table at certain times. That way, people will know there will always be someone available for a conversation.

Anyone can come? Yes, not just people who name themselves as researchers but teachers, parents, children, youth, principals, and others. It needs to be inclusive. There need to be spaces for people just beginning to think about themselves as researchers but also teacher educators so that means parents, families, children, not just the university teacher educators. As well, graduate students and undergraduate students interested in teacher education are invited.

A kind of kitchen table where anyone can come and there will always be tea, a place to sit and talk about important things, at least things that are important to those who are gathered.

And slowly as we imagined and read our favorite authors on imagination and responsibility and community, people like Maxine Greene, Vivian Paley, Elliot Eisner, Nel Noddings, Paula Gunn Allen, and Hanna Arendt, and talked with each other, calling forth other moments and experiences, images began to dance about how to create a structure with dimensions of time, place, people, and events. There was a kind of confidence among us that came from being a community that allowed us to not concern ourselves with how we appeared to others. We did not worry about self-importance, about the norms of research, and what it meant to open up ambiguity and to hold spaces open. Imagining a research centre became a kind of inquiry project itself: what would it look like, feel like'. How would those who came experience it? What edges could we push against as 'we danced at the edge of the world?' (LeGuin, 1989, book title).

In this chapter, we think with Jean's experiences of establishing a research centre. The Centre for Research for Teacher Education and Development (CRTED) came, over many years, to be a homeplace for us, and for many others. The table is critical to the ways that we have come to understand responsibility, commitment and obligations. These notions are fundamental to the relational ontology of narrative inquiry and are grounded in theoretical works of pragmatist and feminist scholars. As we argued elsewhere (Clandinin & Rosiek, 2007) and elsewhere in this book (see Chapter 1), the relational ontology of narrative inquiry

> is to generate a new relation between a human being and her environment – her life, community, world – one that 'makes possible a new way of dealing with them, and thus eventually creates a new kind of experienced objects, not more real than those which preceded but more significant, and less overwhelming and oppressive' (Dewey, 1981b, p. 175).
>
> (Clandinin & Rosiek, 2007, p. 39)

The generation of new relations that are less overwhelming and less oppressive highlights the importance of attending carefully to questions of responsibility and commitment and, perhaps, to obligations. We understand these new relations to be significant to communities, as well as the physical environments of which we are a part.

Turning to Pragmatists

As we have written throughout the book, we see narrative inquiry as grounded in complex ways within the work of pragmatist scholars such as Dewey and Addams who have shaped our ontological stance as narrative inquirers. Grounded, as we are, in pragmatist work keeps our attention firmly on the experiences that people undergo as they live their lives, as well as on what it means to undergo an experience and to live a life. In Chapters 1 and 2, we wrote of our concept of knowledge as experiential, moral, contextual and embodied (Connelly & Clandinin, 1985, 1988). Thinking of knowledge in these ways allows us to acknowledge, attend to and understand the practical consequences and implications for our actions. 'Furthermore, this concept of knowledge as situated within and shaped by experience focuses our attention on the importance of attending to the lives we live within social, cultural, familial, linguistic and institutional narratives' (Clandinin et al., 2018, p. 17). Working with a relational ontology makes evident that we are always working towards new relations among people and within institutional, social, cultural and familial narratives, as well as narratives grounded in place. We are, within narrative inquiry, working to reimagine and recreate worlds that are attentive to the responsibilities, commitments and obligations that are part of living in the world. This sense of reimagining and recreating worlds was strongly present for Jean when she began to imagine the work of the research centre alongside others and with a sense of shaping a community.

As we wrote in Chapter 8, as narrative inquirers, we are attentive to how communities shape us as they prescribe identities on to people and then act upon these prescribed identities. As narrative inquirers, we understand, as does Lindemann Nelson (1995), that 'our communities do more than guide us-they constitute us' (p. 28). As part of worlds and communities, living requires being attentive to who we are within, and to our responsibilities for, the larger worlds and communities, to more than just ourselves.

Working with, and from, a relational ontology calls us to attend to people's ordinary experiences in their everyday lives. A relational ontology highlights, for narrative inquiry, the relationship between knower and what is known, between knowing and action, between how one knows and what one knows, as well as the relationship between knowing and silence. A relational ontological commitment is based in practice, in the living of a life, and calls forth understandings grounded in past and present experience and in relation to an imagined future (Clandinin & Rosiek, 2007).

As we have written elsewhere,

[a]n attentiveness to relational ethics, and the social conditions under which people live, has brought us to feminist philosophers who hold us accountable to understand and hence inquire into experience from a place of social justice and equity. In our work as narrative inquirers a relational ontology therefore allows us to attend to difference and social action rather than compromise. Relational ethics forces us to deal with real issues and social values. Here as Addams (1902) points out, we have to attend to the irritations, uncertainties, and perplexities that we come to know in relation with people.

(Clandinin et al., 2018, p. 19)

In Jean's story of imagining and creating a research centre in teacher education we see her understandings are already shaped by knowing how education and research are part of life-making as she writes about her early work in teacher education as shaped by *collaborative ways of working together across institutions, disciplines, and subject matter areas* and by her knowing that she and *other faculty members, teachers, and pre-service teachers spoke often about responsibilities to children, families, other teachers, and professionals, and to the kind of world we wanted to create through education.*

Turning to Feminist Thinking

What Jean did not know was how to work with the same ideas to create a research centre in teacher education, one which would be congruent with her understandings of the importance of working with others *surrounded by a community of playful colleagues/friends* and one in which she could be *open to being playful, to not knowing, to the surprise of what might be possible.* She knew that the research centre needed to work against the taken-for-granted, the usual, if it was to be a place in which imagining otherwise was possible. She found, as Jane Tompkin's (1997) did in her memoir, *A Life in School*, that she was placing 'herself outside any institutional configuration, virtually leaping into a liminal state' (Heilbrun, 1999, p. 76) in which a research centre would be positioned betwixt and between.

Narrative inquiry's concept of responsibility is grounded in the work of feminist pragmatist scholars such as Addams (2002) who showed, in her writing and her work with Hull House, the need for those in positions of privilege to live in responsible ways with others in society. From a pragmatist view, relationality draws forth responsibilities and commitments for living.

A relational ontology requires us to ask questions of who we each are responsible to, and who we each are responsible for, as well as what our commitments are to others, and to the communities in which we, and they, are embedded. As Jean and her colleagues discuss a centre for research for teacher education, they asked questions of who they were responsible to, and what communities were part of their responsibilities and commitments, deciding that *anyone can come and talk,* that is, that it was a place where obligations and responsibilities were to children, teachers, families and others rather than just to those who were named as researchers.

Addams was not the first philosopher who turned our attention to questions of responsibility and commitment within narrative inquiry. There were others who also called us to think of responsibility such as Greene, Paley, Heilbrun, Noddings and Gunn Allen. But Addams was often mentioned as someone we 'should' read when we spoke of what we were trying to do with narrative inquiry and particularly of our work in establishing a research centre that would be a lived embodiment of pragmatist philosophy and of scholars interested in democracy and dialogue. For example, Heilbrun wrote of Addams in the following way,

> Jane Addams, ill and depressed [...] first observed the squalor of an urban slum from the top of a double-decker bus in London's East End while on a European trip recommended by her physician. At this sight, she wrote in *Twenty Years at Hull House,* she was seized with 'despair and resentment' and was further dismayed to realize that the only context out of which she could respond to disquieting reality was a literary one. We women, Addams thought, waste our time 'lumbering our minds with literature', instead of seeking contact with the real. When, after a second visit to London a few years later, she resolved to begin a settlement house in Chicago, it was as much for the sake of young, middle-class women as for that of the poor: she wanted a place 'in which young women who had been given over to study might restore a balance of activity [...] and learn of life from life itself'.
>
> (Heilbrun, 1999, p. 68)

Addams, as portrayed by Heilbrun, worked from a relational ontology as she highlighted the importance for both residents of the settlement house and the middle class women who worked there to achieve the possibility of learning 'of life from life itself'. She portrayed the importance of seeing the mutuality of the learning for all participants in Hull House. What she was attempting to do appeared to honour our intentions in narrative inquiry and what a research centre in teacher education could be. Drawing on Addams' work at Hull House, McKenna and Pratt noted that Addams illustrated her conception of social change through cooperation and not antagonism.

> Rather than doing good 'for' people, she believed you had to do good 'with' people. The people who were in need of some help or improvement in their lives had to be involved in naming and working for that improvement. Democracy had to be at work in all social relations. This kind of progress was slower but more secure.
>
> (McKenna & Pratt, 2015, p. 50)

And it was this idea that captured what Jean was considering in a research centre in teacher education that invited all to come to the dialogue at a *big table.*

Through her experiences at Hull House, Addams developed her feminist ideas of a social ethic. Critical of using a personal ethics developed in families as the basis of a social ethics, Addams (2002) searched for a social ethics, one that addressed her concern that

> [a]n exaggerated personal morality is often mistaken for a social morality, and until it attempts to minister to a social situation its total inadequacy is not discovered. To attempt to attain a social morality without a basis of democratic experience results in the loss of the only possible corrective and guide, and ends in an exaggerated individual morality but not in social morality at all.
>
> (p. 78)

Like Dewey, and other pragmatist scholars, she looked to everyday experiences as the source of problems and understood that our choice of inquiry problems are ethical decisions that emerge out of our understandings of life.

It was later, as we read Addams, that she helped us shape and name understandings of responsibility and commitment for narrative inquiry. We found her ideas congruent with ours as she expressed a relational ontology in which she was part of the experience with others in inquiry. She wrote, '[w]e are learning that a standard of social ethics is not attained by traveling a sequestered byway, but by mixing on the thronged and common road where all must turn out for one another, and at least see the size of one another's burdens' (Addams, 2002, p. 7).

When we read these lines from Jane Addams we see the parallels with Jean's insistence that any new centre needed *a big table. A table where anyone who wants to can come and talk.* There needed to be an inclusive space for dialogue that was open to many people, *not just people who name themselves as researchers. There need to be spaces for people just beginning to think about themselves as researchers but also teacher educators so that means parents, families, children, not just the university teacher educators. As well, graduate students and undergraduate students interested in teacher education are invited.*

A sense of inclusive spaces so we can learn with each other 'and at least see the size of one another's burdens' (Addams, 2002, p. 7) is a grounding notion for narrative inquiry. It highlights again the relational ontology and the relational ethics of narrative inquiry set within feminist and pragmatist scholarship.

Within narrative inquiry, we cannot think with only a personal ethic but must work with a social ethic that allows us to see ourselves as part of larger communities with responsibilities and commitments to more than ourselves and our personal and familial relationships. As we have written elsewhere,

> a relational ontology requires that we undertake research with an understanding of relational ethics that call us to larger questions of who we are in relation with participants but also who we are in relation with the larger world or worlds that people, including us as researchers, inhabit. This relational ontology interwoven necessarily with a relational ethics calls us to consider mutuality, respect and reciprocity. But it also calls us to questions of responsibility to the person and to the worlds in which we are nested, to questions of complicity in the worlds within which we currently exist as well as to future worlds that our work leads into.
>
> (Clandinin et al., 2018, p. 20)

These questions of who we are in relation to each other and to the worlds that we both live within, and are complicit in, draw us to consider those who are invited to the metaphoric table. Gunn Allen (1998), an Indigenous scholar/poet, calls on us to consider the kinds of dialogue that are called for when we gather. She writes,

> [t]ruth, acceptance of the truth, is a shattering experience. It shatters the binding shroud of culture trance. It rips apart smugness, arrogance, superiority, and self-importance. It requires acknowledgment of responsibility for the nature and quality of each of our own lives, our own inner lives as well as the life of the world. Truth, inwardly accepted, humbling truth, makes one vulnerable. You can't be right, self-righteous, and truthful at the same time.
>
> (p. 64)

This notion of truth and truthfulness is important – it makes us vulnerable, and it also calls us to engage in dialogue and to live up to ways of being in relation. This understanding has called us to revisit the work of Arendt and to think about notions of truth and truthfulness, and of who we are across public and private spaces.

Hannah Arendt: Theoretical Groundings in the Public and Private

Arendt also helped us think of the centrality of dialogue, social equity and social inclusion within narrative inquiry. Arendt (1958) argued that action and speech create spaces for the appearance of individuals at the same time as their lives call forth action in relation to others and to the world. Yet, much of what happens in public spaces is also marked by an absence of action, by a lack of interest in public life. It is important to understand that action takes place between people, which challenges a sense of individualism and requires public spaces and a common world.

Arendt (1958), in capturing the essence of the public realm, made use of the metaphor of a table. She writes,

> [t]o live together in the world means essentially that a world of things is between those who have it in common, as a table is located between those who sit around; the world, like every in-between, relates and separates men at the same time.
>
> (p. 52)

It is not surprising that we were drawn to Arendt's work given her use of a metaphor of a table and Jean's sense of the importance of a *table where anyone who wants to can come and talk*. As Arendt helped us see within narrative inquiry, it was important to make a commitment to each other to gather and to be available for dialogue. In this spirit of gathering around a table, what Arendt (1958, p. 180) names as 'sheer human togetherness', and where 'people are *with* others and neither for nor against each other' (Veck & Gunter, 2020, p. 7; italics for original text), resonated with the concepts of responsibility and commitment within narrative inquiry. As Jean wrote, a research centre needs *A kind of kitchen table where anyone can come and there will always be tea, a place to sit and talk about important things, at least things that are important to those who are gathered.* At this actual physical table that Jean was imagining for the heart of the research centre, she, too, imagined that those who sat at the table would not be in a debate, nor in a 'for or against' discussion but would be in dialogue and conversation with each other, the world and with themselves. As Veck and Gunter (2020) point out, '[w]hat Arendt demonstrates so strikingly is that if we cannot hear others, we cannot really begin to speak. Instead our utterances spill out as just so many assertions' (p. 6). These notions of dialogue and conversation where we engage with each other and ourselves take us back to the importance of engaging with loving perception (Lugones, 1987), in ways that allow us to playfully engage with a sense of what might be possible; a place where human plurality is key. The centrality of understanding a coming together in dialogue is part of narrative inquiry when participants and researchers join with each other to explore experiences.

Within narrative inquiry we draw on Arendt's concept of the importance of spaces of appearance as a way to become human. Engaging in narrative inquiry allows us to understand our, and participants', presence in research as presenting 'a willingness to act and speak at all, to insert one's self into the world and begin a story of one's own' (Arendt 1958, p. 186). As Arendt helps us see, as we enter into dialogue, into 'the disclosure of the "who" through speech, and the setting of a new beginning through action' (p. 184), we always enter in the midst or as Arendt explains we 'fall into an already existing web where the[ir] immediate consequences can be felt' (p. 184). As each person enters, they are nested within an already existing web, and 'start a new process which eventually emerges as the unique life story of the newcomer, affecting uniquely the life stories of all those with whom he comes into contact' (Arendt, 1958, p. 184). In this way, we come to understand the importance of questions of responsibility to, and for, each other and to, and for, our worlds, and our commitments and obligations to act in those worlds with others.

For Arendt, we must, of necessity, attend to responsibility as being responsible for one's actions as well as for, and to, others who share our common world. And in so doing, we need to understand that we are also responsible for what we do not do, for what is not done, for the gaps and silences that persist because we do not act. She directs our attention to the ways that as humans we can come to be 'lovers of the world' (Arendt, 1996, p. 17) and transform the world into an inhabitable place by loving it and by living in it. For Arendt (1996), 'the world consists of those who love it [...] It is the human world, which constitutes itself by habitation and love [....] Love of the world, which makes it "worldly," rests on being "of the world"' (p. 66).

Arendt also helps us see that as we act we have the potential to change situations, not always in ways that we can imagine. In this we see her ideas resonating across pragmatist ideas of forward-looking stories, what is present can shift into unpredicted and perhaps unimaginable future stories. If we are attending closely enough, we make visible the junctures and disruptions, the gaps, silences and inequities that become visible in the interruptions.

Summary

These questions around responsibility, commitment and obligations are part of what it means to think narratively in narrative inquiry. It is these questions that call us to make visible who we are within the experiences of participants, and in relation to, and with, each other and the larger worlds we inhabit. Jemy Rosiek (2018) highlights that our work in narrative inquiry explicitly embodies 'the relational tension between the personal and macrosocial influences on our identity and subjectivity' (p. 206). We are called to help each other make visible the 'personal dimensions of those experiences' (Rosiek, 2018, p. 206) as well as the ways 'the broader social forces bend our feelings, identities, and our sense of right and wrong' (p. 206). Explicit attention to these questions of who we are and what our responsibilities, commitments and obligations are is necessary if we are to engage in the social and political worlds that shape the lives of participants, our lives and our imagined future. We are reminded of the importance of considerations of community and belonging (see Chapter 8) and how we understand the larger narratives within which we live. For Arendt, we are always shaping the world together, at a table where we are, at once, both engaged in the personal, the social, the political, and the spaces between.

Section V

Methodological Notebook

In this methodological notebook we turn to ways in which we live responsibilities and commitments in relation with peoples on diverse political and social landscapes. These commitments run across each narrative inquiry study and continue long after a research study is formally finished (Caine & Estefan, 2011). How we think about our commitments is already visible prior to our engagement with participants. We draw on field texts and fragments of narrative accounts (Clandinin, 2013) as well as narrative threads, and contemplate the personal, practical and social significance of our work (Clandinin & Connelly, 2000) as we make these visible.

A critical piece of our work is understanding that action and consequences are integral to what we do as narrative inquirers. In 2017 Caine et al. wrote,

> we share Rosiek's (2013) view that what we 'use to judge the merits of ontological acts are the consequences – including their effects on our identity, affect, and most fundamental relations – that they precipitate in the ongoing stream of our experience' (p. 697). This future consequential focus shapes the way we think; it shapes our understanding of what we have called living in the midst (Clandinin & Connelly, 2000) and it shapes our understanding of an 'expanded sense of responsibility in our activity of knowing'. (Rosiek, 2013, 700).

> (p. 134)

As we think about this sense of consequent or consequential, we are called to think about how we act and how we engage in action. We are reminded of Beckett' s (1953) play *Waiting for Godot*, in which Vladimir says:

> [l]et us not waste our time in idle discourse! (Pause. Vehemently.) Let us do something, while we have the chance! [...] Let us represent worthily for once the foul brood to which a cruel fate consigned us! What do you say? (Estragon says nothing.) [...] The tiger bounds to the help of his congeners without the

least reflection, or else he slinks away into the depths of the thickets. But that is not the question. What are we doing here, that is the question.

(n.p.)

Situating our Study within the Context of Community

In Methodological Notebook II we make visible how our work is situated alongside people in the community. We also described how we imagined and engaged in the initial aspects of the study alongside COSI, the MCHB and the Syrian Center. We purposefully hired Hanan and Zamard as research assistants who brought their experiences of arriving in Canada as refugees to the study. We knew that it was important to them to have formalized employment.

Our team of researchers included graduate students (Gillian Vigneau and Jennifer Dodd), a postdoctoral fellow (Hiroko Kubota), people who developed and led program development over many years with a focus on diversity in educational contexts (Heather Raymond), and others who worked within the Ministry of Education and were responsible for developing and overseeing initiatives for refugee populations (Kathy Toogood). Yvonne Chiu was part of our research team. In composing this research team we were mindful to work across sectors, that Heather, Kathy and Yvonne were situated in practices that involved refugee families on a daily basis. This was important, not only as we imagined hearing about challenges within school contexts, but that the justifications that developed in response to the narrative threads would be useful.

While we situate our study within the context of community, our commitment to community is more far-reaching. Vera has worked alongside refugees since she was a teenager and also learned from her aunt whose life's work was alongside refugee populations from Eastern Europe and Asia. More recently, Vera became part of COSI and the Alberta Refugee Health Coalition. Within this context Vera worked together with Yvonne and others to develop a community health centre. After several years of work, the community health centre will open its doors in 2021. Both Vera and Jean have engaged with graduate students who are refugees. While we share only some examples, what becomes visible is that the work we do is part of our lives across time, place and social relations. What we learn in our lives shapes how we engage in the study and what we learn as we work alongside participants shapes what we do in life.

Understanding our Commitments within Relationships with Participants

Hiroko, in her narrative account, alongside Maria recounts:

> *'Can you come to our house and teach my mom English?'*
>
> *Elham asked me in an excited, panting breath when we took a short break from running in a big gymnasium. We kicked one of our winter boots in the gymnasium and chased the boot along with other kids. It was in February 2018 […]. On that Friday, we went outside our usual community center for a special activity in a gymnasium: a cooking class. While making hummus in the kitchen connected to the gymnasium, mothers learned English together. They brought their children to the gymnasium, all of whom were excitedly running around and playing with each other in this spacious area.*
>
> *Elham's eyes were sparkling as she curiously looked into my eyes and waited for my response. Her smiling cheeks were fervent and colored in red, after we were absorbed in our improvised boot-kicking game and running excitedly until we lost track of time.*
>
> *'Sure. I will come to your house!' I responded.*
>
> *Elham's smile was even more expanded. Upon hearing my response, she kicked her boot up high in the air […].*

This fragment of a narrative account makes visible how we negotiate with others what the purpose of our research relationships are. While we named our study purpose as learning about the experiences of Syrian refugee families with preschool children, we were wakeful that families might join our study for a different purpose. It is Elham who calls us to remember how important it is to be attentive to multiple reasons why people join research studies.

Being attentive to this ongoing negotiation of purpose shapes the commitment we live alongside participants to the work we undertake, as well as to the unfolding relationships we hold. In narrative inquiry we take risk in the living of a study, that our purpose might change, that wonders and uncertainties arise that call us to negotiate and re-negotiate what we do.

Yet, we do this, because we know that all people hold knowledge. We learned that Elham cared deeply about her mother and that she knew that learning English would be important to her.

Early on it was Coles (1989) who reminded us that the commitment of participants to engage in research studies came with important obligations to us as people in relation.

> What are one's obligations not to oneself, one's career, the academic world, or the world of readers, but to the people who are, after all, slowly becoming not only one's sources or contacts or informants, but one's graciously tolerant and open-handed teachers and friends – there, week after week … there in their available yet so vulnerable and hard-pressed and precarious lives?
>
> (pp. 61–2)

As we think about commitments, we are further pressed to think with and respond to experiences.

Thinking with and Responding to Experiences

As we learn 'week after week' and in close relation we must think carefully of how we respond to experiences in ways that reflect relational ethics (Clandinin et al., 2018). This is not an easy undertaking and it requires us to engage in response communities. Elsewhere, we have written how significant response communities are and how they shape what Arendt (1958) calls spaces of appearance.

> Response communities help us face the world in a different way, one that makes different social, political relationships possible. The space of appearance is not just present in response communities, but is made possible and sustained within the larger world because of response communities.
>
> (Caine, Clandinin, & Lessard, 2020, p. 665).

Vera was present alongside Hiroko during the cooking class when Elham asked Hiroko to teach her mother, Maria, English. The boots were flying high that day and the laughter still echos today. Soon after that day, Elham and Maria joined Hiroko in the study. It was much later that Elham began to tell stories of school.

Particularly, Elham mentioned that her entire impression of the kindergarten was shaped negatively by one teacher in the kindergarten. She slowly and cautiously weaved her words as she recalled her experience. 'My teacher was really ... really mean to me. She didn't call my name correctly. She always changed my name when she called me. When I said to her that is not my name, she said "Go back to where your name is from" I was always sad and cried a lot.'

I [Hiroko] tried to imagine her emotions when she was told 'Go back to where your name is from' by her teacher. Already feeling nervous and lonely in an unfamiliar environment, she must have experienced deep discouragement and perplexity at such a moment. These emotions could even be translated into a sense of disconnection from other students and her school environment, all of which Elham might have truly wished to belong to. [...] When I asked her if there was a happy moment in her kindergarten, Elham quickly replied, 'There was not a happy moment in the kindergarten. I was always sad.'

Each time we read the narrative account a palpable sense of sadness is present; a sense of loss and a sense of betrayal, much like Vera makes visible in Chapter 10 alongside Jaan. As time passses, we recognize that

> it is impossible to predict the ways that stories will be retold and relived. However, we do know that there will be effects 'in the ongoing stream of our experience' (Rosiek, 2013, p. 697), both in our experience as researchers and participants. As narrative inquirers, we are mindful of Dewey's pragmatic argument that amelioration is never permanent or certain because the world is contingent and continually changing, never fixed in place (McKenna & Pratt, 2015).
>
> (Caine et al., 2018, p. 135)

As Hiroko engages with Elham and Maria and as we think with the resonances across the experiences of participants (Clandinin, 2013), we stop to contemplate how important it is to not lose sight of the human potential to act and to imagine differently. It is within the ideas of imagination that we can begin to retell experiences, and that we can imagine otherwise (Brockmeier, 2009). Within this notion of imagination is a sense of agency.

Yet, there is more at play and it is Dewey (1931) who states,

> [p]ragmatism, thus, presents itself as an extension of historical empiricism, but with this fundamental difference, that it does not insist upon antecedent phenomena but upon consequent phenomena; not upon the precedents but upon the possibilities of action. And this change in point of view is almost revolutionary in its consequences. An empiricism which is content with repeating facts already past has no place for possibility.
>
> (pp. 32–3)

Considering Dewey's ideas means that we cannot simply recount experiences, or tell stories as objective units that can be analysed; instead we are asked to create spaces of possibility, of imagination and ultimately of agency. It is here that Lugones' (1987) ideas are most helpful to us as narrative inquirers. Her notion of playfulness is critical as

> we need to challenge racial, social, political, and economic boundaries and social differences in ways that allow researchers and participants to locate themselves in relation to others. Engaging in this manner shows openness to multiple ways of sense making and to creating texts where expectations are broken.
>
> (Dewart et al., 2019, p. 369)

While we are pressed to find ways to respond to Elham in the immediacy of the situation, we also need to think with issues of representation. It is important for us to ensure that the ways in which we represent experiences acknowledge the capacity for growth and that it results in responsive action.

Paying Attention to the Personal, Practical and Social Significance

Each narrative inquiry study must attend to the personal, practical and social significance of the work (Clandinin & Connelly, 2000). We have shown throughout this book how important it is to engage in autobiographical inquiry as a way to attend to the personal significance of our work. Given that we draw often on Addam's work we turn to Rosiek and Pratt (2013) who point out that

> Addam's method of social inquiry, then, had three distinctive elements: a) a commitment to inquiry conducted not prior to, but as part of the fabric of, processes of social amelioration; b) a conception of the subjectivity of the inquirer as an important site of ontological transformation precipitated by the inquiry; and c) a narrative mode of representing the transformation of researcher subjectivity, including transformations of conceptions of self and intimate relations with others.
>
> (p. 584)

While reflecting on the personal significance of our work, we are shaped by our personal, as well as practical and professional experiences. These experiences help us understand the practical significance of our work. In this current study it is important to situate narrative threads within and in relation to schools, settlement organizations, as well as social care agencies whose aim is to develop practices of social inclusion.

The social significance of our work is often framed with further theoretical ideas, such as notions of social inclusion, migration, happiness, home and belonging among others. Yet, it is also important to understand that the social significance of our work is framed within a social justice agenda and that our aim is to build capacity for individual and community well-being (Caine et al., 2018). As we do so we always are concerned about framing our understanding in anticipation of the future (Rosiek, 2013).

And as we consider in this methodological notebook responsibilities and commitments, it is most important that we remember that all of what we do is guided by a relational ethics (Clandinin et al., 2018), it is our ethical understanding that underpins our understanding of democracy and social justice, and most importantly our obligations to the people whose lives become part of ours.

Epilogue

As we come to the end of the book, we are mindful the ideas we outline are still in development, they are, as Greene (1995) noted of people in the making, 'not yet'. Rather than see our work as finished, we see our ideas of narrative inquiry as on the way, on a journey towards thinking narratively. We have not yet arrived, we and narrative inquiry, are what we, and it, are not yet.

We know that the theories we outline in the book are underpinnings of our narrative inquiry work. These are familiar theoretical ideas to us and, as we wrote the book, we sensed we were visiting old friends, as we pulled books off our shelves, reread them and marked favourite passages and concepts. Something similar happened as we retrieved well-worn articles from stacks of paper files and searched online for remembered articles. While we have often turned to these works in the past, we have not brought them all together at the same time. As we brought these theoretical ideas together, we highlighted how our purposes are different for this book. In other books we have written, we forefronted narrative inquiry as methodology or showed resonant narrative threads across participants' experiences of, for example, leaving school early before graduating (Clandinin, Caine & Steeves, 2013). In this book, we are explicit about how theorists shaped our understandings of narrative inquiry as phenomena.

While the theoretical ideas are diverse, they are not eclectic. The defining focus is experience, a concept that shaped our attention towards works that helped us complexify our understandings, and that challenge how we think about, of, and in relation with, experience. And yet, as we noted in the Introduction to the book, we were not applying any particular ideas to the experiences of people. Rather than applying a particular concept or theory to experience, and thus privileging the concept by allowing it to be the starting point for inquiry, we start with experience. This somewhat upside-down view of the relation of theoretical ideas to experience, that is, a view in which experience is the starting point that takes us to different theories, is a kind of counterstory to the more accepted way of using a particular theory or concept as a lens through which to analyse experience. Following Dewey's (1938) ideas, our engagement with theory is marked by placing it in relation to inquiry and experience. In this way it was not only about understanding theoretical ideas, but also about challenging them, understanding them from the vantage point of our own lives and the lives of participants we have come alongside over many years. Who we are, and are becoming, cannot be separated from the theoretical ideas that mark our work, nor the lives we live everyday.

What drew us to writing this book was our desire to show the theoretical bases of our work as narrative inquirers. In writing the book, we remembered how much we enjoyed reading and re-reading, thinking and writing about work that matters to us, work that has shaped us over many years. We were, in many ways, engaging in conversations with theorists, and their ideas, in order to help us understand the philosophical bases for narrative inquiry. It was our desire to show that, in narrative inquiry, experience cannot be understood outside of the context of a relational ontology.

As part of writing this book we sat together reading and talking. We also participated in three different reading groups, with different groups of scholars, focussed on the works of Hannah Arendt, of pragmatist philosophers and of those who write of relational ethics. As we engaged in the writing of this book, Mary Pinkoski (personal note, 2020), a doctoral student, sent the following note to Jean.

> [...] this is a paraphrase of Myles Horton (in an article by Kincheloe, MacLaren, & Steinberg, 2011 on critical theory) and it said: "Myles Horton spoke of the way he read books with students in order "to give testimony to the students about what it means to read a text" (Horton & Freire, 1990). Reading is not an easy endeavor, Horton continued, for to be a good reader is to view reading as a form of research. Reading becomes a mode of finding something, and finding something, he concluded, brings a joy that is directly connected to the acts of creation and re-creation.
>
> (n.p.)

Reading, re-reading and engaging in conversations are critical and ongoing processes that furthered our understandings of narrative inquiry.

Pragmatism and Traditions of Resistance and Radical Theorizing

Pratt (2002) in his book *Native Pragmatism: Rethinking the Roots of American Philosophy* called our attention to the traditions of resistance within pragmatism; something we came to further understand as we engaged with McKenna and Pratt's (2015) more recent work. Rosiek (2013) notes the importance of locating the pragmatist tradition amidst radical theorizing and also political action that is connected to forward-looking stories. This future-oriented thinking has significant implications for the further development of narrative inquiry. While we understand that lives are always in the making, and are lived and told in the midst, Rosiek calls us to attend even more carefully to this notion, by asking: 'So what would a practice of inquiry look like that located its warrant not just in the past or present, but also in the generation of future possibilities for experience?' (p. 697). In showing the theoretical bases for narrative inquiry, we see ourselves as engaging in a practice of inquiry that is forward looking.

As we understand pragmatism and its relation to traditions of resistance, we need to make visible that we understand resistance in a relational way. Addams (2012) calls us to resist hierarchies, to challenge certainties, in order to protect a sense of pluralism. It is here that resistance calls us to engage in dialogue, to acknowledge and make sense of the multiplicity of experience. We are part of the experience and shape the ongoing social contexts in which lives are lived and imagined. Each narrative inquiry study further shapes our understanding of how these traditions of resistance are enacted.

Political Implications: Turning to Feminist Pragmatists

While Dewey (1938) was the first pragmatist we read and the one whose work first shaped our thinking, it was the turn to feminist progamtists, like Addams (2002), who helped us name our work as political. Addams (1930), in her work at Hull House where she engaged with people, also wrote extensively and participated in philosophical thinking. Addams' (1916) focus was on changing the social realities of people. As she worked to change the social realities of people, she relied on the experiences she was part of, or privy to, to shift her philosophical ideas. Feminism and pragmatism were closely intertwined for Addams (2002) and led her to dismiss the universal and instead to acknowledge the plurality and oppression present in ordinary life. She did not turn away from the complexity of people's lives. Addams calls us to continue to think with relational ethics (Clandinin et al., 2018), equity and activism.

As we think about the political implications of our work, we also realize the importance our work holds in relation to historical events and memories. Hampl (1999) reminds us that

> [t]he political implications of the loss of memory are obvious. The authority of memory is a personal confirmation of selfhood, and therefore the first step toward ethical development. To write one's life is to live it twice, and the second living is both spiritual and historical, for a memoir reaches deep within the personality as it seeks its narrative form and it also grasps the life-of-the-times as no political analysis can.
>
> (Hampl, 1999, p. 37)

While Hampl (1999) writes of the political implications of the loss of memory for a person, and for an individual's ethical development, Elder Isabelle Kootenay reminds us of the political implications of the loss of memory for a community. Hampl shows that 'the beauty of memory rests in its talent for rendering detail, for paying homage to the senses, its capacity to love the particles of life, the richness and idiosyncrasy of our existence. The function of memory, while experienced as intensely personal, is surprisingly political' (p. 33). Elder Isabelle Kootenay draws our attention to not only the person's life but to the community's life. In so doing, she teaches us the importance of the political for both person and community. In her teaching, both the person and the community are important. This is different from history, which, 'by contrast, deals primarily with social units, and with individuals only to the extent that their lives and actions are important for the society to which they belong' (Carr, 1997, p.18).

As our work unfolds, we raise questions about current social and political agendas in relation to people's lives and to communities. We engage in thinking about creative ways that continue to place experience at its centre, ways in which staying close to experience challenges and disrupts notions of oppression, ways that allow us to create forward-looking stories.

Temporality, Place and Social Relations

The idea of temporality over time, and in time, is challenging us in new ways. We began writing this book before the 2020 pandemic of Covid-19 changed all of our lives. We read writers such as Arundati Roy (2020) who wrote.

> [h]istorically, pandemics have forced humans to break with the past and imagine their world anew. This one is no different. It is a portal, a gateway between one world and the next. We can choose to walk through it, dragging the carcasses of our prejudice and hatred, our avarice, our data banks and dead ideas, our dead rivers and smoky skies behind us. Or we can walk through lightly, with little luggage, ready to imagine another world. And ready to fight for it.
>
> (n.p.)

Roy turned us back to considerations of temporality, place and social relations that have always been part of our work as narrative inquirers, of seeing our stories as portals, as gateways, of the temporality of being in the midst, neither in one time nor another, neither in one place or social relations, nor another. She reminds us that in times which force us to be different, we can re-imagine and become otherwise. Times which stretch across catastrophes and significant disruption are times of possibility, both real and imagined.

References

Addams, J. (2002). *Democracy and social ethics. Introduction by C.H. Seigfried.1902.* Urbana, IL: University of Illinois Press.

Addams, J. (1930). *Twenty years at Hull House.* New York: Macmillan.

Addams, J. (1916). *The long road of woman's memory.* Urbana, IL: University of Illinois Press.

Ahmed, S. (2010). *The promise of happiness.* Durham: Duke University Press.

Ahmed, S. (1999) Home and away: Narratives of migration and estrangement. *International Journal of Cultural Studies,* 2(3) 329–47.

Ahmed, S., & Stacey, J. (2001). *Thinking through the skin.* London: Routledge.

Andrews, M. (2010). Beyond narrative: The shape of traumatic testimony. In M. Hyvaerinen, L. Hyden, M. Saarenheimo, & M. Tamboukou (Eds.), *Beyond narrative coherence* (pp. 147–66). Amsterdam: John Benjamins.

Anzaldúa, G. (1987). *Borderlands/La Frontera: The new mestiza.* San Francisco: Aunt Lute Books.

Arendt, H. (1996). *Love and Saint Augustine.* In J. Vecharelli Scott & J. Chelius Stark (Eds.), Chicago: The University of Chicago Press.

Arendt, H. (1958). *The human condition.* Chicago: The University of Chicago Press.

Ayers, W. (1995). Social imagination: A conversation with Maxine Greene. *International Journal of Qualitative Studies in Education,* 8(4), 319–28. https://doi.org/10.1080/0951839950080401

Baldwin, S. S. (1999). *What the body remembers.* Toronto: Vintage Canada.

Basso, K. (1996). *Wisdom sits in places: Landscape and language among the western Apache.* Albuquerque, New Mexico: University of New Mexico Press.

Bateson, M. C. (2000). *Full circles, overlapping lives: Culture and generation in transition.* New York: Random House.

Bateson, M. C. (1997). Foreword. In A. Neumann & P. L. Peterson (Eds.), *Learning from our lives: Women, research, and autobiography in education* (pp. vii–viii). New York: Teachers College Press.

Bateson, M. C. (1994). *Peripheral vision: Learning along the way.* New York: Harper Collins.

Bateson, M. C. (1989). *Composing a life.* New York: Grove Press.

Beckett, S. (1953). *Waiting for Godot.* London: Faber & Faber.

Bhabha, H. K. (1994). *The location of culture*. London: Routledge.

Blaise, C. (1993). *I had a father: A postmodern autobiography*. Toronto: Harper Collins.

Blix, B., Caine, V., Clandinin, D.J. & Berendonk, C. (2021) Considering silences in narrative inquiry: An intergenerational story of a Sami family. Journal of Contemporary Inquiry, 50, 4, pp. 580–594.

Brockmeier, J. (2009). Stories to remember: Narrative and the time of memory. *Storyworld: A Journal of Narrative Study*, 1, 115–32.

Buber, M. (1971). *I and thou*. New York: Charles Scribner's Sons.

Bruner, J. (1962/1979). *On knowing: Essays for the left hand*. Cambridge, MA: Belknap Press. (Original work published in 1962)

Bruner, J. (2004). Life as narrative. *Social Research, 71*, 691–710.

Bruner, J. (2002). *Making stories: Law, literature, life*. Cambridge, MA: Harvard University Press.

Bruner, J. (1985). Narrative and paradigmatic modes of thought. In E. Eisner (Ed.), *Learning and teaching the ways of knowing* (pp. 97–115). Chicago, IL: National Society for the Study of Education.

Caine, V. (2010). Narrative beginnings: Travelling to and within unfamiliar landscapes. *Qualitative Health Research*, 20(9), 1304–11.

Caine, V. (2007). *Dwelling with/in stories: Ongoing conversations about narrative inquiry, including visual narrative inquiry, imagination, and relational ethics*. Unpublished doctoral dissertation, University of Alberta, Edmonton, Alberta, Canada.

Caine, V. (2002). *Storied moments: A visual narrative inquiry of Aboriginal women living with HIV*. Unpublished master's thesis, University of Alberta, Edmonton, Alberta, Canada.

Caine, V., Clandinin, D.J., & Lessard, S. (2020). Considering response communities: Spaces of appearance in narrative inquiry. *Qualitative Inquiry*, 27(6), 661–6.

Caine, V., & Estefan, A. (2011). The experience of waiting: Inquiry into the long-term relational responsibilities in narrative inquiry. *Qualitative Inquiry*, 17(10) 965–71. https://doi.org/10.1177/1077800411425152

Caine, V. & Steeves, P. (2009). Imagining and playfulness in narrative inquiry. *International Journal of Education and the Arts*, 10(25),1–14.

Caine, V., Steeves, P, Clandinin, D. J., Estefan, A., Huber, J., & Murphy, S. (2018). Social justice practice: A narrative inquiry perspective. *Journal of Education, Citizenship and Social Justice*, 13(2),133–143. https://doi.org/10.1177/1746197917710235

Carr, D. (1997). Narrative and the real world: An argument for continuity. In L. Hinchman and S. K. Hinchman (Ed.), *Memory, identity, community: The idea of narrative in the human sciences* (pp. 7–25). Albany: State University of New York Press.

Carr, D. (1986). *Time, narrative, and history*. Bloomington, IN: Indiana University Press.

Cisneros, S. (1989). *The house on Mango Street*. New York: Vintage.

Clandinin, D. J. (2013). *Engaging in narrative inquiry*. Walnut Creek, CA: Left Coast Press.

Clandinin, D. J. (1989). Developing rhythm in teaching: The narrative study of a beginning teacher's personal practical knowledge of classrooms. *Curriculum Inquiry*, 19(2), 121–41.

Clandinin, D. J. (1985). Personal practical knowledge: A study of teachers' classroom images. *Curriculum Inquiry*, 15(4), 361–85.

Clandinin, D., & Caine, V. (2008). Narrative inquiry. In Lisa M. Given (Ed.), *The Sage Encyclopedia of qualitative research methods* (pp. 542–545). Thousand Oaks, CA: Sage.

Clandinin, D. J., Caine, V., & Lessard, S. (2018). *Relational ethics in narrative inquiry*. London: Routledge

Clandinin, D. J., & Connelly, F. M. (2000). *Narrative inquiry: Experience and story in qualitative research*. San Francisco: Jossey-Bass.

Clandinin, D. J. & Connelly, F. M. (1995). *Teachers' professional knowledge landscapes*. New York: Teachers College Press.

Clandinin, D. J., & Connelly, F. M. (1994). Personal experience methods. In N. K.Denzin and Y. S. Lincoln (Eds.), *Handbook of qualitative research* (pp. 413–427). Thousand Oaks, CA: Sage.

Clandinin, D. J., Huber, J., Huber, M., Murphy, M. S., Murray Orr, A., Pearce, M., & Steeves, P. (2006). *Composing diverse identities*. New York: Routledge.

Clandinin, D. J., & Rosiek, J. (2007). Mapping a landscape of narrative inquiry: Borderland spaces and tensions. In D. J. Clandinin (Ed.), *Handbook of narrative inquiry: Mapping a methodology* (pp. 35–75). Thousand Oaks: Sage Publishing.

Clandinin, D. J., Steeves, P., & Caine, V. (Eds.). (2013). *Composing lives in transition: A narrative inquiry into the experiences of early school leavers*. London: Emerald.

Coles, R. (1989). *The call of stories: Teaching and the moral imagination*. New York: Houghton Mifflin.

Connelly, F. M. & Clandinin, D. J. (1999). *Shaping a professional identity: Stories of educational practice*. New York: Teachers College Press.

Connelly, F. M., & Clandinin, D. J. (1998). Asking questions about telling stories. In C. Kridel (Ed.), *Writing educational biography: Explorations in qualitative research* (pp. 245–53). New York: Garland.

Connelly, F. M., & Clandinin, D. J. (1990). Stories of experience and narrative inquiry. *Educational Researcher*, 19(5), 2–14.

Connelly, F. M., & Clandinin, D. J. (1988). *Teachers as curriculum planners: Narratives of experience*. New York: Teachers College Press.

Connelly, F. M., & Clandinin, D. J. (1985). Personal practical knowledge and the modes of knowing: Relevance for teaching and learning. *NSSE Yearbook*, 84(2), 174–98.

Connelly, F. M., Fhillion, J., & He, M. F. (2003). An exploration of narrative inquiry into multiculturalism in education: Reflecting on two decades of research in an inner-city Canadian community school. *Curriculum Inquiry*, 33(4), 363–84.

Craig, C.J. (2005) Historical research and narrative inquiry: Striking similarities, notable differences. *American Educational History Journal*, 32(2), 214–18.

Crites, S. (1986). Storytime: Recollecting the past and projecting the future. In T. Sarbin (Ed.) *Narrative Psychology: The storied nature of human conduct*. (pp 152–73). New York: Praeger.

Crites, S. (1979). The narrative quality of experience. In L. Hinchman and S. K. Hinchman (Ed.), *Memory, Identity, Community: The idea of narrative in the Human Sciences*. (pp. 26–50). Albany: State University of New York Press.

Crites, S. (1971). The narrative quality of experience. *Journal of the American Academy of Religion*, 39(3), 291–311.

Cruikshank, J. (1990). *Life lived like a story: Life stories of three Yukon native elders*. Lincoln: University of Nebraska Press.

Dewart, G., Kubota, H., Berendonk, C., Clandinin, D.J., & Caine, V. (2019). Lugones' metaphor of 'world travelling' in narrative inquiry. *Qualitative Inquiry*. https://doi.org/10.1177/1077800419838567

Dewey, J. (1981). Experience and nature: A re-introduction. In J. Ratner (Ed.), *John Dewey, the later works* (Vol. 1, pp. 330–61). Carbondale: Southern Illinois University Press.

Dewey, J. (1958). *Experience and nature*. New York: Dover.

Dewey, J. (1938). *Experience and education*. New York: Collier Books and Macmillan.

Dewey, J. (1934). *Art as experience*. New York: Berkley Publishing Group.

Dewey, J. (1933). Underlying philosophy of education. In J. A. Boydston (Ed.), *John Dewey, the later works* (Vol. 8, pp. 77–103). Carbondale: Southern Illinois University Press

Dewey, J. (1931). The development of American pragmatism. In H. S. Thayer (Ed.), *Pragmatism: The classic writings* (pp. 23–40). In- dianapolis, IN: Hack

Dewey, J. (1916). *Democracy and education: An introduction to the philosophy of education*. New York: The Macmillan Company.

Dewey, J. (1910). *How we think: A restatement of the relation of reflective thinking to the educative process*. Boston, MA: D. C. Heath.

Dillard, A. (1987). *An American childhood*. New York: Harper & Row.

Dillard, A. (1974). *Pilgrim at Tinker Creek*. New York: Harper & Row.

Downey, C. A., & Clandinin, D. J. (2010). Narrative inquiry as reflective practice: Tensions and possibilities. In N. Lyons (Ed.), *Handbook of reflection and reflective inquiry: Mapping a way of knowing for professional reflective practice* (pp. 285–397). Dordrecht, Netherlands: Springer.

Freeman, M. (2010). *Hindsight: The promise and peril of looking backward.* Oxford: Oxford University Press.

Fried, E. (1979). *Liebesgedichte.* Germany: Wagenbach.

Friedman, M. (1993). *Encounter on the narrow ridge: A life of Martin Buber.* New York: Paragon.

Friedman, M. (1989). Friendship and modern friendship: Dislocating the community. *Ethics*, 99(2), 275–90.

Gilligan, C. (1982). *In a different voice: Psychological theory and women's development.* Cambridge, MA: Harvard University Press.

Greene, M. (2007). Imagination and the healing arts. Access 12 December, 2019 at https://maxinegreene.org/uploads/library/imagination_ha.pdf

Greene, M. (2001). *Variations on a blue guitar: The Lincoln Center Institute lectures on aesthetic education.* New York: Teachers College.

Greene, M. (1995). *Releasing the imagination: Essays on education, the arts, and social change.* San Francisco, CA: Jossey-Bass Publishers.

Greene, M. (1994). Carpe Diem: The arts and school restructuring. *Teachers College Record*, 95(4), 494–507.

Gunn Allen, P. (1998). *Off the reservation: Reflections on boundary-busting, border-crossing loose cannons.* Boston, MA: Beacon Press.

Hamington, M. (2004). *Embodied care: Jane Addams, Maurice Merleau-Ponty, and feminist ethics.* Urbana: University of Illinois Press.

Hampl, P. (1999). *Memory and imagination.* New York: Norton & Company.

Heilbrun, C. (1999). *Women's lives. A view from the threshold.* Toronto: University of Toronto Press.

Heilbrun, C. (1988). *Writing a Woman's Life.* New York: Norton & Company.

Hevern, V. W. (1999). Narrative, believed-in imaginings, and psychology's methods: An interview with Theodore R. Sarbin. *Teaching of Psychology*, 26, 300–4.

Hoffman, E. (1994). Let memory speak. In *New York Times*, Section 7, Page 5.

Johnson, M. (2017). *Embodied mind, meaning, and reason.* Chicago: University of Chicago Press.

Johnson, M. (2007). *The body in the mind: The bodily basis of meaning, imagination and reason.* Chicago: University of Chicago Press.

Kearney, R. (1988). *The wake of imagination.* Minneapolis, MN: University of Minnesota.

Kennedy, M. (2001). *Race matters in the life/work of four, white, female teachers.* Unpublished doctoral dissertation, University of Alberta, Edmonton, Alberta, Canada.

Kerby, A. P. (1991). *Narrative and the self*. Bloomington, IN: Indiana University Press.

Lagemann, E. C. (1989). The plural worlds of educational research. *History of Education Quarterly*, 29(2), 185–214.

Lakoff, G., & Johnson, M. (1980). *Metaphors we live by*. Chicago: University of Chicago Press.

Le Guin, U. (1989). *Dancing at the edge of the world*. New York: Perennial Library.

Lessard, S. (2010). *"Two-stones" stories. Shared teachings through the narrative experiences of early school leavers*. Unpublished master's thesis, University of Alberta, Edmonton, Canada.

Lessard, S. (2014). *Red worn runners: A narrative inquiry into the stories of Aboriginal youth and families in urban settings*. Unpublished doctoral dissertation, University of Alberta, Edmonton, Alberta, Canada.

Lessard, S., Kooteray, I., Whiskeyjack, F., Chung, S., Clandinin, D.J., & Caine, V. (2020). Working with Indigenous elders in narrative inquiry: Reflections and key considerations. *Qualitative Inquiry*, 27(1), 28–36.

Lindemann Nelson, H. (1995) Resistance and insubordination, *Hypatia*, 10(2), 23–40.

Lorde, A. (1984). *Sister outsider: Essays and speeches*. Berkeley: Crossing Press.

Lugones, M. (2003). *Pilgrimages/Peregrinajes: Theorizing coalitions against multiple oppressions*. Lanham, MD: Rowman & Littlefield.

Lugones, M. (1987). Playfulness, 'world'-travelling, and loving perception. *Hypatia*, 2(2), 3–19. https://doi.org/10.1111/j.1527-2001.1987.tb01062.x

MacIntyre, A. (1981). *After virtue*. Notre Dame: University of Notre Dame.

Marmon Silko, L. (1997). *Yellow woman and a beauty of the spirit: Essays on Native American life today*. New York: Simon & Schuster.

Marmon Silko, L. (1991). *Almanac of the dead*. New York: Penguin.

Marmon Silko, L. (1977). *Ceremony*. New York: Viking.

Maxwell, R. (2001) *Culture works: The political economy of culture*. Minneapolis: University of Minnesota Press.

McKenna, E., & Pratt, S. (2015). *American philosophy from Wounded Knee to the present*. London: Bloomsbury.

Merleau-Ponty, M. (1968). *The visible and the invisible*. Chicago: Northwestern University Press

Mickelson, J. R. (2015). *Facing the shards*. Bell Canyon, CA: FYD Media.

Min Ha, T. (1989). *Woman, native, other: Writing postcoloniality and feminism*. Bloomington, IN: Indiana University Press.

Mott, R. (2006). Digitizing Leslie Silko's Laguna landscape. *Image & Narrative*, 14.

Neumann, A. (1997). Ways without words: Learning from silence and story in post-Holocaust lives. In A. Neumann & P. L. Peterson (Eds.), *Learning from our lives: Women, research, and autobiography in education* (pp. 91–120). New York: Teachers College Press.

Neumann, A., & Peterson, P. L. (1997). *Learning from our lives: Women, research, and autobiography in education*. New York: Teachers College Press.

Noddings, N. (1983). *Caring: A feminist approach to ethics and moral education*. Berkeley: University of California Press.

Oakley, A. (1992). *Taking it like a woman*. New York: Flamingo.

Okri, B. (1997). *A way of being free*. London: Phoenix.

Oxford Lexico. (n.d.) Wonder. *Oxford English dictionary*. Accessed 5 January, 2020 https://www.lexico.com/definition/wonder

Ozik, C. (1989). *Metaphor & memory. Essays*. New York: Vintage.

Paley, V. (2010). *The boy on the beach: Building community through play*. Chicago: University of Chicago Press.

Paley, V. (1993). *You can't say you can't play*. Cambridge, MA: Harvard University Press.

Paley, V. (1990). *The boy who would be a helicopter*. Cambridge, MA: Harvard University Press.

Paley, V. (1986). *Mollie is three: Growing up in school*. Chicago: University of Chicago Press.

Paley, V. (1984). *Boys and girls: Superheroes in the doll corner*. Chicago: University of Chicago Press.

Pinar, W. (Ed.). (1998). *The passionate mind of Maxine Greene: "I am--not yet"*. Bristol, PA: Farmer Press.

Polanyi, M. (1958). *Personal knowledge: Towards a post-critical philosophy*. Chicago: University of Chicago Press.

Polkinghorne, D. (1988). *Narrative knowing and the human sciences*. New York: SUNY Press.

Pratt, S. (2002). *Native pragmatism: Rethinking the roots of American philosophy*. Bloomington, IL: Indiana University Press.

Ricoeur, P. (1992). *Oneself as another*. Chicago: The University of Chicago Press.

Roger, C., & Buber, M. (1960). Dialogue between Martin Buber and Carl Rogers. *Psychologia*, 3(4), 208–21.

Rosiek, J. (2018). Afterword. In Clandinin, D. J., Caine, V., & Lessard, S. *Relational ethics in narrative inquiry*. (pp. 204–9). London: Routledge.

Rosiek, J. (2013). Pragmatism and post-qualitative futures. *International Journal of Qualitative Studies in Education*, 26(6), 692–705.

Rosiek, J. & Pratt, S. (2013). Jane Addams as a resource for developing a reflexively realist social science practice. *Qualitative Inquiry*, 19(8), 578–88.

Roy, A. (2020). The pandemic is a portal. *Financial Times*.

Rubin, C. (1986). *Autobiographical memory*. New York: Cambridge University Press.

Sandel, M. (1982) *Liberalism and the limits of justice*. Cambridge: Cambridge University Press.

Sarbin, T. (2004). The role of imagination in narrative construction. In Daiute, C., & Lightfoot C. (Eds.), *Narrative analysis: Studying the development of individuals in society.* (pp. 5–20). Thousand Oaks, CA: Sage Publications.

Sarbin, T. (2001). Embodiment and the narrative structure of emotional life. *Narrative Inquiry*, 11(1), 217–25.

Sarbin, T. (1998). Believed-in imaginings. In DeRivera, J., & Sarbin, T. (Eds.), *Believed-in imaginings: The narrative construction of reality*, (pp. 15–30). Washington, DC: American Psychological Association.

Sarton, M. (1980). *Recovering: A journal.* New York: Norton & Company.

Sarton, M. (1987). *At seventy.* New York: Norton & Company.

Sartre, J. P. (1964a). *Nausea.* trans. Lloyd Alexander (New York: New Directions, 1964). First published in French in 1938.

Sartre, J. P. (1964b). *The words.* New York: Braziller.

Schachter, D. L. (1996). *Searching for memory. The brain, the mind, and the past.* New York: Basic Books.

Schön, D. (1983). *The reflective practitioner: How professionals think in action.* New York: Basic Books.

Seigfried, H. (1996). *Pragmatism and feminism: Reweaving the social fabric.* Chicago: University of Chicago Press.

Smith, J. A. (2008). *Qualitative psychology. A practical guide to research questions.* (2nd ed.). Los Angeles: Sage.

Spence, D. (1982). *Narrative truth and historical truth: Meaning and truth in psychoanalysis.* New York: Norton & Company.

Stone, E. (1989) *Black sheep and kissing cousins: How our family stories shape us.* New York: Penguin Books.

Swanson, C. (2019). *A narrative inquiry alongside the familial curriculum making experiences of urban Indigenous children and Families.* Unpublished doctoral dissertation, University of Alberta, Edmonton, Alberta, Canada.

Talpade Mohanty, C. (1993). The epistemic status of cultural identity: On 'beloved' and the postcolonial condition. *Cultural Critique*, 24, 41–80.

Tompkins, J. (1997). *A life in school. What the teacher learned.* New York: Basic Books.

Torgovnick, M. (1994). *Crossing ocean parkway.* Chicago: University of Chicago Press.

Van Gennep, A. (1960). *The rites of passage.* London: Routledge.

Van Wyck, P. (2008). An emphatic geography: Notes on the ethical itinerary of landscape. *Canadian Journal of Communication*, 33(2), 171–91.

Veck, V., & Gunter, H. M. (Ed.). (2020). *Hannah Arendt on educational thinking and practice in dark times. Education for a world in crisis.* London: Bloomsbury.

White, H. (1978). *Topics of discourse: Essays in cultural criticism.* Baltimore and London: John Hopkins University Press.

White, H. (1980). The Value of Narrativity in the Representation of Reality. *Critical Inquiry, 7,* 5–27.

White, H. (1984) The question of narrative in contemporary historical theory. *History and theory,* 23(1), 1–33.

Woolf, V. (1977). *A room of one's own.* London: Grafton Press.

Wright, A. (Ed.). (1986). *The delicacy and strength of lace: Letters between Leslie Marmon Silko and James Wright.* Saint Paul, MN: Graywolf.

Young, M. (2005). *Pimatisiwin: Walking in a good way – A narrative inquiry into language and identity.* Winnipeg, MB: Pemmican Publications.

Index

www.ingramcontent.com/pod-product-compliance
Lightning Source LLC
Chambersburg PA
CBHW071852270326
41929CB00013B/2194